Laughter
the
Best Medicine

A Laugh-Out-Loud Collection
of the Funniest Jokes, Quotes, Stories and Cartoons

Reader's
Digest

The Reader's Digest Association (Canada) Ltd.
• Montreal •

PROJECT STAFF

EDITORS
Pamela Chichinskas-Johnson
Marianne Wait

SENIOR DESIGNERS
Andrée Payette
Elizabeth Tunnicliffe

CONTRIBUTING EDITORS
Robert Ronald
Doug Colligan

COPY EDITORS
Judy Yelon
Jeanette Gingold

COVER AND SPOT ILLUSTRATION
Elwood Smith

PRODUCTION MANAGER
Gordon Howlett

PRODUCTION COORDINATOR
Gillian Sylvain

READER'S DIGEST CANADA

VICE PRESIDENT, BOOK EDITORIAL
Robert Goyette

READER'S DIGEST BOOKS

EDITOR IN CHIEF
Neil Wertheimer

READER'S DIGEST ASSOCIATION, INC.

PRESIDENT AND CHIEF EXECUTIVE OFFICER
Eric W. Schrier

© 2006 The Reader's Digest Association (Canada) Ltd.

All rights reserved. Unauthorized reproduction, in any manner, is prohibited.
No part of this book may be reproduced, stored in a retrieval system, or transmitted in any form or by any means, electronic, electrostatic, magnetic tape, mechanical, photocopying, recording or otherwise, without permission in writing from the publishers.

Reader's Digest and the Pegasus logo are registered trademarks of The Reader's Digest Association, Inc.

Library and Archives Canada Cataloguing in Publication

Laughter, the best medicine: a laugh-out-loud collection of the funniest jokes, quotes, stories and cartoons.

ISBN 0-88850-804-2 (bound)
ISBN 0-88850-805-0 (pbk.)

1. American wit and humour. 2. Canadian wit and humour (English).
PN6153.L39 2006   818'.540208   C2006-900858-2

Address any comments about *Laughter, the Best Medicine* to:
The Reader's Digest Association (Canada) Ltd.
Senior Book Editor, Books and Home Entertainment Division
1100 René-Lévesque Boulevard West
Montreal, QC H3B 5H5

To order copies of *Laughter, the Best Medicine,* call 1-800-465-0780.

Cover illustration © Elwood Smith

For more Reader's Digest products and information, visit our website at: rd.ca

Printed in the U.S.A.
06 07 08 09 / 5 4 3 2 1

About this book

Groucho Marx once said,
"A laugh is like an aspirin, only it works twice as fast."
Every time you laugh, it's like taking a miracle pill for your
health. According to doctors and scientific researchers,
laughter can reduce stress, lower blood pressure, boost the
immune system and improve brain function.
It's no wonder that we lay claim to having a "funny bone," or
that humour is "contagious," and that laughter is "infectious."
So humour is good for your health, and it's also good for your
soul. It's our intent to make you laugh; however humour has been
known to offend, no matter how benignly it's intended.
So we'd like to remind you of the following…

joke \ something not to be taken seriously

Introduction

It was another manic day on the golf course and my new Tiger Woods technology driver was giving me fits off the tee.

Actually, my Fred Flintstone technology irons were giving me equal fits on the fairways, which made me suspect my trouble lay in playing with improperly fitted clubs.

The theory evaporated when I snapped my ball at an impossibly perfect right angle into a nearby pond. The dancing waves seemed to arrange themselves to spell out "sheer incompetence" as they bid my sinking Titleist adieu.

My playing partner, a man with white moustaches that looked like two restful rabbits nuzzling each other's noses on his upper lip, sagely eyed my subsequent five-iron hissy fit.

"Golf is frustrating," he said, "but it is also discouraging."

Having expected to hear some soothing platitude, I began to laugh at the reversed truth of his words.

In laughing, I learned again the great reward of humour in our lives.

Life was, is, and always will be, frequently frustrating, discouraging, infuriating and, as a direct consequence, utterly hilarious. As our new *Laughter* compendium shows on every page, the pell-mell chaos that erupts from our attempts to control the modern world with high technology is fertile ground for the jokes, quotes, anecdotes and laugh lines that bring us back to earth.

Celebrated Canadian humourist Josh Freed proves that even shopping for a new cellphone can be a source of humour—provided it doesn't lead to a padded cell first.

"There were Blackberries, Blueberries, Treos and Oreos—each with enough three-year plans to run the old Soviet Union," Freed writes. "After 90 shopping minutes, I was so exhausted I ordered a phone just to escape the store."

Mary Roach, who writes a humour column for our

American cousins in *Reader's Digest* U.S. edition, points out that even when you escape the madness of the modern high-tech marketplace, it ain't necessarily safer—or saner—at home. Especially when you invite a robot in to do the vacuuming.

"I was on my way out the door to enjoy life when I heard a crash," Roach recounts. "My vacuuming robot had tangled itself up in the telephone cord and then headed off in the other direction, pulling the phone off the nightstand and onto the floor."

And then, cue the danger music, it headed for the bathroom….

Which is where Ottawa writer Scott Feschuk thinks Canadians, Americans and everyone else should go if they feel the urge to buy a brand new Internet Urinal, an actual plastic device marketed on the premise that some people are so stuck on their computers that they won't leave their seats even when nature calls.

In his roundup of the "stupidest of stupid" new products, Feschuk fears the future has been turned over not just to the Internet Urinal but to the likes of

the Electric Marshmallow Toaster, the Tan-Timer Bikini and the Banana Bunker, which "heroically vows to 'keep your fruit safe' so long as it's shaped like a banana."

He may be right, but there will always be safe haven in humour, whatever our shape or size. The evidence for that is the hundreds of contributions in "Life in These Times" that come from *Reader's Digest* readers themselves—ordinary folks who know that the best way to deal with a fruit loops world is to roll with the nuttiness and come up smiling.

It's an attitude best summed up in the riddle posed by an anonymous Canadian, to wit:

Q: "Why did the Canadian cross the road?"

A: "Because that's the direction his car was sliding."

It's about more than just going with the flow. It's living to laugh out loud. We hope this book will fit your need to do just that. Those who need more can always come and watch.

Peter Stockland,
Editor-in-Chief, Reader's **Digest**

Contents

Life in These Times

It keeps us plugged in, turned on and sometimes ticked off.
The ironies, absurdities and marvels of modern-day life.

My boyfriend and I met online and we'd been dating for over a year. I introduced Hans to my uncle, who was fascinated by the fact that we met over the Internet. He asked Hans what kind of line he had used to pick me up.

Ever the geek, Hans naïvely replied, "I just used a regular 56K modem."

— ANNE McCONNE

Kids have a greater need for speed than classroom computers can deliver. Impatient to turn in his term paper, one restless student kept clicking the "Print" command. The printer started to churn out copy after copy of the kid's ten-page report.

The topic? "Save Our Trees."

— KEN CUMMINGS

I am five feet, three inches tall and pleasingly plump. After I had a minor accident, my mother accompanied me to the emergency room.

The triage nurse asked for my height and weight, and I blurted out, "Five-foot-eight and 125 pounds."

While the nurse pondered this information, my mother leaned over to me. "Sweetheart," she gently chided, "this is not the Internet."

— M. M.

Guards escorted a handcuffed prisoner into the courtroom where I stood as the court deputy. "Is this a tough judge?" the prisoner asked.

"Yes," the bailiff said. "A tough but fair judge."

"Yeah? How tough?"

"The toughest judge since Pontius Pilate," the bailiff replied.

"I don't know him," the prisoner replied. "I'm not from around here."

— JOSEPH T. WRIGHT

I was visiting a friend who could not find her cordless phone. After several minutes of searching, her young daughter said, "You know what they should invent? A phone that stays connected to its base so it never gets lost."

— MIRIAM SCOW

Trying to explain to our five-year-old daughter how much computers had changed, my husband pointed to our brand-new personal computer and told her that when he was in college, a computer with the same amount of power would have been the size of a house.

Wide-eyed, our daughter asked, "How big was the mouse?"

— CYNDY HINDS

Learning to use a voice-recognition computer program, I was excited about the prospect of finally being able to write more accurately than I type. First I read out loud to the computer for about an hour to train it to my voice, then I opened a clean page and dictated a nursery rhyme to see the magic.

The computer recorded: "Murry fed a little clam, its fleas was bright and slow."

— CARRIE E. PITTS

Timeless Humour from the '50s

The big electronic computer in the accounting department performed admirably until summer weather arrived. Then it practically quit. A diagnosis of the trouble revealed that the machine was extremely sensitive to changes in temperature, so the only thing to do was to move it into an air-conditioned room.

Now, as we office drones perspire and droop, we are treated to the vision of the computer operating coolly and efficiently beyond the glass wall of its private office. What was that again about men being smarter than machines?

"It's guaranteed for the life of the product, which obviously ended when it broke."

A friend of mine was enjoying his new car's powerful sound system by driving along with the volume way up. At a traffic light, he heard someone shout, "Hey, do you mind?"

Stopped next to him was a young man in an open convertible. He pointed to an object in his hand and said, "Can't you see I'm on the phone?"

— DENNIS DIGGES

I returned from Russia after living there nearly two years. My sister decided to surprise me by creating "welcome home" signs in Russian. She went to a website that offered translations and typed in "Welcome Home, Cole." She then printed the translated phrase onto about 20 coloured cardboard signs.

When I got off the plane, the first thing I saw was my family, excitedly waving posters printed with a strange message. My sister gave me a big hug, and pointed proudly to her creations. "Isn't that great?" she said. "Bet you didn't think I knew any Russian."

I admitted that I was indeed surprised—and so was she when I told her what the signs actually said: "Translation not found."

— COLE M. CRITTENDEN

When my printer's type began to grow faint, I called a local repair shop, where a friendly man informed me that the printer probably needed only to be cleaned. Because the store charged $50 for such cleanings, he told me, I might be better off reading the printer's manual and trying the job myself.

Pleasantly surprised by his candour, I asked, "Does your boss know that you discourage business?"

"Actually it's my boss's idea," the employee replied sheepishly. "We usually make more money on repairs if we let people try to fix things themselves first."

— MICHELLE R. ST. JAMES

A pastor I know of uses a standard liturgy for funerals. To personalize each service, he enters a "find and replace" command into his word processor. The computer then finds the name of the deceased from the previous funeral and replaces it with the name of the deceased for the upcoming one.

Not long ago, the pastor told the computer to find the name "Mary" and replace it with "Edna." The next morning, the funeral was going smoothly until the congregation intoned the Apostles' Creed. "Jesus Christ," they read from the preprinted program, "born of the Virgin Edna."

— ROBIN GREENSPAN

I purchased a new desktop-publishing program that surprised me by containing a make-a-paper-airplane option. I decided to give it a try. After I selected the plane I wanted, the software gave me a choice of accessories available for my plane, including a stick-up tail, adjustable flaps and an AM/FM radio. Out of curiosity I chose the AM/FM radio.

The program responded with a message box stating: "Come on, be serious. These are just paper airplanes."

— GREG SCOTT

Our newer, high-speed computer was in the shop for repair, and my son was forced to work on our old model with the black-and-white printer.

"Mom," he complained to me one day, "this is like we're living back in the twentieth century."

— DENISE PERRY DONAVIN

One cold night my furnace died, so I went to my parents' house. In the morning, a neighbour called to tell me that my water pipes had burst and flooded my townhouse and hers. I raced home—and on the way got a speeding ticket.

Then the furnace repairman arrived and told me he didn't think he had the proper fuse but would check in his truck. Meanwhile, the plumber cut holes in my bathroom wall to locate the leak.

When the furnace repairman returned, he held aloft a fuse. "I had the right one," he said triumphantly. "This must be your lucky day."

— CANDACE M. PRESTWICH

The first Sunday after my husband and I bought a new car, we parked it in the last row of the church lot, not wanting to be ostentatious. While talking with friends, my husband, Byron, accidentally hit the panic button on his electronic key. Immediately our car's horn blared and its lights flashed.

Watching Byron fumble with the button, his friend teased, "Wouldn't it have been in better taste to put a few lines in the church bulletin?"

— DONA A. MOWRY

Working as a telemarketer for MCI Communications, I made a call to a home one evening. When a boy around eight answered the phone, I identified myself, told him I was calling for MCI and asked to speak to his parents.

As he put the phone down, I heard him yell, "Dad! Dad! The FBI wants to talk to you!"

As soon as the father answered the phone in a quivering voice, I said, "Sir, this is not the FBI; this is MCI Communications."

After a long pause, the man said, "This is the first time I am actually glad to hear from you guys."

— LYNDA CYPHER

I was preparing lunch for my granddaughter when the phone rang. "If you can answer one question," a young man said, "you'll win ten free dance lessons."

Before I could tell him I was not interested, he continued. "You'll be a lucky winner if you can tell me what Alexander Graham Bell invented."

"I don't know," I replied dryly, trying to discourage him.

"What are you holding in your hand right now?" he asked excitely.

"A bologna sandwich."

"Congratulations!" he shrieked. "And for having such a great sense of humour..."

— LOLA CANTRELL

My son, Scott, an insurance broker, loves ocean fishing and takes his cellphone along on the boat. One morning we were drifting several kilometres offshore as Scott discussed business on the phone. Suddenly his rod bent double, and the reel screamed as line poured off the spool.

Scott was master of the situation. "Pardon me," he told his customer calmly. "I have a call on another line."

— ART HARRIS

It is so rare to be offered a meal on airlines these days that I was surprised to hear the flight attendant ask the man sitting in front of me,

"Would you like dinner?"

"What are my choices?"
he responded.

"Yes or no,"
she said.

KERVYN DIMNEY

Telephone solicitors are one of my father's pet peeves. He is especially annoyed by those who offer "free gifts" as part of their sales pitch. Late one night, Dad was in bed when the phone rang.

The voice on the end of the line said: "Congratulations, you've just won a free burial plot!"

"Great!" Dad replied. "Send it over." Then he hung up.

— D. VANCE NOONAN

The elevator in our building malfunctioned one day, leaving several of us stranded. Seeing a sign that listed two emergency phone numbers, I dialed the first and explained our situation.

After what seemed to be a very long silence, the voice on the other end said, "I don't know what you expect me to do for you; I'm a psychologist."

"A psychologist?" I replied. "Your phone is listed here as an emergency number. Can't you help us?"

"Well," he finally responded in a measured tone. "How do you feel about being stuck in an elevator?"

— CHRISTINE QUINN

One night, telephone solicitors kept interrupting our supper. When the phone rang yet again, my father answered it. By his remarks, we assumed it was his friend Ed, a notorious practical joker.

Dad kept saying things like, "Cut it out, Ed. This is very funny, but I know it's you. C'mon, stop it or I'll hang up. I'll get you for this."

When Dad hung up, my mom asked, "Was that Ed?"

"No," my father replied. "It was a salesman, and I don't think he'll call back."

— TONI M. VIDRA

I provide technical support for the computer software published by my company. One day, over the phone, I was helping a customer install a product on a Macintosh. The procedure required him to delete an old file. On the Mac there is an icon of a trash can that is used to collect items to be permanently deleted.

I told the customer to click on the old file and drag it to the trash. Then I had him perform a few other steps. As a reminder, I said, "Don't forget to empty the trash."

Obediently he replied, "Yes, dear."

— CYNTHIA KAINU

One Saturday night my boss and her family came to our house to play cards. As they were driving away at the end of the evening, I discovered that she had left her purse in a corner next to the dining-room hutch. I was about to call her house, intending to leave a message on the answering machine, when my son reminded me that they had a cellphone.

As I dialed the number, I marvelled at the technology that would alert them before they had driven all the way home. A few seconds later the purse began to ring.

— PATTY DUNHAM

I'm a police officer and was parked near a motel, running radar checks, when a man approached my vehicle and asked for help. He complained that the volume on the television in the empty motel room next to his was so loud that he and his wife couldn't sleep.

No one was in the motel office. The man's wife was outside when I reached their door. That's when I got my idea. I asked her for their remote control, aimed it through the window of the empty room, and turned off the blaring TV.

— RAY ALLEN

My mother began getting calls from men who misdialed the similar number of an escort service. Mom, who had had her number for years, asked the telephone company to change the organization's number. They refused. The calls kept coming day and night.

Finally, Mom began telling the gentlemen who called that the company had gone out of business. Within a week, the escort service voluntarily changed its number.

— MARIAN BURGESS

What I Really, Really Need Now Is the Padded-cell phone

▶ BY JOSH FREED

I lived the entire 21st-century experience in five hours last week, a modern high-speed mix of anxiety, awe, rage, relief and resignation. I bought a new cellphone.

It all started when I went to repair my old phone, which had died one year and 10 months into its two-year plan. The guy at the store said it was probably the battery. A new one was $70.

"Well, let's try it out and see if it works," I said.

"Sorry, it's in plastic wrapping," he replied. "Once it's open, it's yours."

Naturally, he had another plan: I could get another phone free, just by signing up for a new calling plan. And thus started the most baffling day I've had since—well, I bought my last cellphone.

It began with a staggering choice of some 75,000 models that all sounded like military jets. They had names like the VX8100 Fighter Phone and the SGH-P777 Stealth Phone with Missile Launch Capability. There were BlackBerries, BlueBerries, Treos and Oreos—each with enough three-year plans to run the old Soviet Union.

When I asked why one phone was better than another, the salesman went on about the flash quality and the zoom lens ratio. They don't really sell phones anymore—just cameras that make phone calls.

Each model also came with a wondrous choice of calling plans. Did I want the $500 phone with a 12-month plan, or the free phone with a 36-month plan that would stop working in 20 months, like my last one? Did I want the $30 plan with 400 free monthly twilight weekend minutes, or the $40 plan with unlimited pre-dawn incoming calls, plus free Leap Year text-messaging and online photo development?

After 90 shopping minutes, I was so exhausted I ordered a phone just to escape the store. The salesman couldn't say what would happen to my old phone's leftover minutes, however, so he suggested I call Rogers.

BIG mistake.

I spent the next 15 minutes punching buttons into a pay phone and waiting—until "Patrick" from "Promotions" finally answered. When I said I was at a store buying a phone, he seemed astonished. Didn't I know I could order directly from Rogers and save a fortune? I'd avoid the $35 connection fee and my first $30 monthly fee and countless other fees I'd never heard of.

He spent another 40 minutes outlining all his fabulous calling plan choices and asking me for enough personal data to get me through a U.S. security check in Baghdad.

Finally, I surrendered and said I'd take the same phone as the store had—for about $65 in savings.

"Sorry," Patrick said. "I can't actually sell you a

They don't really sell phones anymore— just cameras that make phone calls.

phone. I can only tell you about it. To purchase, you have to call back and tell 'Sales' what we selected."
Arrrrrrggh.

Ten more minutes of punching numbers and I was talking to Martin in "Sales." I recited the phone model and plan Patrick gave me—but Martin couldn't find it in his computer. After 15 more minutes of searching, he announced that Patrick had made a mistake.

It was impossible to save either the $35 connection fee or my first month's bill. All he could offer was *exactly* the same deal the store had 90 minutes earlier.

At this point, I went ballistic. If I'd have been inside the Rogers office, they'd have had to tie me down with ropes while the police netted me. I had phone rage—double phone rage, where you rage on the phone about the phone.

It took poor Martin five minutes to talk me down, using all the skills of his one-day Psychotic Customer Psychiatry course. Finally, he suggested I contact customer service. Maybe they could help. (Translation: Get off the line, you wacko.)

Later that day, I spoke to a nice woman in customer service who informed me that Patrick, the first salesman, had been right about the $35 connection fee. He was from "Promotions," while "Sales" didn't know about his "special" offer. Patrick was wrong about the free month, however—that wasn't available.

"**Grr-**" I began, but the woman interjected. She knew I'd had a "rough morning," so she would overrule the rules and honour the first deal.

Hallelujah! I had saved my $65, though I'd lost five hours and needed a week of stress leave.

Frankly, if this is cellphone freedom, I prefer a prison cell. Next time I buy a phone, I want a very simple choice: Phone—or no phone. And please, don't even mention the zoom. ▲

"This man here is saying that he stole your identity, got bored, and now wants to return it."

My cellphone quit as I tried to let my wife know that I was caught in freeway gridlock and would be late for our anniversary dinner. I wrote a message on my laptop asking other motorists to call her, printed it on a portable inkjet and taped it to my rear windshield.

When I finally arrived home, my wife gave me the longest kiss ever. "I really think you love me," she said. "At least 70 people called and told me so."

— JARON SUMMERS

The brave new memo about the company's revised travel policy read as follows: We were no longer allowed to buy cheap tickets via the Internet. Instead, we were required to use the more expensive company travel department. Furthermore, to show how much money we were saving, we were asked to comparison-shop for fares—on the Internet.

I thought the typo in the last line of the memo summed it up best: "The new process is ineffective today."

— KIP HARTMAN

Just ahead of me in line at the movie theatre was a woman with a cellphone glued to her ear, arguing with the ticket vendor.

"That movie can't be sold out!" she shouted. "I'm talking to my boyfriend who's sitting in the theatre, and he says there's two empty seats next to him. One ticket, please."

She got her ticket.

— CLAUDIA J. WRAZEL-HOROWITZ

After I bought my mother a compact-disc player and some CDs, she was excited to discover she no longer needed to rewind or fast-forward tapes or move the needle on her record player.

Knowing she was not that technically astute, I called her a few days later to see how she was managing. "Fine. I listened to Shania Twain this morning," she said.

"The whole CD?" I asked.

"No," she replied, "just one side."

— COURTNEY DYER

A phone company representative called to ask if I was interested in caller ID. Since I'm blind, I asked, "Does it come in Braille?"

The rep put me on hold. When she returned, she replied, "I'm sorry, sir, but the caller ID box doesn't come in that colour."

— ED LUCAS

Part of what makes a human being a human being is the imperfections. Like, you wouldn't give a robot my ears. You just wouldn't do that.

— WILL SMITH in InTouch

A computer lets you make more mistakes faster than any invention in human history— with the possible exceptions of handguns and tequila.

— MITCH RATCLIFFE

"If we are a country committed to free speech," asks comedian Steven Wright, "then why do we have phone bills?"

Just think how far we've come in the 20th century. The man who used to be a cog in the wheel is now a digit in the computer.

— ROBERT FUOSS in The Wall Street Journal

Most people hate cellphone use on trains; I love cellphone use on trains. What do you want to do, read that report on your lap, or hear about your neighbour's worst date ever?

— LIZA MUNDY in The Washington Post Magazine

A modern computer is an electronic wonder that performs complex mathematical calculations and intricate accounting tabulations in one ten-thousandth of a second—and then mails out statements ten days later.

— PAUL SWEENEY

You can't write poetry on the computer.

— QUENTIN TARANTINO

You can buy anything on eBay. I bought the world's oldest globe. It's flat.

— BUZZ NUTLEY

Enters Hell

▶ BY STEVE MARTIN

The burning gates of hell were opened, and the designer of CD packaging entered to the Devil's fanfare. "We've been wanting him down here for a long time," the One of Pure Evil said to his infernal minions, "but we decided to wait, because he was doing such good work above, wrapping the CDs with Cellophane and that sticky tape strip. Ask him to dinner, and be sure to invite the computer-manual people too."

The Devil vanished, missing the warm display of affection offered the inventor.

"Beelzebub himself opened a nasty cut on his finger trying to unwrap a Streisand best-of," whispered an imp. A thick snake nuzzled closer, and wrapped itself around the inventor's leg. "He used to be enamoured of the remote-control people, with their tiny little buttons jammed together, and their enigmatic abbreviations," the snake said, "but now all he ever talks about is you, you, you. Come on, let's get you ready for dinner. We can talk about your assignment later."

As the snake led the way to the dressing halls of hell, a yearning, searching look came over its face. "How did you do it?" the snake asked. "You know, invent the packaging? Everyone wants to know."

The inventor, his feet comfortably aflame, and flattered by all the recognition, relaxed into his surroundings. "The original plastic CD "jewel box" was just too damn easy to get into," he explained. "I mean, if we're going to prevent consumer access, for God's sake, let's prevent it! I wanted a packaging where the consumer would run to the kitchen for a knife, so there was a chance to at least slice open his hand."

"Is that when you got the idea for shrink wrap?" said the snake.

"Shrink wrap was nice for a while. I liked that there was absolutely no place to tear into it with a fingernail, but I knew there was further to go. That's when I hit on Cellophane, Cellophane with the illusion of an opening strip, where really none exists."

That night, at the celebratory dinner held once an eon to honour new arrivals, the inventor sat to the Devil's right. On his left sat Cerberus, the watchdog of Hades and noted designer of the pineapple. The Devil chatted with the inventor all night long, then requested that he open another bottle of wine, this time with a two-pronged, sideslip corkscrew. The inventor perspired, and an hour later the bottle was uncorked.

At first, no one noticed the muffled disturbance from above, which soon grew into a sustained clamour. Eventually the entire gathering looked toward the ceiling, and finally the Devil himself noticed that their attention had shifted. He raised his head.

CD buyers are getting a bum wrap, says renowned comedian Steve Martin.

Hovering in the ether were three angels, each holding an object. The inventor knew clearly what the objects were: the milk carton, the Ziploc bag and the banana, all three perfectly designed packages. He remembered how he used to admire them before he fell into evil. The three angels glided toward the dais.

One held the Ziploc bag over the Aspirin-bottle people, and bathed them in an otherworldly light. A yellow glow from the banana washed over the hellhound Cerberus, designer of the pineapple, and the milk carton poured its white luminosity in the direction of the CD packager. The Devil stood up abruptly, roared something in Latin while succubi flew out of his mouth, and then angrily excused himself.

After the fiasco, the inventor went back to his room and fiddled with the five remotes it took to operate his VCR. Frustrated, he closed his eyes and contemplated the eternity to come in the bleakness of hell, and how he would probably never again see a snowflake or a Fudgsicle. But then he thought of the nice meal he'd just had, and his new friends, and decided that snowflakes and Fudgsicles weren't that great anyway. He thought how the upcoming eternity might not be so bad after all. There was a knock at the door, and the snake entered.

"The Devil asked me to give you your assignment," the snake said. "Sometimes he gets powerful headaches. He wants you to be there to open the Aspirin bottle."

"I think I could do that," the inventor replied.

"Just so you know, he likes a fresh Aspirin every time, so you'll have to remove the tamper-resistant collar, the childproof cap and the aluminum seal," said the snake.

The inventor breathed easily. "No problem."

"Good," the snake said, and turned to go.

Just then a shudder rippled through the inventor's body. "Say"—his voice quavered with nervousness—"who will remove the cotton wad from inside the bottle?"

The snake turned slowly, its face contorted into the mask of Beelzebub. Then its voice deepened and transformed itself, as though it were coming from the bowels of hell:

"Why, you will," he said. "Ha, ha, ha, ha, ha!" ▲

"Bobby was caught imposing his values on another student."

The auto auction I attended was selling cars to benefit charity. Vehicles were classified as either "Running" or "No Start." On the block was a No Starter.

It had a shattered windshield, two missing tires, a sagging front bumper, a cockeyed grille, a hood that was sprung up at an angle, and dings and dents all over the body.

Before he started the bidding, the auctioneer announced the car's year, make and model, and then read the owner's comments: "Please note—the radio does not work."

— CHICK MANSUR

Our flight was about to take off when the passenger behind me immediately launched into a loud and annoying conference call on his cellphone. "Sally, get the customer lists. Charlie, pull all the data together we have on… Bob, can you bring us up to date…" and on and on.

As the flight attendant began the preflight safety instructions, the executive's voice was drowned out by the PA system. While the safety speech continued, I heard him mutter into the phone, "Hold on a second. Some people just like to hear themselves talk."

— G. BORMAN

I recently bought a new car that had a faulty light. When, after five visits to the dealer's shop, they were unable to fix it, I tried to get it replaced by threatening to use my province's lemon laws. My calls and letters to the dealer got me nowhere.

I went to a florist, ordered a fruit basket filled with lemons and sent it to the dealer with this poem:

"When I drive my lemon, I'll be thinking of you.

Pretty soon, my attorney will too."

A short time later the dealer called and asked what colour I'd like my new car to be.

— JOHN T. CARROLL

Friends and I were chatting over dinner in a restaurant. A man at the next table told his cellphone caller to hold on. Then he stepped outside to talk.

When he returned, I said, "That was very thoughtful."

"I had no choice," he said to me. "You were making too much noise."

— NORM BLUMENTHAL

After we got broadband Internet, my husband decided to start paying bills online. This worked great; in fact all our bill companies accepted online payments except one—our Internet service provider.

— SARAH LIBERA

I dialed a wrong number and got the following recording: "I am not available right now, but I thank you for caring enough to call. I am making some changes in my life. Please leave a message after the beep. If I do not return your call, you are one of the changes."

— ANTONIO CURTIS

"This tooth will be difficult to remove," the dentist told his patient. "I think you should have an anaesthetic even though it will be a little more expensive." "OK," agreed the patient and began feeling in his pocket for his money. "You needn't pay me yet," said the dentist. "I know," replied the patient. "I'm just counting my money before you put me under."

Security and peace of mind were part of the reason we moved to a gated community. Both flew out the window the night I called a local pizza shop for a delivery. "I'd like to order a large pepperoni, please," I said, then gave him the address of our condominium. "We'll be there in about half an hour," the kid at the other end replied. "Your gate code is still 1238, right?"

— MARY McCUSKER

My mother, a master of guilt trips, showed me a photo of herself waiting by a phone that never rings.

"Mom, I call all the time," I said. "If you had an answering machine, you'd know." Soon after, my brother installed one for her.

When I called the next time, I got her machine: "If you are a salesperson, press one. If you're a friend, press two. If you're my daughter who never calls, press 911 because the shock will probably give me a heart attack."

— SUSAN STARACE BALDUCCI

I realized the impact of computers on my young son one evening when there was a dramatic sunset. Pointing to the western sky, David said, "I wish we could click and save that."

— THERESA KLEIN

Timeless Humour from the '60s

Faculty members at a university were urged to become familiar with the time-saving machines of the brand-new computer centre. Basic courses in their use were given, and research projects were accelerated.

The faculty was enthusiastic—except for one veteran professor. Not only did he flunk the primer course, but on his first project, when he asked the machine simply to separate the names of students by sex, the cards came out in three stacks.

— AMOS MELTON

"I've got to take this call."

My friend always waits until the needle is on empty before filling his gas tank. Finally his car died on him, and we had to push it to the nearest station. After my friend finished pumping gas, the attendant asked if he had learned anything.

"Yeah," my friend muttered, "I learned I have a 50-litre tank."

— EDWARD HYATT

I couldn't decide whether to go to Montreal or Toronto for vacation, so I called the airlines to get prices. "Airfare to Toronto is $300," the cheery salesperson replied.

"And what about Montreal?"

"We have a really great rate to Montreal—$99," she said "But there is a stopover."

"Where?"

"In Toronto," she said.

— CHRIS LEWIS

At the end of her first year at Okanagan University College in Kelowna, B.C., my daughter, Kerrie, decided to stay in town for the summer to work. She moved in with a roommate and a week later she called home. "Mom, I just wanted to apologize," she said. "Apologize for what?" I asked. "For all those times I said to you, 'I'll do it later.'"

— ROBERTA ELCHUK

As an engineer in an upscale hotel, I was asked to repair or replace the television in a guest room. When I arrived, the couple was watching a picture one-third the size of the screen. I knew all our spare sets were in use, so I figured what the heck: I struck the side of the TV with the heel of my hand. The picture returned to full size.

"Look, honey," said the wife to her husband. "He went to the same repair school as you."

— WILLIAM W. OLLER

I was with a friend in a café when a noisy car alarm interrupted our conversation. "What good are car alarms when no one pays any attention to them?" I wondered aloud.

"Some are quite effective," my friend corrected me. "Last summer, my teenager spent a lot of time at the neighbours'. Whenever I wanted him home, I'd go out to our driveway and jostle his car."

— SHEILA MOORE

My husband, a computer-systems troubleshooter, rode with me in my new car one afternoon. He had been working on a customer's computer all morning and was still tense from the session. When I stopped for a traffic light, I made sure to leave a safe distance from the stop line to keep oncoming drivers from hitting the car.

I couldn't help but laugh when my husband impatiently waved at me to move the car forward while saying, "Scroll up, honey."

— GEORGIA M. HARVEY

My wife was in her gynecologist's busy waiting room when a cellphone rang. A woman answered it, and for the next few minutes, she explained to her caller in intimate detail her symptoms and what she suspected might be wrong.

Suddenly the conversation shifted, and the woman said, "Him? That's over." Then she added, "Can we talk about this later? It's rather personal, and I'm in a room full of people."

— ALAN ROBERTS

Opening the box containing my new portable television, I removed the remote and turned it over to install the batteries. Moulded into the device was this message:

"Made in Indonesia— Not Dishwasher Safe."

— MARVIN WIER

I'm Toast

► BY DAVE BARRY

Recently the Washington Post printed an article explaining how the appliance manufacturers plan to drive consumers insane.

Of course they don't SAY they want to drive us insane. What they SAY they want to do is have us live in homes where "all appliances are on the Internet, sharing information" and appliances will be "smarter than most of their owners." For example, the article states, you would have a home where the dishwasher "can be turned on from the office," the refrigerator "knows when it's out of milk," and the bathroom scale "transmits your weight to the gym."

I frankly wonder whether the appliance manufacturers, with all due respect, have been smoking crack. I mean, did they ever stop to ask themselves WHY a consumer, after loading a dishwasher, would go to the office to start it? Would there be some kind of career benefit?

YOUR BOSS: "What are you doing?"

YOU (tapping computer keyboard): "I'm starting my dishwasher!"

YOUR BOSS: "That's the kind of productivity we need around here!"

YOU: "Now I'm flushing the upstairs toilet!"

Listen, appliance manufacturers: We don't NEED a dishwasher that we can communicate with from afar. If you want to improve our dishwashers, give us one that senses when people leave dirty dishes on the kitchen counter and shouts, "Put those dishes in the dishwasher right now or I'll leak all over your shoes!"

Likewise, we don't need a refrigerator that knows when it's out of milk. We already have a foolproof system for determining if we're out of milk: we ask our wife. What we could use is a refrigerator that refuses to let us open its door when it senses that we are about to consume our fourth pudding snack in two hours.

As for a scale that transmits our weight to the gym: Are they NUTS? We don't want our weight transmitted to our own EYEBALLS! What if the gym transmitted our weight to all these other appliances on the Internet? What if, God forbid, our refrigerator found out our weight? We'd never get the door open again!

But here is what really concerns me about these new "smart" appliances: Even if we like the features, we won't be able to use them. We can't use the appliance features we have NOW. I have a feature-packed telephone with 43 buttons, at least 20 of which I am afraid to touch.

In this battle of wits with kitchen appliances…

This phone probably can communicate with the dead, but I don't know how to operate it, just as I don't know how to operate my TV, which has features out the wazooty and requires THREE remote controls. One control (44 buttons) came with the TV; a second (39 buttons) came with the VCR; the third (37 buttons) was brought here by the cable-TV man, who apparently felt that I did not have enough buttons.

So when I want to watch TV, I'm confronted with a total of 120 buttons, identified by such helpful labels as PIP, MTS, DBS and JUMP. There are three buttons labelled POWER, but there are times—especially if my son and his friends, who are not afraid of features, have changed the settings—when I cannot figure out how to turn the TV on. I stand there, holding three remote controls, pressing buttons at random, until eventually I give up and go turn on the dishwasher. It has been, literally, years since I have successfully recorded a TV show. That is how "smart" my appliances have become.

And now the appliance manufacturers want to give us MORE features. Do you know what this means? It means that some night you'll open your "smart" refrigerator, looking for a beer, and you'll hear a cheerful recorded voice—the same woman who informs you that Your Call Is Important when you phone a business that does not wish to speak with you personally—telling you, "Your celery is limp." You will not know how your refrigerator knows this, and, what is worse, you will not know who else your refrigerator is telling about it.

But if you want to make the refrigerator stop, you'll have to decipher an owner's manual written by nuclear physicists. ("To disable the Produce Crispness Monitoring feature, enter the Command mode, then select the Edit function, then select Change Vegetable Defaults, then assume that Train A leaves Chicago travelling westbound at 47 m.p.h., while Train B…")

Is this the kind of future you want, consumers? Do you want appliances that are smarter than you? Of course not.

Your appliances should be DUMBER than you, just like your furniture, your pets and your representatives in government. So I am urging you to let the appliance industry know that when it comes to "smart" appliances, you vote NO. You need to act quickly. Because while you're reading this, your microwave oven is voting YES. ▲

Hee-Hee! Ha! He Hee! Ho! Ha

Jesus and Satan were arguing over who was better with computers. Finally God suggested they settle it: Each would spend two hours using spreadsheets, designing web pages, making charts and tables—everything they knew how to do.

The two sat down at their keyboards and began typing furiously. Just before the two hours were up, a thunderstorm knocked the power out. Once it came back on, they booted up their computers.

"It's gone! It's all gone!" Satan began to scream. "My work was destroyed!"

Meanwhile, Jesus began quietly printing out his work. "Hey, he must have cheated!" Satan yelled. "How come his stuff wasn't lost?"

God shrugged and said simply, "Jesus saves."

— LAURA MASON

Shortly after I had my car repaired, the mechanic who fixed it asked me to bring it back. I watched as he opened the hood and removed a tool he had left behind. In a conspiratorial voice I said, "If you were a surgeon, I'd sue for malpractice."

"Yeah, but if I was a surgeon," he replied, "I'd charge you for having to go back in."

— JEANIE LOVELADY

I'll need to see your licence and registration, "says the policeman after stopping a middle-aged couple. "You were speeding."

"But officer," says the husband, "I was under the speed limit."

"Sir, I measured your speed and you were going too fast."

"I was not speeding!" insists the man. "Your radar gun must be broken."

At this point, the wife leans over. "It's no use arguing with him, officer," she says apologetically. "He always gets this stubborn when he's been drinking."

— LISA MALLETTE

My family has a tradition of naming the cruise control on our cars. We were used to hearing my father proclaim, "Take it, Max," as he flipped on the cruise control during long trips in our station wagon.

Recently, I was travelling with my parents in their new car when we hit a wide-open expanse of highway. My dad leaned back and said, "I think I'll let Tom drive for a while."

"Tom who?" I asked.

My mother translated for me: "Tom Cruise, of course."

— DANA MARGULIES

After shopping at a busy store, another woman and I happened to leave at the same time, only to be faced with the daunting task of finding our cars in the crowded parking lot. Just then my car horn beeped, and I was able to locate my vehicle easily.

"Wow," the woman said. "I sure could use a gadget like that to help me find my car."

"Actually," I replied, "that's my husband."

— KATHY BEHRENBRINKER

My 50-something friend Nancy and I decided to introduce her mother to the magic of the Internet. Our first move was to access the popular "Ask Jeeves" site, and we told her it could answer any question she had.

Nancy's mother was very skeptical until Nancy said, "It's true, Mom. Think of something to ask it."

As I sat with fingers poised over the keyboard, Nancy's mother thought a minute, then responded, "How is Aunt Helen feeling?"

— CATHERINE BURNS

The speaker at my bank's drive-through window had been broken for weeks, and we tellers had to resort to miming or writing notes to communicate with our frustrated customers. One day a sweet elderly lady whom I would see every week pulled up to the window, leaned out of her car and smacked the glass in front of my face.

"Hope this is bulletproof," she yelled.

There had just been a robbery at another bank nearby, so I was touched by her concern. "It is," I yelled back.

"Good," she continued, "because someone is going to shoot you if you don't get that speaker fixed."

— SARAH BANAKOWSKI

Timeless Humour from the '60s

Students at one university proved once and for all that the computer just can't replace human calculations. They held an "IBM mixer" dance, where each student fed his vital statistics and interests into a computer and was then paired off with a member of the opposite sex who, the computer said, was most suited to him.

Imagine the chagrin of one coed who ended up with her twin brother.

— JIM CHAMPION

"I've figured out how to send emails and faxes, take photos, play games, and film videos, but what I'd really like to do is make a phone call."

My sister Darlene has the courage—but not always the skills—to tackle any home-repair project. For example, in her garage are pieces of a lawn mower she once tried to fix. So I wasn't surprised the day my other sister, Jesse, and I found Darlene attacking her vacuum cleaner with a screwdriver.

"I can't get this thing to cooperate," she explained.

"Why don't you drag it out to the garage and show it the lawn mower?" Jesse suggested.

— JUDEE NORTON

After our parents retired, they moved from a busy city in Alberta to a small town in British Columbia. We didn't realize how small the town was until my sister visited the local video store. She selected a movie and told the clerk that she was going to rent the cassette under her parents' name.

The clerk looked at the title and replied, "They already saw that one."

— THERESA COUTCHER SOKOLOWSKI

Bill Gates and the president of General Motors were having lunch. Gates boasted of the innovations his company had made. "If GM had kept up with technology the way Microsoft has, we'd all be driving $25 cars that get 1,000 m.p.g."

"I suppose that's true," the GM exec agreed. "But would you really want your car to crash twice a day?"

My husband works for a high-tech company that uses a sophisticated robotic mail-delivery system. The robot makes mail stops by following a clear painted line on the hallway floor. Recently the line had to be recharged by applying special paint. While it was drying, signs were posted warning, "Please don't step on the invisible line."

— JOELLEN BADIK

The computer in my high school classroom recently started acting up. After watching me struggle with it, one of my students took over. "Your hard drive crashed," he said.

I called the computer services office and explained, "My computer is down. The hard drive crashed."

"We can't just send people

"That sounds expensive. Is there any way you could ship it without handling it?"

down on your say-so. How do you know that's the problem?"

"A student told me," I answered.

"We'll send someone over right away."

— ROLF EKLUND

My wife and I get along just great—except she's a backseat driver second to none. On my way home from work one day, my cellphone rang as I merged onto a freeway bypass. It was my wife. By chance, she had entered the bypass right behind me.

"Honey," she said, "your turn signal is still on. And put your lights on—it's starting to rain."

— WAYNE RAY HAIRSTON

Heard on my cable company's answering machine: "**We realize you are still holding. Please do not hang up, as this will further delay your call.**"

— EDGAR NENTWIG

A helicopter was flying toward the airport when an electrical malfunction disabled all of the aircraft's navigation and communications equipment. Due to the extreme haze that day, the pilot now had no way of determining the course to the airport. All he could make out was a tall building nearby, so he moved closer to it, quickly wrote out a large sign reading "Where am I?" and held it in the chopper's window.

Responding quickly, the people in the building penned a large sign of their own. It read: "You are in a helicopter."

The pilot smiled, and within minutes he landed safely at the airport. After they were on the ground, the co-pilot asked how the sign helped him determine their position.

"I knew it had to be the Microsoft building," the pilot replied, "because like any computer company's help staff, they gave me a technically correct but completely useless answer."

— LINDA A. TOZER

To keep their active two-year-old from roaming onto the busy street in front of their home, my sister and brother-in-law decided to put a gate across the driveway. After working over two weekends on the project, Robert was ready to attach the lock to complete the job. He was working on the yard side of the gate, with his daughter nearby, when he dropped the screwdriver he was using and it rolled under the gate, out of his reach.

"I'll get it, Daddy," Lauren called, nimbly crawling under the newly erected barrier.

— JANICE DECOSTE

Our office building's only elevator was acting up. When I rode it to the lobby on my way to lunch, the door refused to open. Trying not to panic, I hit the emergency button, which triggers an automatic call to the repair service.

Through the speaker in the elevator, I heard the call going through and then a recorded announcement: "The area code of the number you dialed has been changed. The new area code is 450. Please hang up and dial again."

— DIANE MASTRANTONIO

Do We Really Need These?

▶ BY SCOTT FESCHUK

The old saying has it that a fool and his money are soon parted. As modern consumers, we keep that adage alive by repeatedly proving its accuracy.

Day upon day, year after year, we buy more and more stuff—stuff we want, but usually don't need. Having bought all this stuff, we then buy magazines that tell us which stuff to buy to keep all our other stuff organized. If your house is anything like mine, you have enough "storage solutions" from IKEA to qualify for Swedish citizenship.

This circle of strife could never endure without the tireless efforts of entrepreneurs who dedicate their lives to coming up with more useless products for us to buy, use once or twice and then retire to the Great Product Graveyard in the basement.

Let's take a tour of just a sampling of the stupid products—real, actual products—available today.

Pop quiz: While sitting at a computer, have you ever felt the urge to pee? Sure you have! In darker times, before the dawn of the age of the Internet Urinal, you probably responded by doing something crazy such as—oh, I don't know—getting up and going to the bathroom. Welcome to the future! The Internet Urinal is a plastic device into which you can relieve yourself without getting up. Its target market includes enthusiasts of video games, traders on the stock market and, one assumes, people who like to keep their urine in a plastic container.

The Amazin' Beer Chiller is a battery-operated machine into which you pour water and ice and insert a beer can. The can spins quickly, forcing all the liquid into contact with the surface of the can, chilling the contents in minutes. You don't need a cooler. You don't need electricity. Heck, judging from its name, you don't even need the letter *g*. What you do need, however, is a can of beer. And you must need it badly, because if you didn't, you'd put the freaking beer in the fridge and wait 45 minutes like the rest of us.

The basic premise of the propane-fuelled Weed Torch is that the most effective and efficient way to rid your flower beds of small, pesky weeds is to burn them to death wielding the backyard equivalent of a flame-thrower. This may strike some people as overkill. Then again, after enduring sore knees and bad backs in pursuit of tended soil, avid gardeners may well enjoy the novelty of incinerating their feet.

Even as we constantly expand the frontier of human knowledge, there remains so much that we don't know. For instance, despite subscribing to no fewer than three daily newspapers and several news-magazines, I was completely unaware of the growing and senseless tragedy of chronic food squishing.

Apparently, there is a pandemic of squishing, squashing and otherwise flattening of fruit and snack food. How else to explain the invention of the Cup-A-Cake, a gadget that will hold and protect a frosted

The following products are available right now, today! And people who are usually smart are buying them.

cupcake even if it's "bounced (or) jiggled"—perfect when taking your lunch to the Playboy Mansion—and the Banana Bunker, which heroically vows to "keep your fruit safe," so long as it is shaped like a banana.

Speaking of food-related inventions, what kid hasn't experienced the joy of finding the perfect stick to use for toasting marshmallows over the campfire until they're a golden, gooey brown? I'll tell you what kid: the kid of the person who would go out and spend real money to buy the Electric Marshmallow Toaster.

Let's take a moment to compare the two implements. The Electric Marshmallow Toaster is best described as "an automatic, hand-held rotisserie." The stick is best described as a stick. The Electric Marshmallow Toaster features a "sure-grip, heat-shielded, ergonomic handle." The stick features bark.

The same website also offers a Smores Maker. "Nothing brings back childhood memories," declares the website, "like the great taste of s'mores— those fun-to-make campfire creations." Well, guess what? Now they don't have to be fun to make! Now, after toasting your marshmallows on your Electric Marshmallow Toaster, you can make use of the Smores Maker's "central roaster with durable stainless steel grilling surface." Doesn't that sound like a blast? Parents, this is a great product to rob your children of all the joys in life. When the moment is just right, break the news about Santa Claus, too.

Even with all this technology employed in the service of toasting and roasting, you still need to go out and buy the marshmallows at the supermarket—the perfect opportunity to use the Clean Shopper, a cotton liner designed to protect your child by covering the seating area of a shopping cart. Why? Because carts are covered with germs, says the website. You know what else is covered with germs? Children!

The Tan-Timer Bikini is a two-piece swimsuit to which is attached an electronic device that beeps every 15 minutes. This serves as a signal to the wearer: Hey! Turn over now to avoid being burned by the sun! It also serves as a signal to people nearby: Hey! This babe in the bikini is a complete loser!

Despite the evidence presented so far, it's actually not that easy to come up with a truly stupid product. Many strive for stupidity but achieve only pointlessness. The stupidest stupid products fill a niche that we didn't know existed, usually because it shouldn't. Enter the Good Bites Crustless Sandwich Cutter, a gizmo that "removes the crusts, seals the edges and slices a sandwich." It does this all in one motion, freeing you to perform other motions, like the repeated slapping of your forehead with an open palm in memory of your decision to spend $5.95 on a stupid cutter. I'm not sure if this product has a slogan, but I propose: "The Good Bites Crustless Sandwich Cutter: Just in Case You've Forgotten That Knives Exist!" ▲

Over the years I have heard my share of strange questions and silly comments from people who call the computer software company where I work as a tech support telephone operator. But one day I realized how absurd things can sound on the other end of the line when I heard myself say to one caller, "Yes, sir, you must first upgrade your download software in order to download our upgrade software."

— CARLOS MEJIA

As a promotional gimmick for my restaurant, I send out coupons offering people a free dinner on their birthdays. One day an anxious-sounding man called. "I got your card. How did you find me?"

"From a mailing list I purchased from a supplier," I told him. "Why?"

"It used my real name, and I'm in the Witness Protection Program. What's the name of the company?"

I didn't want to say it, but I had to tell him the truth: Moving Targets.

— ROY HARRINGTON

I was delighted to discover that I could play compact discs in the new computer my company had given me. One morning I was enjoying one of my favourite

My wife's car horn began to beep in cold weather and would only stop when she disconnected it. So she disabled the horn and drove to the dealership, whose garage had its door shut to keep out the cold. Outside was a sign: "Honk horn for service."

Jeff Romanczuk

CELLULAR PHONE BOOTH

MUELLER

Beethoven pieces when an administrative assistant stopped by to deliver a stack of papers.

Hearing classical music filling the air, she stopped and exclaimed, "Poor you. They put you on hold?"

— KEITH BRINTON

I thought I had finally found a way to convince Susan, my continually harried friend, that she needed to find ways to relax. I invited her to dinner and, while I was busy cooking, she agreed to watch my videotape on stress management and relaxation techniques. Fifteen minutes later, she came into the kitchen and handed me the tape.

"But it's a 70-minute video," I replied. "You couldn't have watched the whole thing."

"Yes, I did," Susan assured me. "I put it on fast-forward."

— JEAN KELLY

A co-worker asked if I knew what to do about a computer problem that was preventing her from getting email. After calling the help desk, I told my colleague that email was being delayed to check for a computer virus.

"It's a variant of the I Love You virus, only worse," I said.

"What could be worse?" my single co-worker asked wryly. "The Let's Just Be Friends virus?"

— ARTHUR J. ORCHEL

Roomba's Revenge

▶ BY MARY ROACH

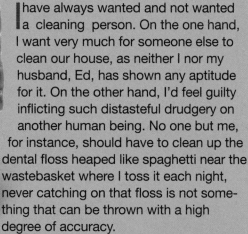

I have always wanted and not wanted a cleaning person. On the one hand, I want very much for someone else to clean our house, as neither I nor my husband, Ed, has shown any aptitude for it. On the other hand, I'd feel guilty inflicting such distasteful drudgery on another human being. No one but me, for instance, should have to clean up the dental floss heaped like spaghetti near the wastebasket where I toss it each night, never catching on that floss is not something that can be thrown with a high degree of accuracy.

You can imagine my joy upon reading that the iRobot company has invented a robotic vacuum. They call it Roomba. Their website plays an animated clip of what appears to be an enlarged CD Walkman scooting across a living room carpet, sucking up conspicuous chunks of unidentified detritus. Meanwhile, sentences run across the screen: "I'm having lunch with a friend"..."I'm planting flowers in the garden." The point is that you can go out and "enjoy life" while your robot cleans up the conspicuous chunks strewn about your living room floor, no doubt rubble tracked in from the garden plot.

Roomba joined our family last week. Right away I changed the name to Reba, in order to indulge my fantasy of having a real cleaning person, yet still respect its incredibly dumb-sounding given name. As techno-gadgets go, the iRobot vacuum is surprisingly simple to use. All you do, beyond switching it on, is tell it the room size. This I calculated in my usual manner, by picturing six-foot guys lying end-to-end along the walls and multiplying accordingly.

I started Reba off in the bedroom. I was on my way out the door to enjoy life, when I heard a crash. My vacuuming robot had tangled itself up in the telephone cord and then headed off in the other direction, pulling the phone off the nightstand and onto the floor. "Maybe Reba needs to make a call," said Ed.

I couldn't, in all fairness, be annoyed, as I'm the sort of person who gets up to go to the bathroom on airplanes without first unplugging my headphones. Only the fact that my head is attached to my neck prevents it from being yanked off onto the floor. Also, it tells you right there in the Owner's Manual to "pick up objects like clothing, loose papers...power cords...just as you would before using a regular vacuum cleaner."

This poses something of a problem in our house. The corners and the floor space along the walls and under the furniture in the office, for instance, are filled with stacks and bags of what I call Ed's desk

Battle over the dental floss

runoff. My husband is a man who does not easily throw things away. Whatever he gets in the mail or empties from his pockets he simply deposits on the nearest horizontal surface.

Once a week, like the neighbourhood garbage truck, I collect Ed's discards and throw them onto a vast, heaping landfill located on his desk. At a certain point, determined by the angle of the slope and the savagery of my throws, the pile will begin to slide. This is Ed's cue to shovel a portion of it into a shopping bag, which he then puts on the floor somewhere with the intent to go through it later, later here meaning "never."

I looked at the floor in our office. There were newspapers, piles of files, socks, pens, not to mention the big guys lying along the floorboards. Picking it all up to clear the way for Reba would take half an hour, which is more time than I normally spend vacuuming. It was the same sort of situation that has kept me from ever hiring an assistant.

It would take longer to explain my filing system to someone else ("Okay, takeout menus and important contracts go in the orange folder labelled 'Bees'...") than it would to do the chore myself.

The bathroom promised to be less problematic. I lifted the hamper into the tub and put the bathroom scale in the sink, where it looked as though maybe it wanted a bath, or maybe it had a date with a vacuum cleaner.

Then I went into the bedroom to fetch Reba, who was at that moment engaged in a shoving match with one of my

Birkenstocks. She had pushed the shoe across the room and under the bed, well into the zone of no-reach.

"Good one," said Ed, who has always harboured ill will toward comfort footwear for women.

I set Reba down and aimed her at the crud-paved crawl space beneath the footed bathtub. I have tried this with Ed and various of my stepdaughters, but it always fails to produce the desired effect.

The wondrous Reba was not only willing but actually enthusiastic about the prospect, motoring full bore across the tile and under the tub and whacking her forehead on the far wall. You just can't find help like that.

The living room was a similar success. Reba does housework much the way I do, busily cleaning in one spot for a while and then wandering off inexplicably in the opposite direction and getting distracted by something else that needs doing. The iRobot people call this an "algorithm-based cleaning pattern," a term I will use the next time Ed catches me polishing silver with the mop water evaporating in the other room.

Halfway across the living room carpet, Reba stopped moving and began emitting undelighted noises. Ed leafed through the troubleshooting guide.

"It's a Whimper Beep," he said, employing the concerned baritone that used to announce the Heartbreak of Psoriasis as though it were the Cuban Missile Crisis. I turned Reba over. Wound around her brushes was a two-foot strand of dental floss. Apparently even robots have their limits. ▲

Our family took shelter in the basement after hearing a tornado warning. My husband told everyone to stay put while he got his cellphone out of the car, in case the lines went dead.

He didn't return for the longest time, so I went looking for him. I was upstairs calling his name, when I heard our answering machine click on.

"Hi," a voice said. "This is Dad. I'm locked out of the house."

— LAURE JORGES

During the mortgage closing on our summer house, my wife and I were asked to sign documents containing small print. When I asked if I should read it, my attorney replied, "Legally, you should. But here's the bottom line: If you pay your installments on time, there is nothing in there that could harm you. Should you stop paying, however, there is definitely nothing in the small print that can save you."

— MILLORAD DEVIAK

My five children and I were playing hide-and-seek one evening. With the lights turned off in the house, the kids scattered to hide, and I was "it." After a few minutes I located all of them. When it was my turn to hide, they searched high and low but could not find me.

Finally one of my sons got a bright idea. He went to the phone and dialed; they found me immediately because my pager started beeping.

— LELAND JENSEN

Timeless Humour from the '70s

A solar-powered computer wristwatch, which is programmed to tell the time and date for 125 years, has a guarantee—for two years.

An IBM exhibit portrayed the advancement in technology of statistical and calculating machines from the abacus to the computer. After completing the tour, I stopped at the reception desk to ask a question. There, a distinguished elderly gentleman was keeping track of the number of visitors in the old tried-and-true method of drawing ~~THI THI~~ on a sheet of paper.

— EMIL L. BIRNBAUM

DID I LEAVE THE IRON ON?

All in a Day's Work

You put a bunch of adults together and tell them to get something meaningful accomplished, and for some reason, it often turns out pretty funny.

"We're considering outsourcing your job. Could you explain to this guy in Guatemala whatever it is you do around here?"

As an airline reservation agent, I took a call from a man who wanted to book a flight for two but wasn't happy with the price of $59 per ticket. "I want the $49 fare I saw advertised," he insisted, saying he would accept a flight at any time. I managed to find two seats on a 6 a.m. flight. "I'll take it," he said, then worried his wife might not like the early hour. I warned there was a $25 fee per person if he changed the reservation. "Oh, that's no problem," he said dismissively. "What's fifty bucks?"

— ANNA ZOGG

I hate the idea of going under the knife. So I was very upset when the doctor told me I needed a tonsillectomy. Later, the nurse and I were filling out an admission form. I tried to respond to the questions, but I was so nervous I couldn't speak. The nurse put down the form, took my hands in hers and said, "Don't worry. This medical problem can easily be fixed, and it's not a dangerous procedure."

"You're right. I'm being silly," I said, feeling relieved. "Please continue."

"Good. Now," the nurse went on, "do you have a living will?"

— EDWARD LEE GRIFFIN

The generation gap proved glaringly obvious at the mail-order music company where my wife works as a customer service representative. Some college students, who were working part-time inputting customer information, wrote the following notes regarding some golden oldies: "Customer is looking for two song titles: 'Shovel Off Two Buffaloes' and 'Honey, Suck a Rose.' "

— JOHN CASARES

Pulling into my service station 45 minutes late one morning, I shouted to the customers, "I'll turn the pumps on right away!" What I didn't know was that the night crew had left them on all night. By the time I got to the office, most of the cars had filled up and driven off. Only one customer stayed to pay. My heart sank. Then the customer pulled a wad of cash from his pocket and handed it to me.

"We kept passing the money to the last guy," he said. "We figured you'd get here sooner or later."

— JIM NOVAK

My fellow teacher called for help—she needed someone who knew about animals. As a science teacher, I filled the bill. "Oh," she added, "bring a net." Expecting to find some kind of beast as I entered her classroom, I was greeted instead by the sight of excited kids watching a hummingbird fly around. Rather than use the net, I suggested they hang red paper by an open door. The bird would be drawn to it, I explained, and eventually fly out. Later, the teacher called back. The trick worked. "Now," she said, "we have two hummingbirds flying around the room."

— RAY POELLET

Most people would be angry if their company was bought and the new owners replaced them with their own people. Not our neighbour Andy. "You know how it goes," he said, waxing philosophical. "Every circus brings its own clowns."

— CHRIS GULLEN

sign language

Noted at the bottom of a receipt for funeral arrangements:
"Thank you. Please come again."

— CARMELA A. HENRIQUEZ

Everyone at the company I worked for dressed up for Halloween. One fellow's costume stumped us. He simply wore slacks and a white T-shirt with a large 98.6 printed across the front in glitter. When someone finally asked what he was supposed to be, he replied, "I'm a temp."

— BRIAN DAVIS

I'm dyslexic, and attended a conference about the disorder with a friend. The speakers asked us to share a personal experience with the group. I told them stress aggravates my condition, in which I reverse words and letters when I'm tense. When I finished speaking, my friend leaned over and whispered to me, "Now I know why you named your daughter Hannah."

— CHARLES JEHLEN

My husband and I are both in an Internet business, but he's the one who truly lives, eats and breathes computers. I finally realized how bad it had gotten when I was scratching his back one day. "No, not there," he directed. "Scroll down."

— CHRISTINE AYMAN

I was on duty as an emergency-room technician when a father brought in his son, who had poked a tire from one of his toy trucks up his nose. The man was embarrassed, but I assured him this was something kids often do. I quickly removed the tire and they were on their way. A few minutes later, the father was back in the ER asking to talk to me in private.

Mystified, I led him to an examining room. "While we were on our way home," he began, "I was looking at that little tire and wondering, how on earth did my son get this thing stuck up his nose and…"

It took just a few seconds to get the tire out of Dad's nose.

— LEAH BEACK

Bad weather meant I was stuck overnight at Pearson International Airport. Along with hotel accommodations, the airline issued each passenger a $10 meal ticket, or "chit." That evening after dinner I presented my meal ticket to the cashier.

"Is this chit worth $10?" I asked.

Looking up nervously, the cashier responded, "I'm sorry, sir. Was the meal that bad?"

— HARRY ANDREWS

Working as a secretary at an international airport, my sister had an office adjacent to the room where security temporarily holds suspects. One day, security officers were questioning a man when they were suddenly called away on another emergency. To the horror of my sister and her colleagues, the man was left alone in the unlocked room. After a few minutes, the door opened and he began to walk out.

Summoning up her courage, one of the secretaries barked, "Get back in there, and don't you come out until you're told!" The man scuttled back inside and slammed the door. When the security people returned, the women reported what had happened. Without a word, an officer walked into the room and released one very frightened telephone repairman.

— RUSS PERMAN

Touring Ireland's countryside with a group of travel writers, we passed an immaculate cemetery with hundreds of beautiful headstones set in a field of emerald green grass. Everyone reached for their cameras when the tour guide said the inventor of the crossword puzzle was buried there. He pointed out the location, "Three down and four across."

— STEVE BAUER

One of my friends, a musician, is always upbeat. Nothing gets her down. But when she developed ringing in one ear, I was concerned it might overwhelm even her. When I asked if her condition was especially annoying to a musician, she shook her head. "Not really," she said cheerfully. "The ringing sound is in the key of B flat, so I use it to tune my cello a half-tone lower."

— KATHLEEN CAHILL

The 104-year-old building that had served as the priory and primary student residence of the small Catholic university where I work was about to be demolished. As the wrecker's ball began to strike, I sensed the anxiety and sadness experienced by one of the older monks whose order had founded the college. "This must be difficult to watch, Father," I said. "The tradition associated with that building, the memories of all the students and monks who lived and worked there. I can't imagine how hard this must be for you."

"It's worse than that," the monk replied. "I think I left my Palm Pilot in there."

— P. J. BROZYNSKI

Timeless Humour from the '50s

When a fellow piano tuner was ill, I took over his assignment of tuning a piano in a girls' boarding house. While I was at work, several of the girls strolled casually through the room in various states of undress. The climax came when a young lady in startling deshabille appeared to pay the bill.

As I was writing the receipt, she suddenly gave me a bewildered look, then fled, screaming, "That's not our regular man!"

Their regular man is blind.

— ALEX BYRNES

Some of my co-workers and I decided to remove the small, wooden suggestion box from our office because it had received so few entries. We stuck the box on top of a seven-foot-high metal storage cabinet and then promptly forgot about it. Months later, when the box was moved during remodelling, we found a single slip of paper inside. The suggestion read, "Lower the box!"

— FRANK J. MONACO

"Ah, the arbitration team is here."

Each year our company holds a training session in the conference room of the same hotel. When we were told we would not be able to reserve our usual location, my secretary, Gail, spent many hours on the phone trying to work out alternative arrangements. Finally, when the details were ironed out, she burst into my office.

"Great news, Scott!" she announced. "We're getting our regular room at the hotel!"

All eyes were on Gail and me as she suddenly realized she had interrupted a meeting with co-workers.

— SCOTT DUINK

A friend and I used to run a small temporary-staffing service. Our agency did mandatory background checks on all job candidates, even though our application form asked them if they'd ever been convicted of a crime. One day after a round of interviews, my co-worker was entering information from a young man's application into the computer.

She called me over to show me that he had noted a previous conviction for second-degree manslaughter. Below that, on the line listing his skills, he had written, "Good with people."

— JANA RAHRIG

The company where I work provides four-foot-high cubicles so each employee can have some privacy. One day a co-worker had an exasperating phone conversation with one of her teenage sons. After hanging up, she heaved a sigh and said, "No one ever listens to me."

Immediately, several voices from surrounding cubicles called out, "Yes, we do."

Jo Jaimeson

Parents are justifiably upset when their children don't get into the college of their choice. As an admissions counsellor for a university, I took a call from an irate mother demanding to know why her daughter had been turned down. Avoiding any mention of the transcript full of D's, I explained that her daughter just wasn't as "competitive" as the admitted class. "Why doesn't she try another school for a year and then transfer?" I suggested.

"Another school!" exclaimed Mom. "Have you seen her grades?"

— SHALONDA DEGRAFFINRIED

I was working as a short-order cook at two restaurants in the same neighbourhood. One night, I was finishing up the dinner shift at one restaurant and hurrying to report to work at the second place. But I was delayed because one table kept sending back an order of hash browns, insisting they were too cold. I replaced them several times, but still the customers were dissatisfied.

When I was able to leave, I raced out the door and arrived at my second job. A server immediately handed me my first order. "Make sure these hash browns are hot," she said, "because these people just left a restaurant down the street that kept serving them cold ones."

— BILL BERGQUIST

"Thanks to wireless technology. I can hate my job almost anywhere."

Public Speaking? No Sweat!

▶ BY STEVE BURGESS

I have lived a long, full life. Most of it was spent one night at the Fairmont Château Whistler Hotel, giving a speech. It was really only a ten-minute talk, but from my perspective it lasted long enough to fill a three-volume biography. That's the worst part of dying onstage—death never actually arrives.

But don't worry. Just because you've reluctantly agreed to an upcoming public-speaking engagement—a wedding toast, perhaps—it's nothing to sweat about. The fact that I suffered like a woodpecker with a migraine doesn't mean you'll do the same. You'll do fine. I can help.

Public speaking can be tough. Apparently there was once a survey of people's greatest fears, in which public speaking ranked higher than death. An even more amazing statistic: 997 out of every 1,000 articles written about public speaking cite that very same survey. Was there ever such a survey? Who knows? Apparently, that oft-repeated story about how we use only ten percent of our brain turned out to be completely bogus. Actually, scientists now say, we use all of our brain. After getting off the stage that night at the Château Whistler, I used mine as a door knocker. Then I assumed the fetal position and whimpered myself to sleep.

The occasion was the Château's popular Christmas craft and home-décor workshops. Someone from the hotel had seen me emceeing an Awards show, crack-ing jokes, and figured I was just the ticket. I was asked to provide some of the after-dinner entertainment. No sweat—give or take six or seven pounds.

My material was suitably festive. I had prepared a Christmas gift-buying guide for people you dislike. There were props and everything. Giant rubber bugs, Pepto-Bismol, coal—oh, it was funny stuff. Killer.

Frankly I don't remember much after the landing craft hit the beach. A lot of noise, a lot of explosions. The noise was all the ladies eating dessert and chatting. The bombs were my jokes. No one could see the props, which was okay because they mostly weren't looking. Poor dears, they just wanted to enjoy their meals and chat with friends. I was like a drunk at a church social. With a microphone.

There is really nothing like standing on a stage, trying to make people laugh and failing miserably. A hundred years ago, Einstein's theory of relativity proved that in certain situations, time can slow. My own work merely confirmed his formulas.

Wedding toasts offer the advantage of a friendly and familiar audience. Long ago I was asked to give a toast to the bride. It was certainly an honour. Unfortunately, I hadn't known her that long. One thing I did know was that the groom was an undertaker. So I focused on that. "All of this must seem familiar to Kevin," I offered. "People saying, 'Look at Kevin— he's smiling. He looks so peaceful. I've never seen

Ha, Ha, Ha! Tee-Hee! Ho!

When toasting the bride, it's best to omit her former association with a biker gang!

him in a suit before…'" People seemed to like it. All except the woman I was supposed to be discussing, who must have wondered if I had missed the fine print on the "Toast to the Bride" contract.

Humour is your biggest trap. Everyone wants to be funny, and generally speaking, audiences appreciate a joke. It's the specifics that can get you in trouble.

Amusing stories about the bride/groom/guest of honour are fine—maybe. The groom's fit of nerves before proposing is cute. The best man's private prediction that the marriage won't last six months is not. Groom's cooking skills/laundry disasters—cute. Bride's former association with the Hell's Angels—not. It's a good idea to run your material past some friends or family members first. The practice helps, and their occasional looks of horror can provide important clues.

Profanity ought to be avoided, unless you know your audience particularly well. Every situation is different, of course—when speaking to a gathering of newspaper people, it might be a good idea to speak entirely in profanities. Knowing your audience is important. For a sports crowd, lots of talk about scoring and giving 110 percent. At a wedding, however, this could be misconstrued.

If possible, it's a good idea to tell jokes at your own expense—although not jokes that refer to your own case of nerves. Joking about your own nervousness makes the audience nervous for you, starting a deadly feedback loop. Project confidence. Your audience can smell fear, and they'll tear you apart like sharks in a feeding frenzy.

Actually, your audience wants you to succeed. If you're giving a wedding toast, odds are you are not even the most frightened person at the head table. At least one half of the happy couple will probably be in worse shape than you. And the other half will be drunk.

Which, by the way, you shouldn't be. Tempting as it might seem to take the edge off with a few martinis or a bottle of wine or a large hose attached to a keg of Guinness, resist. As a general rule, the less you remember about your speech, the more appallingly memorable it's likely to be. Legendary, even.

Try not to worry. Your time in the spotlight may loom large on your personal horizon, but most of your audience will forget about your big moment almost as soon as it ends.

And even if things go horribly wrong, it's not all bad. Look at me. I lost seven pounds. ▲

On duty as a customer-service representative for a car-rental company, I took a call from a driver who needed a tow. He was stranded on a busy highway, but he didn't know the make of the car he was driving. I asked again for a more detailed description, beyond "a nice blue four-door."

After a long pause, the driver replied, "My car is the one on fire."

— DAEMIEN O'KEEFFE

"We're going to have to let you go, but I'm confident that you'll land on your feet."

Ever wonder what medical personnel scribble on those clipboards attached to the foot of the bed? Here are some incredible comments taken from hospital charts:

"The patient refused autopsy."

"The patient has no previous history of suicides."

"She's had no rigours or shaking chills, but her husband states she was very hot in bed last night."

"She is numb from her toes down."

"Patient has two teenage children but no other abnormalities."

"Discharge status: Alive but without my permission."

— WILLIAM D. J. MURPHY

Hospital regulations require a wheelchair for patients being discharged. However, while working as a student nurse, I found one elderly gentleman already dressed and sitting on the bed with a suitcase at his feet—who insisted he didn't need my help to leave the hospital. After a chat about rules being rules, he reluctantly let me wheel him to the elevator.

On the way down I asked if his wife was meeting him. "I don't know," he said. "She's still upstairs in the bathroom changing out of her hospital gown."

— PATSY R. DANCEY

My father is a skilled CPA who is not great at self-promotion. So when an advertising salesman offered to put my father's business placard in the shopping carts of a supermarket, my dad jumped at the chance. Fully a year went by before we got a call that could be traced to those placards. "Richard Larson, CPA?" the caller asked.

"That's right," my father answered. "May I help you?"

"Yes," the voice said. "One of your shopping carts is in my yard and I want you to come and get it."

— MATTHEW LARSON

During a business trip to Boeing's Everett, Wash., factory, I noticed several 747 and 777 airliners being assembled. Before the engines were installed, huge weights were hung from the wings to keep the planes balanced. The solid-steel weights were bright yellow and marked "14,000 lbs." But what I found particularly interesting was some stencilling I discovered on the side of each weight. Imprinted there was the warning: "Remove before flight."

— KEVIN N. HAW

Anytime companies merge, employees worry about layoffs. When the company I work for was bought, I was no exception. My fears seemed justified when a photo of the newly merged staff appeared on the company's website with the following words underneath: "Updated daily."

— DIANNE STEVENS

A Catholic priest I once knew went to the hospital to visit patients. Stopping at the nurses station, he carefully looked over the patient roster and jotted down the room number of everyone who had "Cath" written boldly next to his name. That, he told me, was a big mistake.

When I asked why, he replied, "It was only after I had made the rounds that I learned they were all patients with catheters."

— DENNIS SMYTH

I was halfway through a meeting with a photocopy salesman, when he suddenly mentioned his wife and children, and how contented he was. I was puzzled, but let him continue. It was only when I glanced down that I understood his reason for imparting this personal information: The table leg against which I had been rubbing my itchy foot wasn't a table leg at all!

— EILEEN GASKIN

I'm a police officer and occasionally park my cruiser in residential areas to watch for speeders. One Sunday morning I was staked out in a driveway, when I saw a large dog trot up to my car. He stopped and sat just out of arm's reach. No matter how much I tried to coax him to come for a pat on the head, he refused to budge. After a while I decided to move to another location. I pulled out of the driveway, looked back and learned the reason for the dog's stubbornness. He quickly picked up the newspaper I had been parked on and dutifully ran back to his master.

— JEFF WALL

"Since my office went business casual, I've been having this identity crisis. I mean, am I still a suit?"

Don't Let
Email Become an
Ejail

▶ BY JOSH FREED

If you sit down at your computer in the morning and there are 35 new messages in your email, which of the following do you do?

A) Answer every message politely, including all your junk mail.

B) Erase them all, without reading any.

C) Turn off your computer and deal with it later.

If you answered C, you're a typical cyberspace junkie, caught between the lure of email and the horrors of ejail. Your complex feelings can be summed up in two sentences:

1: Email is great because it allows me to communicate instantly with friends and acquaintances anywhere, anytime.

2: Email is awful because it allows me to communicate instantly with friends and acquaintances anywhere, anytime.

Email has become so much of a good thing it's overwhelming us. It's more addictive than chocolate and spreads faster than the flu. In the last year, my mailbox and my telephone messages are drying up as email becomes my only link with the outside world. That's how I get all my personal letters, work notes, jokes, junk mail, party invites, film and gallery invitations and 200-page manuscripts people want me to "browse."

Lately, I'm even getting birth, death and wedding announcements by email. How long before you'll be able to split up with your spouse by sending them a public email saying: "I divorce thee," three times.

Old-fashion letters took days to arrive so you had days to reply—and if you took longer, people blamed Canada Post. But email arrives instantly and many people expect instant replies.

I know this because their email is marked with little red flags, or flashing messages that say: URGENT! PRIORITY LEVEL: EXTREMELY HIGH! READ NOW OR DIE!

I've learned to ignore these alerts because they're mostly sent by people who consider everything urgent, including a note about their son's coming trumpet recital.

I set my own priorities for dealing with mail. First, I answer messages from good friends and colleagues. Second, I ignore most letters from strangers, like this morning's message from Mrs. Luz Stella Cabrillon in Colombia who is undergoing kidney treatment and was "divinely inspired to pick Josh Freed's name for financial help, after a series of prayers and fasts, she asked God for direction." Apparently, God gave her my email address.

Hardest to deal with are letters that require quick decisions that I may not want to make that day—or even think about. But if I don't answer, I'll just get more nervous messages saying: "I emailed you

27 minutes ago. Could you please confirm that you received it."

That's because many people with portable Black-Berries answer every email they get the second they get it: "Dear Ms. Cabrillo: I regret to say I will not be able to contribute to your Colombian kidney treatment at this time..."

I don't know how these people get any work done. Ideally, I try to wait for the end of the day to answer my mail so it doesn't take over my whole day and distract me from work. But part of me wants to be distracted from work, too.

Every time I hear that BOING sound of a letter arriving I'm tempted to take a fast glance. Then I find myself reading letters and writing back and the next thing I know, I've spent two hours on email and no time working. I've become an email writer, instead of a real one.

What to do? I guess I could find an email withdrawal program and go cold turkey. But like any addict, I'm not ready to give up all the highs. I love getting emails from family and friends thousands of miles away. I like getting a good ejoke amid many bad ones.

I enjoy getting emails from readers, because they're unexpected and demand nothing—and I try to reply to each one. But here, too, there can be too much of a good thing. In one of my recently published pieces, I cited Churchill's famous quote about "nothing to

URGENT! PRIORITY LEVEL: EXTREMELY HIGH! READ NOW OR DIE!
...email arrives instantly and many people expect instant replies.

fear but fear itself." Instantly, I received a flood of emails reminding me that it was actually Roosevelt who said that, not Churchill.

So, you see, email can be helpful for keeping writers on their toes—but I didn't send everyone a reply. I couldn't face writing all those apologies.

Mea culpa. My mistake. As Shakespeare said: "To forgive is human, To err divine."

Er... it was something like that, wasn't it? ▲

**"I want to try something, Caruthers—
come at me like you're asking for a raise."**

My husband, Daniel, had been promoted to a newly created position. He was eager to find out what his official title was, so when his business cards finally arrived, I was surprised that he seemed reluctant to show me. After some persuasion, Daniel gave me a card, naming him director of product efficiency. "Wow," I responded, "that sounds impressive."

"Not really," Daniel replied as he removed my thumb from the acronym underneath. It read DOPE.

— SANDY GERVAIS

The chef of the upscale restaurant I manage collided with a waiter one day and spilled coffee all over our computer. The liquid poured into the processing unit, and resulted in some dramatic crackling and popping sounds. After sopping up the mess, we gathered around the terminal as the computer was turned back on.

"Please let it work," pleaded the guilt-ridden waiter.

A waitress replied, "Should be faster than ever. That was a double espresso."

— BRIAN A. KOHLER

One of my pet peeves as a musician in a symphony orchestra is trying to follow the erratic beat of famous guest conductors. I didn't realize how strongly the rest of the musicians felt until we were talking to someone from a university physics department at a reception. When I asked him what his field was, he answered, "I work with semiconductors." "So do we," I heard a colleague mutter.

— BERNARD GOLDSTEIN

During the latter stages of my pregnancy, I brought a cushion to work to make my chair more comfortable. One afternoon I returned from lunch to find my chair had been pushed to the far side of my work area.

"Looks like someone's been sitting in my chair," I commented to one of my co-workers.

Glancing down at my stomach, she said, "Looks like someone's also been sleeping in your bed."

— RUTH MALLARD

Excerpts from actual employee evaluations. Hope none of these rings a bell:

- "Works well when under constant supervision and cornered like a rat in a trap."
- "His men would follow him anywhere, but only out of morbid curiosity."
- "When she opens her mouth, it is only to change feet."
- "He doesn't have ulcers, but he's a carrier."
- "If you see two people talking and one looks bored, he's the other one."

My father began teaching business classes at the local prison through a community college. On his first night of class, he started a chapter on banking. During the course of his lecture, the subject of ATMs came up, and he mentioned that, on average, most machines contain only about $1,500 at a given time.

Just then a man in the back raised his hand. "I'm not trying to be disrespectful," he told my father, "but the machine I robbed had about $5,000 in it."

— JENNIFER JOHNSON

It was an unusually hectic evening at the emergency clinic where I work. The doctor on duty was simultaneously bombarded with questions, given forms to sign, and even asked for his dinner order.

I was in the next room, cleaning up a newly sutured wound, when I realized he hadn't given instructions for a bandage. I poked my head out the door and asked, "What kind of dressing do you want on that?"

"Ranch," he replied.

— BRENDA TODD

As a 911 dispatcher, I speak to people in various states of panic. One day, a woman called saying that a family member had fallen and needed help.

"Do you know what caused the fall?" I asked.

"No," the woman nervously replied. "What?"

— REBECCA PARKS

I work at a department store where every night at closing time one of our customer-service representatives reminds shoppers over the public-address system to finish their shopping. One evening, a woman who had recently worked at a Kmart opened the announcement by saying, "Attention Kmart shoppers…"

Quickly realizing her mistake, she tap-danced her way out of trouble by adding, "You are in the wrong store."

— MATTHEW PERENCHIO

Our copier was on the fritz so I put a note on it: "Service has been called." When the technician told me he had to order parts, I added a second note: "Parts have been ordered."

During the next five days, when we had to use an older, slower copier on the other side of the building, someone taped a third note to the machine: "Prayers have been said."

— JENNIFER HARRISON

Timeless Humour from the '70s

A favourite story among colour-film processors concerns the negative of a poodle which a woman sent to a photo-finishing lab. When the print was made, the dog came out looking green. Figuring that there must have been a mistake in the colour balance, a problem which plagues colour processors, the lab tried again and again, and finally got the dog to come out a kind of improbable tan.

The woman who sent in the negative was furious when she got the picture of the tan poodle, which, she informed the lab, she had dyed green.

— DONALD M. SCHWARTZ

The aquarium shop where I work has been in business for more than 20 years. One Sunday a customer called wanting to buy a larger aquarium. "And by the way, I've spent a lot of money at your store over the years," he said. "I think I should get a discount."

"Only our owner can give a discount," I explained, "and he won't be in until tomorrow."

When the customer said that he'd come in the next day, I asked him if there was anything else I could help him with.

"Sure," he said. "Where is your store located?"

— DAVID A. BILLINGTON

QUOTABLE QUOTES

The squeaky wheel may get the most oil, but it's also the first to be replaced.
— MARILYN VOS SAVANT, Of Course I'm for Monogamy (St. Martin's)

You're not famous until my mother has heard of you.
— JAY LENO

The grass may be greener on the other side, but it's just as hard to cut.
— LITTLE RICHARD

A peacock that rests on his feathers is just another turkey.
— DOLLY PARTON

It was while making newspaper deliveries, trying to miss the bushes and hit the porch, that I first learned the importance of accuracy in journalism.
— CHARLES OSGOOD, Defending Baltimore Against Enemy Attack (Hyperion)

When people ask if I do my own stunts, I always answer, "Not on purpose."
— BILLY BOB THORNTON

You've got to be original, because if you're like someone else, what do they need you for?
— BERNADETTE PETERS on "Inside the Actors Studio" (Bravo)

If you can see a bandwagon, it's too late to get on it.
— JAMES GOLDSMITH

Each new patient at the clinic where I work must fill out a questionnaire asking basic health and personal-history questions. One query that inevitably gets a "No" answer is, "Do you now use or have you ever used recreational drugs?"

We were unprepared for the response of a young newlywed who wrote: "Yes—birth-control pills."

— FRANCES BOWEN

My nephew, a flight attendant, split the back of his pants one day during a flight. To save embarrassment, he decided to work in front of the beverage cart, facing forward.

The arrangement worked perfectly until he got to the last row and a passenger leaned over to him and said in a low voice, "Your fly is open."

— RICHARD F. MARKS

One of my customers at the department of motor vehicles wanted a personalized licence plate with his wedding anniversary on it. As we completed the paperwork he explained, "This way I can't forget the date."

A few hours later, I recognized the same young man waiting in

"Damn it, Peterson, you've got to try and fit in!"

my line. When his turn came, he said somewhat sheepishly, "I need to change the numbers on that plate application."

— N. V. GOODMAN

While on vacation, my wife and I stopped for lunch at a diner. We sat at the counter, right next to the grill. The cook was a young man who was very busy flipping pancakes. Every so often, he would stop and hit the grill with the handle of the spatula. Finally I asked him facetiously, "Does that improve the taste of the pancakes?"

"No," he replied. "That keeps the handle from falling off."

— NORMAN SMEE

When a woman came through my cashier's line at Wal-Mart, her purchase came to twenty dollars. "That's what I had in my hand. You must be psychic," she joked.

"I am," I teased. "I knew exactly how much you wanted to spend."

The next customer stepped up and, looking at me with a big grin, pulled out a loonie.

— MELISSA MORSE

The insurance agency I work for draws business from a retirement community. Once, when applying for auto insurance for a client, I asked him how many kilometres he drives in a year. He said he didn't know.

"Well, do you drive 10,000 kilometres a year?" I asked, "or 5,000?"

He said the numbers sounded high. "What month is this?" he asked. I told him it was July.

"Maybe this will help," he said. "I filled the car with gas in February."

— LYNN BEBEE

Overheard: "Yesterday I got my tie stuck in the fax machine. Next thing I knew, I was in Red Deer."

— STEVE HAUPT

How many chiropractors does it take to change a light bulb?

Only one, but it takes six visits.

"We need to focus on diversity. Your goal is to hire people who all look different but think just like me."

It was our new receptionist's very first job, and it showed in the way she dressed—her revealing clothes screamed "college" more than "office." As diplomatically as he could, our boss sat her down and told her that she would have to dress more appropriately. "Why?" she asked. "Are we going out to lunch?"

— CLAUDIA SMELKO & MARION ABEL

The salesman at the megastore had only one sale that day, but it was for a staggering $158,762. Flabbergasted by such a massive sale, the manager asked him to explain. "First, I sold the man a fishhook," the salesman said. "Then I sold him a rod and reel. When I found out he was planning on fishing down the coast, I suggested he'd need a boat. Then I took him to the automotive department and sold him our biggest SUV to pull the boat."

"You sold all that to a guy who came in for a fishhook?" asked the boss.

"Actually," said the salesman, "he came in for a bottle of Aspirin for his wife's migraine. I told him, 'Your weekend's shot. Might as well go fishing.'"

Our nephew was getting married to a doctor's daughter. At the wedding reception, the father of the bride stood to read his toast, which he had scribbled on a piece of scrap paper. Several times during his speech, he halted, overcome with what I assumed was a moment of deep emotion. But after a particularly long pause, he explained, "I'm sorry. I can't seem to make out what I've written down." Looking out into the audience, he asked, "Is there a pharmacist in the house?"

— TONY BELMONTE

As my husband, the county highway commissioner, was driving to the hospital for treatment of his painful leg, he decided to use the valet parking service so he wouldn't have to walk far. Staring at his official-looking vehicle, one of the valets asked my husband if he was driving a government car. "Why, yes," my husband replied, surprised by the question. "In fact it's an unmarked police car."

"Wow!" the young man said, sliding behind the wheel. "This will be the first time I've been in the front seat."

— PATTY ANN HEINEMANN

I thought I wanted a tattoo, so I had a friend come with me to the tattoo parlour. As I nervously paused outside the door, I noticed the T had slipped off their sign. Now it read "Creative ouch."

— KAREN BLOUNT

Doctors are used to getting calls at any hour. One night a man phoned, waking me up. "I'm sorry to bother you so late," he said, "but I think my wife has appendicitis."

Still half asleep, I reminded him that I had taken his wife's inflamed appendix out a couple of years before. "Whoever heard of a second appendix?" I asked.

"You may not have heard of a second appendix," he replied, "but surely you've heard of a second wife."

— JAMES KARURI MUCHIRI

Finishing up our work at a trade show in San Diego, my co-worker Maureen and I decided to go sightseeing across the border in Tijuana, Mexico. While there, we went shopping and bought a few pieces of clay kitchenware. As we crossed back into the United States, a customs official asked if we had anything of value to report. "Not really," Maureen replied, digging in her bag for the bean crock she had purchased. Everyone around us froze as she continued, "I only bought a little pot."

— RUSS TOMPKINS

My wife and I run a small restaurant where we often name our specials after our employees—dishes like "Chicken Mickey," after our dishwasher who gave us the recipe, and "Rod's Ribs," after a waiter who had his personal style of barbecue. One evening after rereading the menu, I broke with this tradition and changed the description of the special we had named after our chef.

Despite her skills and excellent reputation, somehow I didn't think an entrée named "Salmon Ella" would go over big with our customers.

— BRETT LEHIGH

Timeless Humour from the '50s

An acquaintance of mine was hired as a research assistant by a university physics department to investigate the thermodynamic properties of wood. Two weeks after starting work he was approached by an encyclopedia salesman who explained that purchase of the encyclopedia entitled the buyer to have any three special questions answered completely. To save himself a great deal of work, the researcher bought the encyclopedia, stipulating for his first free question a full dissertation on the thermodynamic properties of wood.

Three weeks later the head of the physics department called the research assistant into his office and said, "We have a request from an encyclopedia company. One of their customers has asked for a report on the thermodynamic properties of wood. Please prepare the report for them."

— JOHN F. MELLOR

"Do you want a **salary** or benefits?"

Walking through the hallways at the high school where I work, I saw a new substitute teacher standing outside his classroom with his forehead against a locker. I heard him mutter, "How did you get yourself into this?"

Knowing he was assigned to a difficult class, I tried to offer moral support. "Are you okay?" I asked. "Can I help?"

He lifted his head and replied, "I'll be fine as soon as I get this kid out of his locker."

— HELEN BUTTON

Because I was processing my first accident report at the transport company where I worked, I was being particularly attentive. The driver had hit a deer on the highway, and the result was a severely damaged hood and fender. My serious mood was broken, however, when I reached the section of the report that asked, "Speed of other vehicle?"

The driver had put "Full gallop."

— DOUGLAS WAKEHAM

On the afternoon of Administrative Professionals Day, my co-worker and I finally found the time to get gifts for our secretaries. While at the store, my colleague noticed my disappointment when I discovered the shop didn't provide gift wrapping.

After being on the phone forever with a customer who had been having difficulties with a computer program, a support technician at my mother's company turned in his report: "The problem resides between the keyboard and the chair."

Nicole Milligan

"What's wrong?" he asked.

"They won't wrap the gifts for us," I answered.

"No problem," he said quickly. "I'll ask my secretary to do it."

— WENYAN MA

The college football player knew his way around the locker room better than he did the library. So when my husband's co-worker saw the gridiron star roaming the stacks looking confused, she asked how she could help. "I have to read a play by Shakespeare," he said.

"Which one?" she asked.

He scanned the shelves and answered, "William."

— SANDRA J. YARBROUGH

As a high-school football coach, I'm aware that student athletes tend to focus too much on sports. A fellow coach, Bob, was talking about one such player, who called him at home one night. When his wife informed the kid that Bob wasn't home, he became frantic and said he had to speak to the coach right away.

"Just calm down, and I'll have him call you as soon as he gets home," the coach's wife told him. "What's your number?"

The flustered kid replied, "Three."

— ALLAN FLOYD

"I'll need the saw again, sir."

I'm a life-and-career coach and one morning, when a prospective client called for an appointment, I asked him what he wanted to get out of our sessions. "Clarity," he said very firmly.

"And on what issues are you looking for clarity?" I probed.

"Well," he said in a less confident tone, "I really don't know."

— SHANA SPOONER

Four students walked in halfway through the Canadian history test my father was giving at the local community college. "Sorry," they said, "we had a flat tire."

An understanding man, Dad said that if they could all answer just one question correctly, he would give them each an "A" for the exam. The students agreed. So my father handed each one a piece of paper, placed them in four separate corners and said, "Write down which tire was flat."

— KURT SMITH

My husband and I arrived at the auto dealership to pick up our new car, only to be told that the keys had been locked inside. We went to the service department, where a mechanic was working to unlock the driver's side door. Instinctively, I reached for the passenger door and—voilà!—it was unlocked. "Hey," I shouted to him. "It's open!"

"I know," yelled the mechanic. "I already got that side. Now I'm working on this door."

— BETTY M. PHILLIPS

Hal's handyman wasn't the swiftest guy on earth. But he was cheap, and so was Hal, which is why he hired the guy to paint his porch for $50. "You tightwad," scolded Hal's wife. "Our porch covers half of the house! He'll be there for days." Hal simply smirked.

An hour later, there was a knock at the door. The handyman had finished. "How did you get done so quickly?" Hal asked.

"It was a piece of cake," the handyman replied. "Oh, and it's a Ferrari, not a Porsche."

My buddy applied for a job as an insurance salesperson. Where the form requested "prior experience," he wrote "lifeguard." That was it. Nothing else.

"We're looking for someone who can not only sell insurance, but who can sell himself," said the hiring manager. "How does working as a lifeguard pertain to salesmanship?"

"I couldn't swim," my pal replied. He got the job.

— TEDD C. HUSTON

sign language

On the door of a rural post office:

PULL. If that doesn't work, PUSH. If that doesn't work, we're closed. Come again.

— VERA KASSON

60

A first-grader came to the ophthalmology department where I work for his checkup. He sat down and I turned off the lights. I switched on a projector that flashed the letters F, Z and B on a screen. I asked the boy what he saw.

Without hesitation he replied, "Consonants."

— STEPHEN DOWNING

Hard to believe, but many of our customers at the bank still don't know how to swipe their card through the ATM card reader. Because of this, my fellow tellers and I often find ourselves having to explain how it's done. One teller complained that she kept getting odd looks every time she explained it. I found out why when I overheard her tell one man, "Strip down facing me."

— VICKI STONE

While editing announcements for a newspaper, I came across an item promoting a camp for children with asthma. Aside from all the wonderful activities the kids could enjoy, such as canoeing, swimming, crafts and more, it promised that its lakefront property offered something the kids probably did not expect: "breathtaking views."

— CHRISTY NICHOLS

A neighbour had invited some friends, including our minister, over for dinner. On the menu were mashed potatoes, stuffing, peas and baked chicken. As we prepared to eat, we were serenaded by a crowing rooster. "Listen to that rooster," said one of the guests.

Glancing at our pastor digging into his chicken, the host said, "You'd crow too if your child was going into the clergy."

— E. LENORE MILLER

Unfortunately, we humans don't come equipped with delete buttons for our mouths. My friend and his rock band were playing a concert at the psychiatric hospital where he worked as a musical therapist. The audience was a little too quiet for his taste, so the guitarist decided to do something about it. He grabbed the microphone, pointed to the group and yelled, "Are you ready to get a little crazy?"

— STEPHAN DERVAN

A guy shows up late for work. The boss yells, "You should've been here at 8:30!"

The guy replies, "Why? What happened at 8:30?"

"Good news, Mr. Hawkins. Companies have laid off too much deadwood, and now there's a shortage."

Caddy Hack

▶ BY RICK REILLY

I know I'll never play golf like the great golfers, pro or celeb. I'll never play it like those guys' gardeners. But in golf, more than in any other sport, I can get close to great athletes without actually being one: I can be a caddy.

I persuaded Jack Nicklaus, the greatest golfer in history, to let me carry his bag for him at the grand opening of The Summit at Cordillera, a course he designed near Vail. I felt stupid caddying for Jack Nicklaus, really. I mean, the man had two U.S. Amateur titles, 71 Tour wins, six Masters, four U.S. Opens, was eight times the leading money winner and now, at age 63, builds some of the finest golf courses around. What is the point of telling Jack Nicklaus, "Okay, this is a little 389-yard dogleg with a pond guarding the green left," when the guy designed and built the freaking thing?

It rained most of the day. And that, combined with trying to caddy and interview him, plus the ridiculous distances between green and tee, plus the altitude, plus the bottles of wine the night before—well, these things started to chip away at my skills. And that's about when it happened.

On the 15th hole, the rain was coming in sideways and the wind was serious. Nicklaus's umbrella had been a pill. It kept trying to poke me in the eye or fake a "click," making me think it was locked open and then nearly collapsing. This time, it went too far.

Jack was giving some folks in the gallery a chipping lesson and I was standing on a hill trying to write, not realizing I had the bag a little upside down, and perhaps I forced the umbrella too hard, because suddenly it folded up the wrong way. And as I looked on in horror, the bag toppled over backward, sending some of the clubs flying and, unfortunately, some of the balls out of the unzipped pouch—oops—just as Nicklaus asked me for another ball to chip. Busted. Jack looked at me, waited for the laughter to die down and then said, "Don't quit your regular job."

On the day I'm caddying for Donald Trump at his preposterously wonderful Trump National Golf Club in Briarcliff Manor, N.Y., there's a problem. Trump wants me to play instead of caddy. He's already got his usual caddy, Billy, ready to go— "Best caddy in the world!" he declares—and he won't play by himself under any circumstances. You don't get the feeling Trump is a guy who requires a lot of personal quiet time. I ask him, "Any chance maybe you'd have a game tomorrow I could caddy for?"

Trump looks at me. "Believe me," he says, "one day of me is enough."

Hauling bags for the stars

Just a word on Trump's hair. There are those who do not like it. And I admit, when I asked Trump if I could caddy for him, I was wondering if we would need a separate caddy for the hair. Up close, though, it is much less threatening and possibly real. It resembles red cotton candy. It seems to have been spun off a wheel and fired. Maybe the hair is fibreglass. I cannot imagine the teams of artists it must take to do Trump's hair each day, but I know they must arrive by the bus-load. And somehow they've managed to make his hair look like the moment when you open a bottle of Aspirin and you can't quite get the cotton ball out and it comes partially out, all teased. That's Trump's hair.

Trump plays golf fast, and well. Mostly he hits the ball low, far and straight. He owns the joint, so he parks the cart where he wants the rest of the world not to—edges of greens, backs of tee boxes. We will end up going 18 holes in three hours and 15 minutes and that includes stopping

often to harangue the stonemason and the greenskeeper to re-do the bricks or re-trim a tree that is not absolutely, immaculately Trumpalicious. Before long, the bricks have been ripped out and the stonemason is starting over.

When Trump sees work that is Trumpalicious, he is practically moist. Just now he saw five workers doing a job he liked on a cart path. "Beautiful!" he says. So we gotta go over and tell them. They're from Chile, and they don't speak a syllable of English. He whips out three $100 bills and gives them out. The workers smile melon slices, shocked at their good fortune. Trump climbs back in the cart, pleased mightily. "Now those guys are the Donald Trumps of Chile!" he says.

Before caddying for Bob Newhart—the former accountant turned genius stand-up comic, TV psychologist and Vermont inn owner—I had lunch with him in the grill overlooking the first tee at Bel-Air, L.A.'s club of the stars. Soon enough,

What is the point of telling Jack Nicklaus, "Okay, this is a little 389-yard dogleg with a pond guarding the green left," when the guy designed and built the freaking thing?

▶ Caddy Hack

people were wondering why a caddy was having lunch with Bob in the grill, so we set out. Bob said we'd start on the back nine and then play the front nine. But somebody was playing the 10th and 11th, so we started on 12. I asked Bob what his handicap was. "Nine," he said. "I say I'm a nine no matter what I am. I like being a nine."

Right off, Bob proved he wasn't a nine. He was more like a four. He hit a perfect drive and then a perfect five-wood toward the Mae West green at 12. It's called that because it used to have two huge humps guarding it. The humps are gone now, but then so is Mae West. Bob was on in two strokes but three-putted. "Does golf drive stars crazy too?" I asked.

"Oh, yeah," he said. "Like, I'll come home after a bad round, swearing. And my wife will say, 'I thought you played golf to relax!' and I'll snap, 'Dammit, honey, you don't know the first thing about the game!'"

Bob lives among the mansions in the Bel Air hills. "We live next to the house Dean Martin owned," he said. "Dean sold it to Tom Jones, who sold it to Nicolas Cage. Next to that is the house that Clark Gable and Carole Lombard lived in. It sounds glamorous, I guess. But sometimes I'll be doing some menial task and I'll say to my wife, 'Hon, do you think Carole Lombard ever asked Clark Gable to take out the recycling?'"

By the round's end, Bob hit 7 out of 13 fairways, 6 out of 16 greens, and shot what probably would've been an 88 if we'd counted everything and played 18 holes. On the second ball he hit, though, Bob was probably more like an 81. But then, aren't we all?

Oh, one last thing. You're thinking, "How come you didn't ask Tiger Woods if you could caddy for him?" I did. I asked him 100 ways. And he always said no. "Why not?" I wondered.

"Because," Tiger explained, "I suck. I need good help." ▲

I admit, when I asked Trump if I could caddy for him, I was wondering if we would need a separate caddy for the hair.

Responsible, who wants to be responsible? Whenever something bad happens, it's always, Who's responsible for this?

— JERRY SEINFELD

You're never allowed to step on people to get ahead, but you can step over them if they're in your way.

— STAR JONES on "The View"

If an idea's worth having once, it's worth having twice.

— TOM STOPPARD, Indian Ink

The key to success? Work hard, stay focused and marry a Kennedy.

— ARNOLD SCHWARZENEGGER

If men can run the world, why can't they stop wearing neckties? How intelligent is it to start the day by tying a little noose around your neck?

— LINDA ELLERBEE in The Seattle Post-Intelligencer

Money doesn't talk, it swears.

— BOB DYLAN, "It's Alright Ma (I'm Only Bleeding)"

Many an optimist has become rich by buying out a pessimist.

— ROBERT G. ALLEN, Multiple Streams of Income (John Wiley & Sons)

When I hear about people making vast fortunes without doing any productive work or contributing anything to society, my reaction is, How do I get in on that?

— DAVE BARRY in The Miami Herald

I feel inadequate when talking with a mechanic, so when my vehicle started making a strange noise, I sought help from a friend. He drove the car around the block, listened carefully, then told me how to explain the difficulty when I took it in for repair. At the shop I proudly recited, "The timing is off, and there are premature detonations, which may damage the valves."

As I smugly glanced over the mechanic's shoulder, I saw him write on his clipboard, "Lady says it makes a funny noise."

— KATE KELLOGG

My musical director wasn't happy with the performance of one of our percussionists. Repeated attempts to get the drummer to improve failed. Finally, in front of the orchestra, the director said in frustration, "When a musician just can't handle his instrument, they take it away, give him two sticks and make him a drummer!"

A stage whisper was heard from the percussion section: "And if he can't handle that, they take away one of his sticks and make him a conductor."

— QUINCY WONG

Desperate for registered nurses, my colleagues and I in hospital administration often share ideas to recruit employees. Out of exasperation, I made a joking plea to two of my colleagues, asking them to send me six nurses from each of their hospitals. That request prompted one of them to suggest a unique solution: "Send six nurses to the top three names on the list of hospital administrators, and then send your request to five other colleagues. In 14 days you will have received 1,567 nurses."

— DAVID PARKS

A Toronto retail clerk was suffering from aching feet. "It's all those years of standing," his doctor declared. "You need a vacation. Go to Miami, soak your feet in the ocean and you'll feel better."

When the man got to Florida, he went into a hardware store, bought two large buckets and headed for the beach.

"How much for two buckets of that seawater?" he asked the lifeguard.

"A dollar a bucket," the fellow replied with a straight face.

The clerk paid him, filled his buckets, went to his hotel room and soaked his feet. They felt so much better he decided to repeat the treatment that afternoon. Again he handed the lifeguard two dollars. The young man took the money and said, "Help yourself."

The clerk started for the water, then stopped in amazement. The tide was out. "Wow," he said, turning to the lifeguard. "Some business you got here!"

— CARL D. KIRBY

sign language

Seen on the door of a repair shop:

WE CAN FIX ANYTHING. (Please knock on the door—the bell doesn't work.)

— VICTORIA GOLDEN

On the job as a dental receptionist, I answered the phone and noticed on the caller-ID screen that the incoming call was from an auto-repair shop. The man on the line begged to see the dentist because of a painful tooth. "Which side of your mouth hurts?" I asked the patient.

He sighed and answered, "The passenger side."

— CHERYL PACE SATTERWHITE

I am a deputy sheriff assigned to courthouse security. As part of my job, I explain court procedures to visitors. One day I was showing a group of ninth-graders around. Court was in recess and only the clerk and a young man in custody wearing handcuffs were in the courtroom. "This is where the judge sits," I began, pointing to the bench. "The lawyers sit at these tables. The court clerk sits over there. The court recorder, or stenographer, sits over here. Near the judge is the witness stand and over there is where the jury sits. As you can see," I finished, "there are a lot of people involved in making this system work."

At that point, the prisoner raised his cuffed hands and said, "Yeah, but I'm the one who makes it all happen."

— MICHAEL McPHERSON

A livestock truck overturned in my town, and the accident made the local news. The young reporter who covered the story declared on camera, "Two cows, Black and Gus, escaped into nearby woods."

At the studio there was muffled laughter as they cut to a commercial. After the break, the reporter sheepishly added, "About that overturned truck—make those Black Angus cattle."

— JULIANA KEMP

The boss placed a sign directly over the sink in the men's room at work. It had a single word on it: think!

The next day when the boss went to the men's room, he saw another sign had been placed immediately above the soap dispenser.

It read: thoap!

— MURIEL NAYLOR

Timeless Humour from the '60s

Another man and I share a locker at work. Noticing that it needed a new combination lock, my partner said he would pick one up on his way to work the next day. It occurred to me later that I might not see him in the morning. How would I find out the combination? I needn't have worried.

When I arrived at work I found that he had used the locker before me and had left a note reading: "To find the first number subtract 142 from your high score the last time we went bowling. The second number is 16 less than that. To find the third number subtract 1.87 from the amount you owe me."

— MICHAEL KLABER

"Technically, we're not firing you. We're just moving you into an exit-level position."

A client recently brought her two cats to my husband's veterinary clinic for their annual checkup. One was a small-framed, round tiger-striped tabby, while the other was a long, sleek black cat. She watched closely as I put each on the scale. "They weigh about the same," I told her.

"That proves it!" she exclaimed. "Black does make you look slimmer. And stripes make you look fat."

— SUSAN DANIEL

I was inspecting communications facilities in the Yukon. Since I had little experience flying in small planes, I was nervous when we approached a landing strip in a snow-covered area. The pilot descended to less than 100 metres, then gunned both engines, climbed and circled back. While my heart pounded, the passenger next to me seemed calm. "I wonder why the pilot didn't land," I said.

"He was checking to see if the landing strip was plowed," the man replied.

As we made a second approach, I glanced out the window. "It looks plowed to me," I commented.

"No," my neighbour replied. "It hasn't been cleared for some time."

"How can you tell?" I asked.

"Because," the man informed me, "I'm the guy who drives the plow."

— LAWRENCE D. WEISS

"How much do you charge?" a man asked a lawyer.

"I get $50 for three questions," the lawyer answers.

"That's awfully steep, isn't it?" says the man.

"Yes, it is," replies the lawyer. "Now, what's your final question?"

At the busy dental office where I work, one patient was always late. Once when I called to confirm an appointment, he said, "I'll be about 15 minutes late. That won't be a problem, will it?"

"No," I told him. "We just won't have time to give you an anaesthetic."

He arrived early.

— TERRI SPACCAROTELLI

Corporate managers are always a good source of memorable quotes. Here are some examples of mediocrity rising to the top.

- "As of tomorrow, employees will only be able to access the building using individual security cards. Pictures will be taken next Wednesday, and employees will receive their cards in two weeks."
- "What I need is a list of specific unknown problems we will encounter."
- "Email is not to be used to pass on information or data. It should be used only for company business."
- "This project is so important, we can't let things that are more important interfere with it."
- "We know that communication is a problem, but the company is not going to discuss it with the employees."

— E. T. THOMPSON

The customer ordering a floral arrangement from my shop was giving me very specific guidelines. "Nothing fragrant," she instructed. "Nothing too tall or too wild. And no bright colours, please. My house is decorated in beige and cream. Here is a wallpaper sample." She handed me a plain square of tan-coloured paper.

"Your name?" I asked.

"Mrs. Bland," the woman replied.

— STEPHEN STANLEY

A teller at the bank where I work noticed that a drive-in customer was writing something on one of the documents he was going to place in the transaction basket. As she looked at the contents of the basket, she saw "This is robbery!" printed on one of his bills to be paid.

She panicked, looked up at the man in the car and asked in a shaky voice, "What do you want?" The customer, realizing the teller's apprehension, began apologizing. "I'm so sorry! That wasn't for you—it's a message for the electric company."

— JIM CHOMA

My brother Jim was hired by a government department and assigned to a small office cubicle in a large area. At the end of his first day, he realized he couldn't see over the panels to find his way out, so he waited until he saw someone else leaving and followed him. He did the same the next day. On the third day he had to work late, long after his colleagues had left. He wandered around lost in the maze of cubicles and corridors, but then, just as panic began to set in, he came upon another employee in a cubicle.

"How do you get out of here?" Jim asked.

The fellow looked up from his desk, smiled and said, "No cheese for you."

— CHRISTINE PROBASCO

Giving a sermon one Sunday, I heard two teenage girls in the back giggling and disturbing people. I interrupted my sermon and announced sternly, "There are two of you here who have not heard a word I've said." That quieted them down.

When the service was over, I went to greet people at the front door. Three adults apologized for going to sleep in church, promising it would never happen again.

— WILLIAM C. RUSS

My brother-in-law, head chef in a high-end restaurant, underwent major surgery. His wife, who spent anxious hours awaiting news, supposed that the atmosphere in the operating room was comparable to what she was experiencing. Things obviously were less tense there than she had pictured.

When they wheeled my brother-in-law out, this memo was pinned to his hospital gown: "Don't forget to give operating-room nurse recipe for remoulade sauce."

— MRS. E. G. LEBLANC

"There's an important job I'd like you to tackle, Haffner—yours."

Me and My Big Mouth

▶ BY TERRY BRADSHAW WITH DAVID FISHER

When my football-playing career ended, I had no idea how I wanted to spend the rest of my life. Fortunately for me, there is a fine tradition in this country that if you are a successful athlete or performer, people supposedly want to eat the same peanut butter that you do, drink the same beer, wear the same pants, etc. That's how I got involved in the worst product endorsement I ever did. I am bald and I agreed to be the spokesman for a toupee company. The basic concept of the campaign was that if a he-man football player like Terry Bradshaw was not embarrassed to wear a toupee, no one else should be. To show potential customers how good I looked with hair, the company made and distributed to salons all over the country a plastic model of my head. These salons then stuck a toupee on the model and put it on the counter or in the front window. They made the mold for my head at a Holiday Inn near the Shreveport Regional Airport. I lay down on a bed while people stuck straws up my nose so I could breathe, and then covered my entire head with plaster.

The plaster began drying too quickly, and they had trouble getting it off my head. In the meantime I was having difficulty breathing. There are lots of bad ways to die, but being suffocated by plaster while getting your head duplicated for a toupee display is high on the list. Eventually, they mass-produced my head, and it did look just like me. The toupee people were so proud of the plastic bust, they mailed one to my dad. The problem was I didn't tell him it was coming. This big box arrived at my parents' house, and my father opened it up. He was shocked to see me looking right back at him. "Novis," he yelled to my mother, "you better get in here. They sent us Terry's head in a box." It bothered my mother so much that they put it back in the box and stored it in the attic. As another part of the deal, I filmed several toupee commercials. In one, I swam with a hairpiece on as an announcer said, "You, too, can have a full robust life with our toupee. Look how natural it looks." Then I surfaced with what looked like road kill stuck to my head.

Maybe the worst part of the deal was that I agreed to wear a toupee whenever I appeared in public. One day I was playing in a pro-am golf

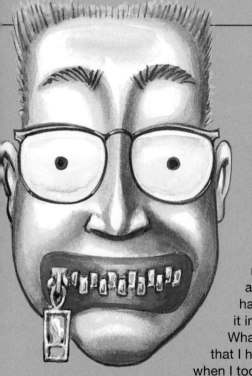

How Terry Bradshaw fumbled his way to success

tournament on a hot afternoon. Sweat was pouring out from under the dense synthetic wig. Finally I just couldn't take it anymore; I went behind a tree, ripped off the hairpiece and shoved it into my back pocket. What I didn't realize was that I had cut my head when I took it off, so my scalp was bleeding. I spent the rest of the tournament walking around with blood running down my face and the hairpiece hanging out of my back pocket like a squirrel's tail. After that, for some reason, the company decided I was not a proper spokesman for their toupee and fired me. I had to hand in my hair. Once again I needed to find a way to make a living. Talking is what I do best, and I like to make people smile. When I was playing, reporters liked to interview me because I gave them good sound bites.

Luckily this had attracted the attention of TV network executives. One day my phone rang. A CBS executive asked, "Want $5,000 just for talking?" And that is how I got into the broadcasting business long-term.

When I signed with CBS, Terry O'Neil, the executive producer of CBS Sports, teamed me with veteran play-by-play announcer Verne Lundquist. Verne was facing a big challenge; he had to teach me how to do my job before I destroyed his career. My first broadcast was a preseason game in San Diego between the Chargers and some other team. As a quarterback, the big picture had been the only thing that mattered to me, but as a broadcaster I soon learned it was the small frames that make up the big picture. I didn't know the players and their assignments; I didn't know when to talk and when to keep quiet. I didn't know what to look at, how to describe what I was seeing. There was so much I didn't know, I didn't even know it. I would not describe my first game as a disaster, mostly because that would be understating how truly bad I was. For example, in about the middle of the first quarter it became obvious to me that in addition to a lack of knowledge and preparation, I had a serious problem. "Verne," I said, "I can't see a thing down there." I had never watched a football game from that distance in my life. All I could see

▶ Me and My Big Mouth

The first few games I was probably more nervous than at any time during my entire playing career. I would always bring two clean shirts with me, because I knew I was going to sweat through one of them.

was a bunch of people with numbers I couldn't read running around.

"Really," said Verne, amazingly calm, considering that the broadcasting partner he was depending on for insightful commentary had just announced he was basically useless. "We've got to get you binoculars for the next game." Gradually I got better. Very, very gradually. The first few games I was probably more nervous than at any time during my entire playing career. I would always bring two clean shirts with me, because I knew I was going to sweat through one of them. Maybe I was so nervous because I really cared. I worked hard. I wanted to be good, to please the viewers. And I needed that job. With a lot of help from Verne, I guess I did okay because CBS eventually offered me another job as co-host of "The NFL Today" with Greg Gumbel. I'd be the analyst.

Before the first show I was extremely nervous. Then, minutes before we went on the air, a heavy boom microphone smacked me upside the head so hard it nearly knocked me out. I felt dizzy, sick to my stomach, and my ears rang. In a strange way, that hit in the head relaxed me. Being in the studio was brand-new to me, but I could relate to a pain in my head. During my playing career, there had been many games when I had to play hurt, but as one reporter wrote, this was the first time I had to talk hurt.

Fortunately all went well. Since then I've gone from CBS to Fox, and have made the transition from football player to football entertainer. My role on TV is not to be serious. People do not want to hear me speak football, things like "That's the old sixty-six inside release." They expect to hear me say things like "The Giants are having a bad offensive day, and they've got to make some changes. It's like when I went fishing with my dad last week and we were catching a lot of fish and all of a sudden we couldn't catch mud. Then my daddy said to me, 'Son, either these fish got real bright all of a sudden or they're not interested in these lures. We got to change lures.' When the defensive isn't biting, you've got to change your offensive at halftime. You got to change lures." For a man who thought his best talent was throwing an inflated ellipsoid a long way, I've been fortunate in my career. In the end I discovered my real talent—just being myself. ▲

"Wouldn't it be easier if you just took my salary out of the taxes?"

Being the office supervisor, I had to have a word with a new employee who never arrived at work on time. I explained that her tardiness was unacceptable and that other employees had noticed that she was walking in late every day. After listening to my complaints, she agreed that this was a problem and even offered a solution. **"Is there another door I could use?"**

— BARBARA DAVIES

I n my job as an electronics salesman, I've seen the rise in popularity of sport-utility vehicles and minivans, which has created a market for rear-seat entertainment. Monitors that keep passengers occupied with movies and television have been selling like crazy. One day as I was showing a young couple how a monitor could play videos, DVDs, and even pick up local TV stations, the husband asked matter-of-factly, "Does it get cable?"

— JOSEPH WADE

"Sanders, I just sold your soul. You weren't using it, were you?"

D uring a shopping trip to a department store, I was looking around for a salesperson so I could pay for my purchase. Finally I ran into a woman wearing the store's ID tag. "Excuse me," I said. "I'm trying to locate a cashier."

"I can't help you," she briskly replied, barely slowing down. "I work in customer service." And she walked away.

— SERENA HEARTZ

A fter harvesting the usual bumper crop of squash last year, I took a half-dozen to the office. I piled them on the table in the break room, and posted a sign advertising them as free. The next day I noticed an addition to my sign. Below "Free Zucchini," someone had written, "Save the Whales."

— DAN ARCHEY

I 'm an attendant in a laundro-mat. A woman came in, sat near my counter and chain-smoked cigarette after cigarette. The smoke was bothering me, so I turned on a fan. "Could you please point that thing in another direction?" she asked. "I'm just getting over pneumonia and the last thing I need is a breeze blowing on me."

— HOLLY SNAPP

A young man asked for a job with the circus, any job at all. The manager decided to give him a chance to become an assistant lion tamer and took him to the practice cage.

The head lion tamer, a beautiful young woman, was just starting her rehearsal. Entering the cage, she removed her cape with a flourish and, standing in a gorgeous costume, motioned to a lion. Obediently the lion crept toward her and then rolled over twice.

"Well," said the manager to the young man, "do you think you can learn to do that?"

"I'm sure I could," he replied, "but first you'll have to get that lion out of there."

— SCOTT M. RIVA

As an obstetrician, I sometimes see unusual tattoos when working in labour and delivery. One patient had some type of fish tattoo on her abdomen. "That sure is a pretty whale," I commented.

With a smile she replied, "It used to be a dolphin."

— RON NORRIS

Late one night I stopped at one of those 24-hour gas station mini-marts to get myself a cup of fresh brewed coffee. When I picked up the pot, I could not help noticing that the brew was as black as asphalt and just about as thick. "How old is the coffee you have here?" I asked the woman who was standing behind the store counter.

She shrugged. "I don't know. I've only been working here two weeks."

— PETER CULVER

When employees of the restaurant where I work attended a fire-safety seminar, we watched a fire official demonstrate the proper way to operate an extinguisher. "Pull the pin like a hand grenade," he explained, "then depress the trigger to release the foam."

Later, an employee was selected to extinguish a controlled fire in the parking lot. In her nervousness, she forgot to pull the pin.

Our instructor hinted, "Like a hand grenade, remember?"

In a burst of confidence, she pulled the pin—and hurled the extinguisher at the blaze.

— BECKI HARRIS

Timeless Humour from the '70s

My friend John and I, determined to see the world, signed on a Norwegian freighter as deckhands. We were being trained as helmsmen, and John's first lesson was given by the mate, a seasoned but gentle white-haired seafarer. John was holding the heading he had been given, when the mate ordered, "Come starboard."

Pleased at knowing immediately which way starboard was, John left the helm and walked over to his instructor.

The mate had an incredulous look on his face as the helm swung freely, but he merely asked politely, "Could you bring the ship with you?"

— BRUCE INGRAHAM

I got stuck in a traffic jam while commuting into Vancouver one day. The woman in the SUV in front of me took full advantage of the slowdown. She whipped out her eyebrow pencil, lip gloss and a mirror, applying the finishing touches on her face in the ten minutes it took us to creep across the bridge.

Finally, the traffic broke up and as she zoomed away, I caught a glimpse of her vehicle's licence plate: NTRL BTY.

— CHRIS DURMICK

Students in the adult French class I teach include quite a few health-care professionals. During one class, I was coughing so badly a doctor in the class raised her hand. "If you like, I could give you a prescription for that," she offered. Another hand shot up. "I could fill it for you," said a pharmacist's assistant. Not to be outdone, a paramedic added, "And I can take you there to pick it up!"

— JOANNE DUGUAY

A man rushed to the jewellery counter in the store where I work soon after the doors opened one morning and said he needed a pair of diamond earrings. I showed him a wide selection, and quickly he picked out a pair.

When I asked him if he wanted the earrings gift-wrapped, he said, "That'd be great. But can you make it quick? I forgot today was my anniversary, and my wife thinks I'm taking out the trash."

— ANDRE F. PAYSON II

sign language

Posted in a dental office:

"Be kind to your dentist. He has fillings too."

— CHRISTY CRITCHFIELD

When my daughter was preparing for her school's "career week," a time when career options are discussed and often led by representatives of different professions, we talked about my job as an airline customer-services representative. I mentioned that one of my responsibilities was to load passengers' luggage at the check-in counter. I later found out to my dismay that my daughter had listed my occupation as "Bag Lady."

— VICKI FREEMAN

76

A Kid's World

They're innocent, earnest and accidentally hilarious. The priceless things kids say, the unlikely things they do and the brain-squashing challenges they pose to us unsuspecting adults.

"Can you hear me now?"

I was on family leave, spending my days caring for my two-year-old son while pregnant with my second. To kill some time, I began watching The Game Show Network, and I got hooked. One afternoon my husband came home from work to find the house in complete disarray and me plopped in front of the TV. "So that's what you do while I'm at work?" he said, smirking.

"I just happened to have it on," I lied.

The next day we were watching Prime Minister Harper give a speech. As Harper stepped out of his car and waved to his cheering supporters, my son shouted, "Look, Mommy, he won the car!"

— CRYSTAL PELLEGRINI

My mother is a cleaning fanatic. One Saturday she told me and my brother to get down to the playroom and straighten it up. We had had a party there the previous evening and she was none too happy about the mess. As she watched us work, it was clear Mom was completely dissatisfied with our cleaning efforts and let us know it.

Finally my brother, exasperated with having to do it all over, reached for a broom and asked, "Can I use this or are you planning to go somewhere?"

— MARK BERMAN

Because it was my brother's birthday, our mom wanted to do something special. She called his fraternity house and said she wanted to bring a cake. The young man who took the call was very excited. "Hey, Mrs. Schaeffer," he said, "that would be great!"

The next day she drove to the fraternity and rang the doorbell. The same boy answered the door. When he saw the cake, his face fell. "Oh," he said, clearly disappointed. "I thought you said 'keg.'"

— MARY SCHAEFFER

One evening after dinner, my five-year-old son Brian noticed that his mother had gone out. In answer to his questions, I told him, "Mommy is at a Tupperware party."

This explanation satisfied him for only a moment. Puzzled, he asked, "What's a Tupperware party, Dad?"

I've always given my son honest answers, so I figured a simple explanation would be the best approach. "Well, Brian," I said, "at a Tupperware party, a bunch of ladies sit around and sell plastic bowls to each other."

Brian nodded, indicating that he understood. Then he burst into laughter. "Come on, Dad," he said. "What is it really?"

— KENNETH W. HOLMES

One day I went to the mall for a beauty makeover. Afterward, I stopped at the photo gallery to have pictures taken of my new look. When I got home, my eight-year-old stared at me wide-eyed and exclaimed, "You look divorced!"

— BECKY MILLER

My husband and I had been trying to have a third child for a while. Unfortunately, the day I was to take a home pregnancy test, he was called out of town on business. I had told our young daughters about the test, and they were excited. We decided if it was positive, we would buy a baby outfit to surprise their father when he got home. The three of us stood in the bathroom eagerly waiting for the telltale line to appear.

When it did not, my thoughtful seven-year-old gave me a hug. "It's okay, Mom," she said. "The next time Daddy goes out of town, you can try and get pregnant again."

— JUANITA MACDONALD

While waiting in line for the Tilt-A-Whirl, I overheard my two nephews arguing. "Aunt Staci's going with me!" insisted Yoni. "No," said his brother, "She's going with me!"

Flattered at being so popular, I promised Yoni, "You and I can go on the merry-go-round."

"But I want you on this ride," he protested.

"Why?"

"Because the more weight, the faster it goes."

— STACI MARGULIS

My 12-year-old daughter asked me, "Mom, do you have a baby picture of yourself? I need it for a school project." I gave her one without thinking to ask what the project was.

A few days later I was in her classroom for a parent-teacher meeting when I noticed my face pinned to a mural the students had created. The title of their project was "The oldest thing in my house."

— AIMEE KENT

"As your mother, I took the liberty of making your wishes and blowing out your candles."

My niece, delivering her first child, requested that her mother and I come into the labour room with her. During one violent contraction she looked up at my sister and said, "Mom, please help me. The pains are really bad."

"Honey," my sister replied, "there isn't anything I can do."

My niece then turned to me. "Marisela, please help me," she implored. "Mom doesn't understand what I'm going through."

— MARISELA BOBO

Luke, our venturesome 14-month-old son, was at my mother-in-law's house. He was playing with her car keys when the phone rang. After hanging up, my mother-in-law realized that Luke had put the keys down someplace, but she couldn't find them anywhere. Thinking quickly, she gave him another set of keys.

As she pretended not to look, Luke toddled around the corner and into her bedroom. Then she watched as he carefully placed the second set of keys under her bed—right next to the original car keys.

— TONY BECKER

I began thinking about my own mortality after I became a widow. One day my daughter called home from college, and I announced to her, "I think it's time for us to talk about where I would like to be buried."

"It's way too soon to even think of anything like that," she snapped indignantly. Then there was a brief silence. "Wait a minute, did you say married or buried?"

When I repeated buried, she said, "Oh, okay, sure."

— WILMA L. WEINERT

My teenage niece, Elizabeth, was nervous as she took the wheel for her first driving lesson. As she was pulling out of the parking lot, the instructor said, "Turn left here. And don't forget to let the people behind you know what you're doing."

Elizabeth turned to the students sitting in the back seat and announced, "I'm going left."

— RACHEL NICHOLS

Our high school has lots of spirit, but that didn't help the football team, who had yet to win a game. So when our principal saw some cheerleaders sitting in the stands, he asked, "Don't you think you girls should be down there cheering for your team?"

"I think," one of them said, "we should be down there playing for our team."

— EMILY KARNES

Before heading on vacation, I went to a tanning salon. I was under the lights so long the protective eye shades I wore left a big white circle around each eye. Gazing at myself in the mirror the next day I thought, "Man, I look like a clown."

I had almost convinced myself I was overreacting—until I was in line at the grocery store. I felt a tug at my shirt and looked down to see a toddler staring up at me, "Are you giving out balloons?" he asked.

— NINA SECVIAR

Driving with my two young boys to a funeral, I tried to prepare them by talking about burial and what we believe happens after death. The boys

behaved well during the service. But at the grave site I discovered my explanations weren't as thorough as I'd thought.

In a loud voice, my four-year-old asked, "Mom, what's in the box?"

— GINNY RICHARDS

My girlfriend took her five-year-old daughter shopping with her. The little girl watched her mother try on outfit after outfit, exclaiming each time, "Mommy, you look beautiful!"

A woman in the next dressing room called out, "Can I borrow your daughter for a moment?"

— JEAN STAMMET

Timeless Humour from the '50s

I work as a nurse's aide in a large hospital. One morning as I began to bathe one of my patients, she put out her hand to stop me.

"Do you have a small boy in your family?" she asked.

"Why yes," I said, looking rather puzzled.

"I thought so," my patient said. "That's exactly the way you're washing my face."

— MRS. J. L. MILLER

"Bobby has a Global Positioning System on his scooter. Can I?"

My 16-year-old son was getting his learner's permit, and I never missed an opportunity to remind him about seat-belt safety. Riding in the car one day, I started my lecture: "When you or your friends are in your car, do not start driving until everyone is strapped in! Understand?"

Instead of giving me the usual "I know," he said, "Mom, say that again."

So I warned again: "Whenever you're in your car, don't start driving…"

He asked me to repeat it three more times, until I finally asked what was wrong.

"Nothing," he said. "I just love hearing you say, 'your car.'"

—ANITA ROBBINS

Not long after we moved to our new home, I bought a bird feeder and hung it in front of my kitchen window. One day I looked out to see a spectacular variety of birds perched on it. I called to my 18-year-old daughter. "Kelly, come and see the birds!"

From the other room I heard, "I'm not that old yet, Mom."

— CARROLL J. SCHWING

When we moved cross country, my wife and I decided to drive both our cars. Nathan, our eight-year-old, worriedly asked, "How will we keep from getting separated?"

"We'll drive slow so one car can follow the other," I reassured him.

"Yeah, but what if we get separated?" he persisted.

"Then I guess we'll never see each other again," I quipped.

"Okay," he said, "I'm riding with Mom."

— JAMES C. BUSH

One afternoon while I was visiting my library, I noticed a group of preschoolers gathered for story time. The book they were reading was "There Was an Old Lady Who Swallowed a Fly."

"I've discovered that I'm homework intolerant."

After the librarian finished the first page, she asked the children, "Do you think she'll die?"

"Nope," a little girl in the back said. "I saw this last night on 'Fear Factor.'"

— BRIANNE BURCL

I was telling my three boys the story of the Nativity and how the Wise Men brought gifts of gold, frankincense and myrrh for the infant Jesus.

Clearly giving it a lot of thought, my six-year-old observed, "Mom, a Wise Woman would have brought diapers."

— ANGIE FLAUTE

My retired husband, Jim, has been attending a beginning watercolours class. During one session the instructor asked the class what they planned to do with their paintings when they were finished.

Virtually all of the students were undecided, but Jim knew exactly what he would do with his.

"I'm going to send them to my children," he said with a smile, "so they can put them on their refrigerators."

— BEVERLY D. LEE

QUOTABLE QUOTES

My perspective on my mother has changed immensely. She was a lot taller when I was younger.

— HOWIE MANDEL in I Love You, Mom! by Kelly Ripa and Others (Hyperion)

A perfect parent is a person with excellent child-rearing theories and no actual children.

— DAVE BARRY

All mothers have intuition. The great ones have radar.

— CATHY GUISEWITE, quoted in The Joys of Motherhood by Jane Hughes Paulson (Andrews McMeel)

Having a family is like having a bowling alley installed in your head.

— MARTIN MULL

Nowadays they say you need a special chip to put in the TV so kids can't watch this and that. In my day, we didn't need a chip. My mom was the chip. End of story.

— RAY CHARLES in Esquire

There's no such thing as fun for the whole family.

— JERRY SEINFELD

Raising kids is part joy and part guerrilla warfare.

— ED ASNER

Just be good and kind to your children. Not only are they the future of the world, they're the ones who can sign you into the home.

— DENNIS MILLER

How Did That Get There?

▶ BY LINDA M. SCHMITZ

My son, Adam, has always been an industrious child. One time, when he was four years old, he set out to invent a paper airplane with egg-carton wings. But he didn't just make one proto-type—he mass-produced an entire fleet. Don't get me wrong. I loved those airplanes . . . for several days. With two creative kids in the house, however, Adam's crafts had plenty of company—Popsicle-stick sculptures, rubber-band contraptions and polystyrene peanut people, to name just a few. So in an effort to declutter our home, I decided it was time for the last of the jumbo jets to be stored in its final hangar, if you know what I mean. After all, I told myself, we really can't keep everything.

After making sure the kitchen was child-free, I discreetly squashed the airplane deep into the trash can. As a precaution, I camouflaged it with a cereal box and a few carrot peelings.

Why did I think I could get away with it? I should know that no matter how sly I am, my kids always know when I'm trashing their treasures. And sure enough, just when I'd slid the garbage can back into place, in walked Adam. Right away he noticed something was amiss. Must be some kind of preschool radar, I figured.

He headed to the trash can, tossed in a tissue and trotted off to play. Whew, I thought, I'm in the clear. But suddenly he turned around and went back for a closer inspection.

Imagine my horror as I peered over his shoulder to see that the silly aircraft had wriggled its way out from under the cereal box, waving its feeble egg-carton wings in a last-ditch effort to be saved. Carrot peelings dangled accusingly from the tail.

"Mommmm! My airplane!" Adam howled. I quickly realized I had two choices: 1) feign disbe-lief—"How did that land there?"—and resurrect the aircraft, or 2) explain the impracticality of keeping everything he ever made.

I went for No. 1 this time. Gingerly I gathered up the smelly, broken jet in my arms as if it were museum-worthy and placed it on top of the refrig-erator. I'll get you next time, I said under my breath.

The other person who knows instinctively when I'm trashing something "valuable" is my daughter, Emily, who is three years older than Adam. Emily has saved everything from the moment she could wrap her fingers around it. A while ago, a survey of her "treasure boxes" revealed a foil candy wrapper dating back to Christmas '96, a napkin from a friend's birthday party, and a vast assortment of plastic pinkie rings.

But the real problem is her photographic memo-ry of the loot.

There's no sneaking a kid's "treasure" into the trash

She once asked me, "Mom, do you know where my plastic pinkie ring is that Aunt Laura gave me on my second birthday?"

Gulp. "Hmm..." I muttered thoughtfully, stalling for time.

"You know, it was in my heart-shaped box next to the friendship bracelet Suzanne gave me last May."

Of course. How could I forget? "Umm...I think the dog ate it."

"Mom, we don't have a dog!"

"Yes, but did I mention that Daddy and I are thinking of getting one?"

Even recycling isn't simple anymore. Adam once brought home a Styrofoam turtle he'd made at Bible school. We oohed and aahed appropriately. A few days later I encouraged the turtle to take a little swim in the recycle bin marked Styrofoam. Then I forgot all about it.

Three weeks later, off we went to the recycling centre to do our part as responsible citizens. My kids love to help dump the containers, something that turtle was apparently counting on. It waited until just the right moment to tattle on me as it tumbled out of our bin. "She threw me away-ay! She threw me away-ay," it seemed to chant.

My children stared at me in disbelief. There goes that Mother of the Year Award, I thought as I escorted the turtle back to the car.

After that incident I decided on a new plan: 1) wait till the kids are at school, 2) use a trash bag separate from the kitchen one, and 3) fill 'er up!

With twisted glee, I set about my task. Into the bag marched toilet-paper-tube soldiers, soggy party-favour blowers and a pink plastic alligator. I strangled the bulging bag with a knot even Houdini couldn't untie and tossed it into the garage. As I patted myself on the back that Tuesday morning, I failed to recognize the flaw in my plan: trash pickup wasn't for three more days.

By the time Friday rolled around, that annoying pink alligator from Chuck E. Cheese's had worked a hole in the bag with its pointy snout. Of course, I wasn't the only one to notice this, but you already guessed that. It was that preschool radar again.

My mom has been warning me for years that this, too, shall pass. All too soon I'll have a show-room-worthy refrigerator that won't double as an art gallery.

The dust bunnies under my kids' beds will long for the company of a rolled-up sock or half a crayon. Worst of all, this mom's trash will be painfully ordinary—banana peels, milk jugs, soup cans.

So with a tear in my eye—born partially of defeat, but mostly of sentiment—I rescued the struggling alligator from the garbage bag. For more than a year it sat proudly on a kitchen shelf.

But I didn't see it as just another piece of clutter. It served as a reminder to enjoy my children and their treasures today. Because the day will come when I'll throw something away, and it will actually stay there. ▲

I am an oral surgeon, and once I was scheduled to extract four wisdom teeth from Jim, a high-school football player, who had opted to be sedated for the procedure. As the IV anaesthesia was being administered, I asked Jim how he was feeling.

"Man," he replied, struggling to keep his eyes open, "I feel like I'm in English class."

— THOMAS F. KELLY, D.D.S.

During our computer class, the teacher chastised one boy for talking to the girl sitting next to him.

"I was just asking her a question," the boy said.

"If you have a question, ask me," the teacher tersely replied.

"Okay," he answered. "Do you want to go out with me Friday night?"

— TRACY MAXWELL

On a demographics survey given at our high school, students were asked, "What disadvantages do you see in having children?" Usual answers included "It's expensive to raise kids" and "They take up a lot of your time."

But one boy was not worried about money or responsibility. He wrote, "If I have children, I might have to drive a minivan."

— CHERITH DIEMERT

On vacation my nine-year-old son, Ryan, and I were at the pool, where two attractive young women wearing thong bikinis were sunning themselves. I noticed that Ryan kept staring at them, but he would occasionally glance back at me.

When they got up to leave, Ryan watched them particularly closely. I was bracing myself for questions he might have when he turned to me and whispered, "Dad, can I take that candy bar those girls left behind?"

— PAUL DELUCA

It began as an innocent game with my toddler son, Robert. I'd get in the fighter's stance and start shadowboxing. Jabbing with both fists, I'd say, "One-two, one-two," and he would imitate me over and over.

I never thought about the consequences of this little exercise until my wife took our son to a birthday party. When the boy's mother was handing out noise-makers she leaned over to Robert and asked, "Would you like one too?"

It took my wife a while to explain her way out of what happened next.

— ALFRED ISNARDI

My two-year-old cousin scared us one summer by disappearing during our lakeside vacation. More than a dozen relatives searched the forest and shoreline, and everyone was relieved when we found Matthew playing calmly in the woods.

"Listen to me, Matthew," his mother said sharply. "From now on when you want to go someplace, you tell Mommy first, okay?"

Matthew thought about that for a moment and said, "Okay. Disney World."

— LEAH HALLENBECK

Mel's son rushed in the door. "Dad! Dad!" he announced. "I got a part in the school play!"

"That's terrific," Mel said proudly. "What part is it?"

"I play the part of the dad"

Mel thought this over. "Go back tomorrow," he instructed, "and tell them you want a speaking role."

— DERLEEN GIANNINI

sign language

Sign above the scale in a doctor's office:
"Pretend it's your I.Q."

— LYNN MICLEA

Rushing to get to the movies, my husband and I told the kids we had to leave "right now"—at which point our teenage daughter headed for the bathroom to apply makeup. Her dad yelled for her to get in the car immediately, and headed for the garage grumbling.

On the way to the multiplex my husband glanced in the rearview mirror and caught our teen applying lipstick and blush, which produced the predictable lecture. "Look at your mom," he said. "She didn't put on any makeup just to go sit in a dark movie theatre."

From the back I heard, "Yeah, but Mom doesn't need makeup."

My heart swelling with the compliment, I turned back to thank this sweet, wonderful daughter of mine just as she continued, "Nobody looks at her."

— DELORES BREWINGTON

Our family was dazzled by the sights and the bustling crowds during a visit to Calgary. "This is the city that never sleeps," I told my eleven-year-old daughter.

"That's probably because there's a Starbucks on every corner," she observed.

— LINDA FOLEY

THE KIDS ARE ASLEEP. LET'S GO TO EUROPE.

MUELLER

While I sat in the reception area of my doctor's office, a woman rolled an elderly man in a wheelchair into the room. As she went to the receptionist's desk, the man sat there, alone and silent. Just as I was thinking I should make small talk with him, a little boy slipped off his mother's lap and walked over to the wheelchair.

Placing his hand on the man's, he said, "I know how you feel. My mom makes me ride in the stroller too."

— STEVE ANDERSON

When my neighbour's grand-daughter introduced me to her young son, Brian, I said to him, "My grandchildren call me Mimi. Why don't you call me that too?"

"I don't think so," he retorted, and ran off after his mother.

Later I was asked to baby-sit for Brian, and we hit it off wonderfully. As he snuggled up to me, he said, "I don't care what your grandchildren say. I love you, Meanie."

— MARILYN HAYDEN

Our teenage son, Marc, never misses an opportunity to remind us that he needs his own car. One morning as I drove him to school, it was apparent that we would be late. I asked him to write a note, which I would sign when we arrived.

At school, he handed me a pen and the note, which read: "Marc is late this morning due to car trouble. The trouble is, Marc doesn't have his own car, and his mom drives too slowly."

— LAURA Z. SOWERS

Since I am a busy mom of four, I rely on my children to help me out with everyday chores around the house. One morning I was running around trying to get the children and myself ready, when I suddenly realized it was trash pick-up day. So I handed a bag of garbage to my sleepy seven-year-old son and told him to toss it in the trash bin on his way out the door.

Glancing out my window moments later, I saw him wearily boarding the bus. He was carrying his backpack, his lunchbox and a big white bag of garbage.

— LYNN PAREJKO

After years of using the same perfumes, I decided to try something different and settled on a light, citrusy fragrance. The next day I was surprised when it was my little boy, not my husband, who first noticed the change. As he put his arms around me, he declared, "Wow, Mom, you smell just like Froot Loops!"

— TRINA MULDOON

My older son loves school, but his younger brother absolutely hates it. One weekend he cried and fretted and tried every excuse not to go back on Monday. Sunday morning on the way home from church, the crying and whining built to a crescendo. At the end of my rope, I finally stopped the car and explained, "Honey, it's a law. If you don't go to school, they'll put Mommy in jail."

He looked at me, thought a moment, then asked, "How long would you have to stay?"

— TRINA REES

One night about 10 p.m., I answered the phone and heard, "Dad, we want to stay out late. Is that okay?"

"Sure," I answered, "as long as you called."

When I hung up, my wife asked who was on the phone.

"One of the boys," I replied. "I gave them permission to stay out late."

"Not our boys," she said. "They're both downstairs in the basement."

— LAWRENCE M. WEISBERG

Timeless Humour from the '60s

My son, age 13, was sick in bed with bronchitis, and although he showed some general improvement, his harsh cough persisted and could be heard all over the house. Worried, too, that he was missing so much school, I went into his room to see how he felt.

There he was, propped up in bed, earphones on, listening to a baseball game—while the tape recorder coughed on and on. The next morning he was in school.

— JAMES S. WOODS

"It's a painting. There is no sound."

Meow, Mmmeow, Meaow

The Cat Years

▶ BY ADAIR LARA

I just realized that while children are dogs—loyal and affectionate—teenagers are cats. It's so easy to be a dog owner. You feed it, train it, boss it around. It puts its head on your knee and gazes at you as if you were a Rembrandt painting. It bounds indoors with enthusiasm when you call it.

Then, around age 13, your adoring little puppy turns into a big old cat. When you tell it to come inside, it looks amazed, as if wondering who died and made you emperor. Instead of dogging your footsteps, it disappears. You won't see it again until it gets hungry—then it pauses on its sprint through the kitchen long enough to turn its nose up at whatever you're serving. When you reach out to ruffle its head, in that old affectionate gesture, it twists away from you, then gives you a blank stare, as if trying to remember where it has seen you before.

You, not realizing that the dog is now a cat, think something must be desperately wrong with it. It seems so antisocial, so distant, sort of depressed. It won't go on family outings.

Since you're the one who raised it, taught it to fetch and stay and sit on command, you assume that you did something wrong. Flooded with guilt and fear, you redouble your efforts to make your pet behave.

Only now you're dealing with a cat, so every-thing that worked before now produces the oppo-site of the desired result. Call it, and it runs away. Tell it to sit, and it jumps on the counter. The more you go toward it, wringing your hands, the more it moves away.

Instead of continuing to act like a dog owner, you can learn to behave like a cat owner. Put a dish of food near the door, and let it come to you. But remember that a cat needs your help and your affection too. Sit still, and it will come, seeking that warm, comforting lap it has not entirely for-gotten. Be there to open the door for it.

One day, your grown-up child will walk into the kitchen, give you a big kiss and say, "You've been on your feet all day. Let me get those dishes for you." Then you'll real-ize your cat is a dog again. ▲

Adair Lara is the author of Hold Me Close, Let Me Go, *a memoir about raising a teenager (Broadway Books)*

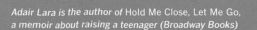

"What? I thought I *was* wearing it backwards."

QUOTABLE QUOTES

Setting a good example for your children does nothing but increase their embarrassment.

— DOUG LARSON, United Feature Syndicate

No matter how old a mother is, she watches her middle-aged children for signs of improvement.

— FLORIDA SCOTT-MAXWELL,
The Measure of My Days (Knopf)

If pregnancy were a book, they would cut the last two chapters.

— NORA EPHRON, Heartburn (Knopf)

Without enough sleep, we all become tall two-year-olds.

— JOJO JENSON, Dirt Farmer Wisdom (Red Wheel)

Like all parents, my husband and I just do the best we can, and hold our breath and hope we've set aside enough money for our kids' therapy.

— MICHELLE PFEIFFER

You know your kids are growing up when they stop asking you where they came from and refuse to tell you where they're going.

— P. J. O'ROURKE in First for Women

When it comes to raising children, I believe in give and take. I give orders and they take 'em.

— BERNIE MAC in People

There's an upside to grandparenthood. You play, you give, you love, then you hand them back and go to an early movie.

— BILLY CRYSTAL in Good Housekeeping

"It's hard to believe that in just a few weeks, I'll be refusing to eat it."

Being a teenager and getting a tattoo seem to go hand in hand these days. I wasn't surprised when one of my daughter's friends showed me a delicate little Japanese symbol on her hip. "Please don't tell my parents," she begged.

"I won't," I promised. "By the way, what does that stand for?"

"Honesty," she said.

— LINDA SINGER

Blood may be thicker than water, but hockey beats them both. I learned this after explaining to my two boys that they were half-Lithuanian on their father's side, and half-Yankee, meaning their other set of parents came from an old New England family.

My younger son looked worried. "But we're still a hundred percent Oilers, right, Mom?"

— GAYLA BIEKSHA

Visiting his parents' retirement village in Florida, my middle-aged friend, Tim, went for a swim in the community pool while his elderly father took a walk. Tim struck up a conversation with the only other person in the pool, a five-year-old boy. After a while, Tim's father returned from his walk and called out, "I'm ready to leave."

Tim then turned to his new friend and announced that he had to leave because his father was calling. Astonished, the wide-eyed little boy cried, "You're a kid?"

— JANICE PALKO

One night our local newscaster was reading about an allegation that two Sesame Street characters, Bert and Ernie, were gay. The show's producer refuted this, pointing out that they were only puppets, not humans. They argued a lot and then made up to show children how to resolve conflicts and stay friends.

While watching this report, my wife, Donna, noticed that our seven-year-old daughter was also listening. As Donna struggled to come up with an explanation for the term "gay," our crestfallen daughter said in dismay, "They're puppets?"

— BILL DOERING

As she slid behind the wheel for her first driving lesson, my daughter couldn't contain her excitement. "You need to make adjustments so the car is comfortable for you, the driver," I began. "Now, what's the first thing you should do?"

"Change the radio station," she said.

— RHONDA BUCALO

While doing renovations in our house, one of the workmen paused to look at a flattering photo of me wearing makeup and a fancy gown. I heard him let out a low whistle and ask my son, Joshua, "Who's that?"

"That's my mom," Joshua answered.

"Wow," the man said, "my mother doesn't look like that."

"Yeah," my son said, "well, neither does mine."

— TAMMY L. VITULANO

My sister had been ill, so I called to see how she was doing. My ten-year-old niece answered the phone. "Hello," she whispered.

"Hi, honey. How's your mother?" I asked.

"She's sleeping," she answered, again in a whisper.

"Did she go to the doctor?"

"Yes. She got some medicine," my niece said softly.

"Well, don't wake her up. Just tell her I called. What are you doing, by the way?"

Again in a soft whisper, she answered, "Practising my trumpet."

— SHARRON DISBRO

As my five-year-old son and I were heading to McDonald's one day, we passed a car accident. Usually when we see something terrible like that, we say a prayer for whoever might be hurt, so I pointed and said to my son, "We should pray."

From the back seat I heard his earnest voice: "Dear God, please don't let those cars block the entrance to McDonald's."

— SHERRI LEARD

Preparing my son for his first day of kindergarten, we were reviewing numbers and counting. Suddenly he asked, "What is the biggest number in the world?"

As briefly as possible, I tried to explain the concept of infinity. I thought I had done pretty well, but then he said, "Dad, what number comes just before infinity?"

— SHAWN FOSTER

For years I had been telling my friend Pete that he ate too much fast food, but he always denied it. One day he admitted I was right.

"What changed your mind?"

"My grandson. When my daughter told him I was coming to visit, he asked, 'Grandpa from Florida, or Grandpa from Pizza Hut?' "

— STEVE FRANK

I am a first-grade teacher and a new empty nester. One night I was trying out an art project: making a person with simple materials. I took a coat hanger, attached a paper-plate face, put a shirt on the hanger and stuffed it. Then I sat it on the couch to see how it looked.

Later that evening my son walked in the door, home for a surprise visit. Taking one look at my coat-hanger friend sitting on the couch, he said, "Mom, it's not that bad, is it?"

— LINDA ADAMS

"Go ask your mother."

I was teaching a life-skills class to my high school students one day, and we were discussing the various terms one might encounter in a restaurant. I asked,

"What does the phrase 'à la carte' mean?"
"It means," a student said, "you're in the wrong restaurant."

— ALBERT T. GRANDE

Time for "The Talk"

▶ BY BRET LOTT

"Boys pupate at around age 15," my older son, Zeb, said matter-of-factly one day after school.

"They what?" I asked.

"Pupate," he said. "Your voice changes. You get hair." He paused. "A lady from the medical school talked to our class today."

It was then I remembered that the month before, he'd come home and told us about metamorphosis in butterflies, the whole business of worms turning into miraculous flying creatures.

Holding back laughter, I said, "You mean puberty."

"Yeah," he replied, shrugging, "that's it."

"'Pupate,'" I said, "that's good."

"Actually," my wife, Melanie, added, "that's a pretty good idea of what happens."

Zeb, at ten, knows more about sex than I did at his age. I am certain of this because Melanie and I took it upon ourselves to have The Talk with Zeb the summer before he started fourth grade. Our decision to tell him the truth about where babies come from was a direct result of the mutant facts that Melanie and I had been given as kids.

We told our younger son, Jake, seven, he could watch TV in our bedroom, a treat that would assure our privacy in the kitchen. Then we got out our copy of ABC's of the Human Body and had Zeb sit with us at the kitchen table.

"There are some things we want you to know about before you start school this fall," Melanie said.

Zeb crossed his arms and looked at us with the level stare he employs when he suspects trouble: eyes half-closed, lower jaw jutting forward.

"Do you know where babies come from?" Melanie went on.

"Yes," he said, too quickly. "I know." He held his arms tighter.

"Where?" I asked. I smiled, trying hard to soften what sounded like a cross-examination.

He shrugged.

"We want to explain it to you," Melanie said, "so that if kids try to tell you something crazy at school, you'll know the truth." Then, slowly, she turned to me. "Bret?"

I took a breath, swallowed and turned to Zeb.

He put his hands up to his ears and covered them.

I remember looking at my mom one night during dinner and asking flat out, "Where do babies come from?" This must have been in fourth grade, right about the time I picked up the facts of life "on the street." I'll never forget my dad's reaction.

"Hey!" he shouted, leaning toward me, a fork in one hand, a knife in the other. "Don't talk like that!"

I am not kidding. That's what he said.

Mom defended me, saying, "He just asked."

Dad sat straight in his chair. We four children were looking at him, waiting. Then he put his fork and knife to the pork chop on his plate. "Well, this isn't the time or the place. It's rude."

I wouldn't get The Talk

A defining moment of parenthood had arrived

for another four years. By that time some friends and I had built a fort where we huddled and joked about creased pages torn out of *Playboy*.

Then one day Mom suddenly said, "You and your father need to have a talk." Dad looked at her, swallowed and said to me, "All right, let's go," then headed down the hall toward their bedroom.

He sat down on the bed. His eyes hadn't yet met mine. He put his hands on his thighs, lifted them, let them drop. "Well," he said. "Okay."

I had him in a way I'd never known before: powerless, stunned. So, to make matters worse, I said, "Go ahead. I'm listening."

He looked at me. "Well, what do you want to know?"

I shrugged, then let the question hang in the air a few moments before saying, "I already know."

"Okay," he said, and breathed out. "Good. That's good." Then he laughed. It was a nice, solid laugh, a kind of laugh I hadn't heard before.

That was The Talk for me, the one everyone either gets or doesn't get.

I got one, but it gave me nothing, only a glimpse of my dad without armour, defenceless.

Zeb surrendered his hands from his ears once we brought out the diagrams and photos, his eyes wide open, taking in the images. I don't remember what we said, but the words lined up in a semblance of factual order.

Zeb finally started laughing. It was laughter like what my dad had shared with me: laughter of relief about this whole huge mystery—sex.

We finished off this astonishing set of facts by revealing to Zeb the greater truth behind it all: that this is all a result of love and respect. We told him this is part of what it means to be a husband and wife. Sex is a sacred act, a gift from God, carried out after love has been secured through marriage.

Now Zeb knows the truth. At least—and at best—both his mom and dad have had a hand in how he came to find out.

The mystery of it all is still

revealing itself to me, here in my own marriage. One evening we were in the van, backing down the driveway.

"Wait," Melanie said, "my sunglasses." I stopped; she climbed out and headed toward the front door. There was something about the way her hair fell, something about the back of her neck, that made me say, "She's beautiful, isn't she?"

The boys were quiet behind me. Finally Zeb said, "Yeah."

Then came Jake's voice: "Hubba-hubba," he said. I turned around and looked at him. He was grinning. "Ooh, baby," he said.

"Where'd you hear that?" I asked, trying not to laugh.

"My friend Garrett," Jake said, still grinning. "He says that all the time about Sarah and Elizabeth."

I shook my head. One down, one to go. ▲

Football players at the high school where I worked were stealing the practice jerseys, so the coach ordered a set with "Property of Central High School" emblazoned on them. When the thefts continued, he ordered a new batch that had the imprint "Stolen From Central High School." But the jerseys still kept disappearing.

The larceny finally stopped after he changed the wording to "Central High School 4th String."

— HAL OLSEN

When my daughter was little, we took a vacation to P.E.I. Seated on the airplane near the wing, I pointed out to Rhonda that we were above the ocean. "Can you see the water?" I asked her.

"No," she said, peering out the window at the wing, "but I can see the diving board."

— REBECCA RICCI

My husband, a big-time sports fan, was watching a football game with our grandchildren. He had just turned 75 and was feeling a little wistful. "You know," he said to our grandson, Nick, "it's not easy getting old. I guess I'm in the fourth quarter now."

"Don't worry, Grandpa," Nick said cheerily. "Maybe you'll go into overtime."

— EVELYN BREDLEAU

Thinking his son would enjoy seeing the reenactment of a colonial battle, my niece's husband took the boy, Will, to the event. But the poor child was terrified by the booming cannons. During a lull, Will's dad finally got him calmed down.

That's when the British general hollered,

"Fire at Will!"

Betty Ammar

While driving on the highway, my daughter noticed a child in the window of a car in the next lane, holding up a handwritten sign that read "Help."

A few minutes later, the car passed her and she again glanced at it. The little boy held up the same sign and this time followed it with another, which read "My mother is singing!"

— LIL GIBSON

The board of education in a nearby town sold off a building that had been a one-room schoolhouse. The buyer converted it to a tavern. One day an elderly man was walking by the place with his grandson and pointed to the building.

"That's where I went to school when I was your age."

"Really," said the boy. "Who was your bartender back then?"

— DUANE SMITH

It was the first day of high school basketball practice. The coach handed a ball to each player. "Fellas," he said, "I want you to practise shooting from the spots you might expect to be in during the game."

The No. 12 sub immediately sat down on the bench and began arcing the ball toward the basket.

— HERMAN L. MASIN

On our way to my parents' house for dinner one evening, I glanced over at my 15-year-old daughter. "Isn't that skirt a bit short?" I asked. She rolled her eyes at my comment and gave me one of those "Oh, Mom" looks.

When we arrived at my folks' place, my mother greeted us at the door, hugged my daughter, then turned to me and said, "Elizabeth! Don't you think that blouse is awfully low-cut?"

— ELIZABETH SCOTT

After registering for his high school classes, my son burst into the house, filled with excitement. "Dad," he announced in one breath, "I got all the classes I wanted. But I have to have my school supplies by tomorrow. I need a protractor and a compass for geometry, a dictionary for English, a dissecting kit for biology—and a car for driver's ed."

— JIM TIMMONS

My cooking has always been the target of family jokes. One evening, as I prepared dinner a bit too quickly, the kitchen filled with smoke and the smoke detector went off. Although both of my children had received fire-safety training at school, they did not respond to the alarm. Annoyed, I stormed through the house in search of them. I found them in the bathroom, washing their hands.

Over the loud buzzing of the smoke alarm, I asked them to identify the sound.

"It's the smoke detector," they replied in unison.

"Do you know what that sound means?" I demanded.

"Sure," my oldest replied. "Dinner's ready."

— DEBI CHRISTENSEN

Timeless Humour from the '70s

Toward the end of the school year, the sixth-grade teachers decide which of their students should be accelerated in certain subjects in the seventh grade. When a child is chosen, his parents are notified. When one boy was accelerated in science and math, his mother wrote to the teacher: "I think this is quite an honour for someone who just tried to make two litres of lemonade in a one-litre pitcher!"

— MRS. MARVIN PADNICK

"Do you win every time?"

I had finished my Christmas shopping early and had wrapped all the presents. Having two curious children, I had to find a suitable hiding place. I chose an ideal spot—the furnace room. I stacked the presents and covered them with a blanket, positive they'd remain undiscovered.

When I went to get the gifts to put them under the tree, I lifted the blanket and there, stacked neatly on top of my gifts, were presents addressed to "Mom and Dad, From the Kids."

— LORALIE LONG

As I was nursing my baby, my cousin's six-year-old daughter, Krissy, came into the room. Never having seen anyone breastfeed before, she was intrigued and full of all kinds of questions about what I was doing.

After mulling over my answers, she remarked, "My mom has some of those, but I don't think she knows how to use them."

— LOIS SINGER

My husband and I both work, so our family eats out a lot. Recently, when we were having a rare home-cooked meal, I handed a glass to my three-year-old and told her to drink her milk.

She looked at me bewildered and replied, "But I didn't order milk."

— JANET A. NUSSBAUM

One of my fourth graders asked my teacher's assistant, "How old are you, Mrs. Glass?"

"You should never ask an adult's age," I broke in.

"That's okay," Harriett said smiling. "I'm fifty."

"Wow, you don't look that old," the boy said. I was breathing a sigh of relief when another child chimed in, "Parts of her do."

— KATHERINE NORGARD

I was having lunch with my daughter Rachel, who's three, at our local mall and was feeling particularly macho for a 46-year-old. All morning, women had been smiling at me and giving me the eye.

Getting up to leave the table, I ran my fingers through my hair—and discovered two yellow-ducky barrettes that had been lovingly placed there hours before.

— PAUL J. MEYER

My mother was away all weekend at a business conference. During a break, she decided to call home collect. My six-year-old brother picked up the phone and heard a stranger's voice say, "We have a Marcia on the line. Will you accept the charges?"

Frantic, he dropped the receiver and came charging outside screaming, "Dad! They've got Mom! And they want money!"

— RODNEY HOWELL

"I remind you that my client is nice until proven naughty."

Dumb and Dumber

People do dumb things—the dumber, the funnier.
Here are the verbal flubs, social gaffes and fix-it fiascos
we love to laugh at—as long as they're not ours.

"But I have a witness. Here, talk to her yourself."

My wife received a credit-card application in the mail that she had not requested. She didn't want it, but I did. So I crossed off my wife's name on the form, entered my own and returned the application. I soon got a phone call from a woman saying my application had been rejected.

I asked her why, and she told me the card could only be issued to the person originally solicited by the offer. However, she invited me to reapply, which I did during the same telephone call.

A few days later I got another call to tell me my second application had been rejected.

Why? The woman told me their files showed that I had previously applied for a card and had been denied.

— SANFORD P. BLANK

When the skipper of an Icelandic trawler accidentally rammed Englishman Jim Hughes's yacht, he caused $30,000 worth of damage. Exactly a year and a day before, reported the London *Times*, the skipper, Eriker Olafsson, had hit the same boat, causing $40,000 in damage.

What are the odds of this happening twice? Pretty good, since Olafsson purposely steered toward Hughes to apologize for the previous year's collision.

— KIRSTY SCOTT

During our church service one Sunday, a parishioner was speaking about an emotionally charged topic and had trouble controlling her tears. Finishing her remarks, she told the congregation, "I apologize for crying so much. I'm usually not such a big boob."

The bishop rose to close the session and remarked, "That's okay. We like big boobs."

— L.S.

My family was in a celebrating mood, so we decided to go out to a fancy steakhouse. As our waiter stood there ready to take our orders, I was caught up listening to the background music that was piped into the restaurant. "What CD is this?" I asked him.

Apparently my accent confused him, because he leaned over and answered, "Calgary."

— JULIE A. FOLGER

On vacation in Hawaii, my stepmom, Sandy, called a café to make reservations for 7 p.m. Checking her book, the cheery young hostess said, "I'm sorry, all we have is 6:45. Would you like that?"

"That's fine," Sandy said.

"Okay," the woman confirmed. Then she added, "Just be advised you may have to wait 15 minutes for your table."

— KELLY FINNEGAN

Calling for information about one of my credit cards, I got the following recorded prompt: "Please enter your account number as it appears on your card or statement."

I did as instructed, and the system said, "Please enter your postal code."

After I put that in, I got a third message: "If you would like your information in English, press one."

— MICHELLE GOLF

Timeless Humour from the '60s

As a salesman, I was searching for a certain company in unfamiliar territory. I came to a likely-looking road marked with a small red sign reading: Industrial Centre. I was not certain that this was the right road, so I drove back to a gas station to inquire.

The attendant took my arm and pointed to the sign that I had just read, now barely discernible in the distance. "See that little sign about three blocks away?" he asked.

"You mean the red one that says industrial centre?" I asked.

"Man!" he exclaimed. "You've got eyes like an eagle!"

— EDWARD M. LONGAN

My husband decided life would be easier if he wired a new light switch in the master bedroom to save us from fumbling in the dark for the lamp. He cut through the drywall and found a stash of bottles and small boxes inside the wall. "Honey!" he called excitedly. "Come see what I found!" I ran in and quickly realized that his next task would be to fix the hole that now led into the back of our medicine cabinet.

—NOLA PIRART

It was the standard series of check-in questions that every traveller gets at the airlines counter, including, "Has anyone put anything in your baggage without your knowledge?"

"If it was put there without my knowledge," I asked, "how would I know?"

The agent behind the counter smiled smugly. "That's why we ask."

— KATE VETTER

sign language

Sign in front of golf shop:

"Golf Balls the Size of Hail."

— EMILY WIRTES

"It says, 'Separate two eggs.' Is that far enough?"

When I moved to the west coast, I was a nervous wreck about earthquakes. My friend Linda, who was born and raised there, was completely blasé. I remember once when we pulled up to a light, her Honda began to shake.

She looked worried until I stammered, "I think that we're having an earthquake."

"Thank goodness," Linda said. "I thought something was wrong with my car."

— DYAN ARNOLD

My mother, a meticulous housekeeper, often lectured my father about tracking dirt into the house. One day he came in to find her furiously scrubbing away at a spot on the floor and launching into a lecture. "I don't know what you've brought in," she said, "but I can't seem to get this out."

He studied the situation for a moment and, without a word, moved a figurine on the windowsill where the sun was streaming in. The spot immediately disappeared.

— MICHELE DONNELLY

During weekly visits to my allergist, I've noticed a lot of inattentive parents with ill-behaved children in the waiting room. So I was impressed one day to see a mother with her little boy, helping him sound out the words on a sign.

Finally he mastered it and his mother cheered, "That's great! Now sit there. I'll be back in 15 minutes."

What did the sign say? "Children must not be left unattended."

— DARLENE HOVEL

On my way to a picnic, I stopped at a fast-food place to order a litre of potato salad. "We don't sell it by the litre," the clerk snapped.

"Okay, then give me two pints, please," I replied.

I'm proud to say I held my tongue when she asked, "Do you want it in one container?"

— JULIE GUITERREZ

An aching back sent me stumbling to the drugstore for relief. After a search I found what I was looking for: a selection of heating pads specifically for people with back pain—all on the bottom shelf.

— KATHERINE JOHNSON

While rummaging through her attic, my friend Kathryn found an old shotgun. Unsure about how to dispose of it, she called her parents. "Take it to the police station," her mother suggested.

My friend was about to hang up when her mother added, "And Kathryn?"

"Yes, Mom?"

"Call first."

— KAREN WHEDON

An unintentional double entendre from a local flyer: "Mixing bowl set designed to please a cook with round bottom for efficient beating."

— C. P. LEWIS

One day while at the doctor's office, the receptionist called me to the desk to update my personal file. Before I had a chance to tell her that all the information she had was still correct, she asked, "Has your birthdate changed?"

— MARGARET FREESE

Dining out one evening, I noticed some teenagers celebrating at a nearby table. When one girl pulled out a camera, I offered to take a picture of the group. After one photo, I suggested taking another just in case the first one didn't come out.

"Oh, no, that's okay," she said, as she took back her camera. "I always get double prints."

— DEANNA GUY

"Reservations? No, we definitely want to eat here."

Ha, Ha, Ha! Tee-Hee! Ho

Clumsy Crooks

▶ BY DANIEL BUTLER, ALAN RAY AND
LELAND GREGORY

Police work, like any other stressful profession, is full of moments when situations take a turn toward the absurd. Here are a few criminals who, through selfishness, ignorance or greed, proved themselves not just dumb, but dumber:

Positive ID

"We got a call that a woman's purse had been stolen," recalls Detective Chris Stewart of Brunswick, Georgia. "A short time later we saw a man who fit the description the victim gave us. So we picked him up and took him back to the scene of the crime."

Stewart explained to the suspect that when they arrived he was to exit the vehicle and face the victim for a positive ID. The suspect did exactly as he had been told. He stepped from the car, looked at the victim and blurted out, "Yeah, that's her! That's the woman I robbed."

Run of Bad Luck

When the robber from Pensacola, Florida, entered a liquor store to hold it up, he found too many people around. So he switched to Plan B. Fishing in his pocket for a piece of paper, he scrawled a note demanding money. The cashier quickly handed over all the money in the drawer, and the man was out the door in a flash. He seemed to have pulled off the robbery with flawless precision.

Except for one important little detail. He had written the note on the back of a letter from his probation officer—complete with his own name and address.

Right on His Heels

Outside Lawrence, Kansas, an all-night market had just been robbed. Police units in the area responded quickly to the alarm, but the fleeing thief wasn't worried. It was dark, he was a fast runner, and he knew the neighbourhood like the back of his hand.

It didn't take long for the thief to leave the first pair of officers behind. But more officers joined in the chase. Each time the frustrated suspect would elude one pursuer, he would be spotted by another, until he was finally captured.

He really hadn't been hard to find. Pursuing officers had simply followed the red lights on his heels—the ones that blinked on and off every time his high-tech running shoes hit the ground.

Clothes Make the Man

One day an apartment-complex maintenance man in Virginia Beach decided to supplement his income by robbing a 7-Eleven store. He wore a ski mask and made his voice deep as he ordered, "Give me all the money." Staring, the clerk handed it over.

When the police arrived, they asked the 7-Eleven employee to describe the robber. "He was wearing a ski mask," said the clerk, "and a blue maintenance uniform." On the front of the uniform were the name of an apartment house and the man's name.

Ha, Ha! Hee Hee! Ho! Ha

A lineup of fumbling felons, and bumbling bad guys

The two officers looked at each other. Surely not. But when they appeared at the maintenance man's apartment, he hadn't even changed clothes. The ski mask? In his back pocket. The money? In his front pocket.

Winner Loses

When the woman hit the California state lottery for thousands, she was thrilled. It seemed things were really looking up. Her picture appeared in the local newspaper, and people on the street recognized her. Unfortunately for her, so did the police. A local cop remembered her as the woman wanted by authorities on an eight-month-old shoplifting warrant.

Some of the money she had just won went toward paying her fine.

AND IF YOU THINK ONLY AMERICAN CROOKS ARE DUMB, READ ON...

Lost, Found—and Jailed
BY BONNIE MUNDAY

It happened in Winnipeg, just before Christmas. A guy lost $91,000 in illegal drug money in a shopping mall—then went personally to the lost-and-found office the next day to try to get it back!

Most shoppers in the Polo Park mall would have had visions of sugar plums dancing in their heads, and Christmas wish lists in their wallets and purses. But 30-year-old Richard Wong, sitting in the food court, presumably enjoying some refreshments, must have had other things on his mind—cocaine dealing—and he carried more than a wish list. Inside his black backpack were 91 rolls of $1,000 each wrapped in elastic bands. That could buy a lot of Christmas presents, but Wong's next move would make for a decidedly unhappy holiday season. For reasons unfathomable, the Vancouver native didn't remember to take that backpack with him when he left the food court.

Most drug dealers worth their salt would have, when they realized what they'd done, cut their losses and laid low. Not Wong. The next day he actually returned to the mall's lost-and-found office.

Then—get this—when police showed up, after mall security called them, Wong was found in possession of a Palm Pilot that contained a list of drug transactions. To top it off, he'd brought along the key to a locker that contained almost two kilos of cocaine and three quarters of a kilo of crack.

"It appears he is totally inept," said Crown attorney Paul Jensen during Wong's trial. "The way he conducted himself shows that he's really not, from what I can see, a seasoned drug dealer. His practices seem to indicate that if he wasn't caught this time, it was inevitable he would get caught sometime."

Wong pleaded guilty to possession for the purpose of trafficking in cocaine and was sentenced to five years in prison. ▲

A man played golf every Saturday and always got home around 2:00 in the afternoon. One Saturday, however, he rushed in at 7:30 p.m and blurted to his wife. "I left the course at the normal time, but on the way home I stopped to change a flat for a young woman. She offered to buy me a drink, one thing led to another, and we spent the afternoon in a motel. I'm so sorry. I'll never do it again." "Don't hand me that malarkey," the angry wife shouted. "You played 36 holes, didn't you?"

— GEORGE W. EDWARDS

Sometime around two in the morning our phone rang, waking us out of a sound sleep. "Wrong number," my husband growled and slammed down the receiver.

A few minutes later it rang again. I heard him say, "One with pepperoni and extra cheese and one with sausage. Pick up in 20 minutes."

"What was that?" I asked.

"I took his order. Now we can sleep."

— JACKIE HUTH

I was getting
into my car when
I noticed a dent.
On the windshield
was a note and a
phone number from
the driver.
"I feel terrible," the
woman apologized
when I called.
"I hit your car as I
was pulling into the
next parking spot."

"Please, don't worry,"
I said to her.
"I'm sure our insur-
ance companies
will take care of
everything."

"Thank you for your
understanding," she
said. "You're so
much nicer than
the man I hit on the
way out."

Laurie Payne

After I asked for a 250-gram trout fillet at my supermarket's seafood counter, the clerk picked one out of a pile and set it on the scale. It weighed precisely 250 grams.

Impressed, I asked, "How did you know?"

Looking pleased with himself, he declared, "I'm psychotic."

— GLADYS HOCUTT

While on the freeway in Oakville, I was behind a pack of cars. The last driver was on the phone and drifting all over the road. This did not escape the attention of an OPP officer, who snuck up behind her and said over his loudspeaker, "If you can't stay in your lane while on the phone, pull over until the call is completed."

Immediately eight cars pulled over.

— GREG ASH

I was preparing to teach a college course on the history of movie censorship and went to the library to take out films that had been censored. "Do you have any banned movies in your collection?" I asked the librarian.

"Oh yes," she answered. "We have some really good ones. What would you like: Tommy Dorsey? Glenn Miller?"

— PAUL H. STACY

The first day at my new health club I asked the girl at the front desk, "I like to exercise after work. What are your hours?" "Our club is open 24/7," she told me excitedly, "Monday through Saturday."

— APRYL CAVENDER

Stormy weather diverted our Vancouver-bound flight to another airport. As we approached the runway, the pilot came on the intercom: "For those of you who are not familiar with the area, this is Kelowna."

Then he paused. "And for those of you who are familiar with this area, I *think* this is Kelowna."

— DARRELL BURTON

No one is more cautious than a first-time parent. After our daughter was big enough to ride on the back of my bicycle, I bought a special carrier with a seat belt and got her a little helmet. The day of the first ride I put her in the seat, double-checked all the equipment, wheeled the bike to the end of the driveway, carefully looked both ways and, swinging my leg up over the crossbar, accidentally kicked her in the chin.

— ZACHARY GIBBS

Living in a dry county was the bane of my friend Robert's existence. He was complaining to me one day about having to make a 75-kilometre round trip to get his favourite brand of rye. "I buy it by the case," he said.

"Are you addicted to that stuff?" I asked.

Robert thought for a second. "I don't know. I've never run out."

— RICK WORKMAN

For my grandmother's 80th birthday, we had a huge family celebration and even managed to get a photo announcement printed in the local paper. "That was a nice shot," I commented.

"It's my passport picture," she revealed.

"Really?" I stared in amazement at my homebody grandma. "Where did you go?"

"The Bay," she replied.

— KAREN THOMPSON

My mother is always trying to understand what motivates people, especially those in her family. One day she and my sister were talking about one relative's bad luck. "Why do you suppose she changed jobs?" Mother asked my sister. "Maybe she has a subconscious desire not to succeed."

"Or maybe it just happened," said my sister, exasperated. "Do you know you analyze everything to death?"

Mother was silent for a moment. "That's true," she said. "Why do you think I do that?"

— BOBBIE S. CYPHERS

Our pastor was winding down. In the back of the church the fellowship committee stood to go to the church hall and prepare snacks for the congregation. Seeing them get up, Pastor Michel singled them out for praise.

"Before they all slip out," he urged, "let's give these ladies a big hand in the rear."

— GORDON MOORE

Recently my wife was behind a car with three bumper stickers: "Don't be fooled by genetically engineered food—demand labels and safety testing for food"; "Eat for the health of it"; and "Support organic farmers."

The car was in front of her at a McDonald's drive-through.

— BROOKS MONK

Low on gas while on a vacation trip to Ottawa, I pulled my van into a service station. As I was turning in, I spied lying on the ground a gas cap that looked like it might replace my missing one. I hurriedly parked by the pump, jumped out of the van, ran over and picked up the cap. I was pleasantly surprised to find that it screwed easily onto my tank.

A perfect fit, I thought. And then I noticed the keyhole in the top of the cap.

— BOB SJOSTRAND

New to Canada, I was eager to meet people. So one day I struck up a conversation with the only other woman in the gym. Pointing to two men playing racquetball in a nearby court, I said to her, "There's my husband." Then I added, "The thin one—not the fat one."

After a slightly uncomfortable silence she replied, "And that's my husband—the fat one."

— NITYA RAMAKRISHNAN

My new credit card arrived in the mail with a large sticker on it, giving the phone number to activate the card. I called the number and got one option: "Press One" to activate the credit card. That led me to a live person, who answered with her first name and the title "Credit Card Activator."

As I got ready to give her the necessary information, she interrupted me, asking, "How can I help you?"

— ANGELA NOLAN

---

sign language

On a plumbing contractor's truck:

"You Don't Have to Sleep With That Drip Tonight."

— CARL C. WURST

I am full-figured, and when I dine in restaurants, I often find the chairs too small and uncomfortable. The last time I ate out, I filled in a comment card, saying that while the food and service were wonderful, the chairs did not accommodate anyone over a size 14.

Several weeks later I received a note of apology—and a coupon for a free dessert.

— PAT BALLARD

The road by my house was in bad condition after a rough winter. Every day I dodged potholes on the way to work. So I was relieved to see a construction crew working on the road one morning.

Later, on my way home, I noticed no improvement. But where the construction crew had been working stood a new, bright-yellow sign with the words "Rough Road."

— SARAH KRAYBILL LIND

A couple of hours into a visit with my mother she noticed I hadn't lit up a cigarette once. "Are you trying to kick the habit?"

"No," I replied, "I've got a cold and I don't smoke when I'm not feeling well."

"You know," she observed, "you'd probably live longer if you were sick more often."

— IAN A. HAMMEL

For our honeymoon my fiancée and I chose a fashionable hotel known for its luxurious suites. When I called to make reservations, the desk clerk inquired, "Is this for a special occasion?"

"Yes," I replied." It's our honeymoon."

"And how many adults will there be?" she asked.

— LARRY REEVES

My father and I belong to the religion of Sikhism. We both wear the traditional turban and often encounter strange comments and questions. Once, in a restaurant, a child stared with amazement at my father. She finally got the courage to ask, "Are you a genie?"

Her mother, caught off guard, turned red in the face and apologized for the remark. But my dad took no offence and decided to humour the child.

He replied, "Why, yes I am. I can grant you three wishes."

The child's mother blurted out, "Really?"

— MANVIR KALSI

Over the years, my husband and I have usually managed to decode the cute but confusing gender signs they sometimes put on restroom doors in restaurants (Buoys & Gulls, Laddies & Lassies, etc.), but every so often we get stumped. Recently my husband, Dave, wandered off in search of the men's room and found himself confronted by two marked doors. One was labelled "Bronco" and the other was designated "Cactus."

Completely baffled, he stopped a restaurant employee passing by. "Excuse me, I need to use the restroom," Dave said. Gesturing toward the doors, he asked, "Which one should I use?"

"Actually, we would prefer you to go there," the employee said, pointing to a door down the hall marked "Men." "Bronco and Cactus are private dining rooms."

— SHERRIE LEE

An author was coming to my local bookstore to discuss her novel set in the Prairies. The main character was "a strong-willed heroine fighting to survive the hardships of the times."

When I went to the reading, I was disappointed to learn the writer had cancelled her appearance. The reason? She didn't want to drive in the rain.

— DIANE MARSHALL

Our first day at a resort my wife and I decided to hit the beach. When I went back to our room to get something to drink, one of the hotel maids was making our bed. I grabbed my cooler and was on my way out when I paused and asked, "Can we drink beer on the beach?"

"Sure," she said, "but I have to finish the rest of the rooms first."

— LOUIS ALLARD

A friend of ours was puzzled with the odd messages left on his answering machine. Day after day friends and family would talk and then say, "Beep." He discovered the reason for the joke when he decided to listen to his greeting.

"Hi," it said. "I'm not in right now, so please leave a beep after the message."

— SHEEBA MATHEW

After a recent move, I made up a list of companies, agencies and services that needed to know my new address and phoned each to ask them to make the change. Everything went smoothly until I made a call to one of my frequent-flyer accounts. After I explained to her what I wanted to do, the woman I reached in customer service told me, "I'm sorry; we can't do that over the phone. You will have to fill out our change-of-address form."

"How do I get one of those?" I asked.

"We'd be happy to provide you with one," she said pleasantly. "Can I have your new address so I can mail it to you?"

Bad weather had backed up all flights, and as a result our plane sat on the runway for three hours. All attempts to placate the passengers weren't working. Then the pilot came on the intercom to announce his umpteenth update: "We'll be getting permission to take off, but I have to tell you that we're 26th in line for departure."

As a collective groan filled the aircraft, a flight attendant took the mike and added, "Ladies and gentlemen, please close your window shades. We'll soon be showing our almost-inflight hit movie, *Anger Management*."

— STEVE NORTH

After booking my 90-year-old mother on a flight from Halifax to Winnipeg, I called the airline to go over her needs. The woman representative listened patiently as I requested a wheelchair and an attendant for my mother because of her arthritis and impaired vision. I also asked for a special meal and assistance in changing planes.

My apprehension lightened a bit when the woman assured me everything would be taken care of. I thanked her profusely.

"Why, you're welcome," she replied. I was about to hang up when she cheerfully asked, "And will your mother be needing a rental car?"

— THOMAS A. CORBETT

During a beautiful spring afternoon, I was attending a folk music festival. Just as I stopped to listen to a folk singer, a group of exhibitors, dragging out tools and sawhorses, began setting up their display booth nearby. All their shouting and hammering made it difficult to enjoy the music. The noise they made got louder and even more obnoxious and intrusive as time went on.

Finally, to everyone's relief, they completed the construction. As a finishing touch, they hung a sign on their booth. It read "Silent Auction."

— JIM TRUMAN

Timeless Humour from the '70s

One October my wife and I spent a vacation in British Columbia. We were eager to visit the rainforests near the coast, but we heard that snowslides had made some of the roads impassable. Although apprehensive about the conditions we might run into, we drove on.

Sure enough, we had gone only a short way on the highway when we saw a sign: "Ice 10 kilometres."

Five kilometres farther on there was another: "Ice 5 kilometres."

The next one was: "Ice 1 kilometre." We practically crept that last kilometre.

Then we came to the last sign. It was outside a small grocery store, and it read: "Ice 50¢."

— GIFFORD S. WALKER

115

There's a scar on my face from a car accident. A customer came into the gas station where I work, glanced at me and exclaimed, "My God, what happened to you?" I told him and hoped that would be the end of it. But he kept pressing me for more information.

Finally, he made his purchase and, just before walking away, said, "Hey, don't worry about it. It's not that noticeable."

— ROBERT GOEBEL

At 82 years old, my husband applied for his first passport. He was told he would need a birth certificate, but his birth had never been officially registered. When he explained his dilemma to the passport agent, the response was less than helpful.

"In lieu of a birth certificate," the agent said, "you can bring a notarized affidavit from the doctor who delivered you."

— ELGARDA ASHLIMAN

One day my wife and I came home to find a message from a friend of hers on our answering machine. She said she had applied for a job and needed a character reference—basically someone to verify she was honest and trust-

"Of course, it's nothing serious, honey... just a flooded engine."

worthy—and had given the interviewer my wife's name. Also, she said, there was a form for my wife to sign.

"But I couldn't find you," the friend concluded, "so I forged your signature."

— WILL PETERS

When I walked up to the ATM at my bank, I noticed someone had left his card in the slot. Since it was a Friday evening, I thought the Good Samaritan thing to do was try to find the card's owner so he wouldn't go the weekend without it. I looked up the

person's name in the phone book and gave him a call.

"I found your ATM card," I told the man who answered.

He then asked hopefully, "You didn't happen to find my sunglasses too?"

— G. DAVID PETERSON

My friend Ann and I were eating at a Chinese restaurant. When an elderly waiter set chopsticks at our places, Ann made a point of reaching into her purse and pulling out her own pair. "As an environmentalist," she declared, "I do not approve of destroying bamboo forests for throwaway utensils."

The waiter inspected her chopsticks. "Very beautiful," he said politely. "Ivory."

— ERICA CHRISTENSEN

I played for a semipro baseball team. At every game we sold raffle tickets. Half the money paid the team's expenses and the other half went to the winning ticket holder. One day they held the drawing just as I was stepping up to bat.

The home plate umpire pulled the winning ticket, and then turned to me. "Could you read me the number?" he asked. "My vision's not too good."

— EDWARD NANDOR

A co-worker of mine was admiring a pair of delicate white earrings that Sue, another co-worker, was wearing. "Those are lovely," the woman said. "Are they ivory?"

Appalled at the suggestion, Sue replied, "I would never consider wearing anything made by killing innocent elephants. These are bone."

— HEATHER WILLIAMS

Thanks to my daughter, I have become thoroughly sensitized to environmental issues. Recently I purchased a greeting card, and when the cashier started to place it in a plastic bag, I remembered my daughter's repeated warnings and immediately declined its use.

"I'll be mailing that quickly," I told the clerk. "You can take the bag back."

"Okay. Have a good day," she said with a smile. Then I watched as she scrunched the bag into a ball and tossed it into the garbage.

— ARLENE KUSHER

My three sisters and I have weight problems and are always sharing diet tips. One day my oldest sister was showing us a low-fat cookbook and pointed out a chicken dish she had tried the night before. Reading the ingredients, I commented, "It looks like it would taste really bland."

"It did," she replied, "until I added cheese and sour cream."

— PATRICIA LAANSMA

While away on business, a colleague and I decided to catch a movie. As we approached the theatre, we read the marquee. It bore the name of the feature film followed by the numbers "7," "5," and "9." Assuming these were the show times, we were somewhat perplexed by their order.

I went inside to ask about it. "Our next show is at eight o'clock," the woman in the box office announced.

"Eight o'clock?" I said, surprised. "But the marquee says seven, five and nine."

"Right," she agreed. "That's 7:59. We lost our number eight."

—DIANE CLANCY

After shopping for weeks, I finally found the car of my dreams. It was only two years old and in beautiful condition. The salesman asked if I would like to take it for a test drive. We had travelled no more than a kilometre when the car broke down. The salesman called for a tow truck.

When it arrived, we climbed into the front seat. While the driver was hooking up the car, the salesman turned to me with a smile and said, "Well, now, what is it going to take to put you behind the wheel of that beauty today?"

— JAN BAIRD

117

Dad is from the old school, where you keep your money under the mattress—only he kept his in the underwear drawer. One day I bought my dad an unusual personal safe—a can of spray paint with a false bottom—so he could keep his money in the workshop. Later I asked Mom if he was using it.

"Oh, yes," she replied, "he put his money in it the same day."

"No burglar would think to look on the work shelf!" I gloated.

"They won't have to," my mom replied. "He keeps the paint can in his underwear drawer."

— JUDEE MULVEY

My very pregnant sister-in-law had just returned from another disappointingly uneventful trip to the hospital when she went into true labour. With no time to make it back to the hospital, my brother called 911. In shock, he followed the telephone instructions of the operator to deliver the baby. He even tied the umbilical cord with a string.

The Emergency Medical Service team arrived shortly thereafter, only to see an exhausted mother holding her beautiful daughter—with a tennis shoe dangling on the cord between them!

— SABRINA FORD

There was a notice that appeared in my mailbox. It told me I was required to go to court as a witness against someone whose name I did not recognize. Calling for more information, I found out my notice was for reporting a driver who had illegally passed my stopped school bus—ten years ago when I had been driving a bus part-time.

The appearance date was the same time as my night class, so I called to see if my court appearance could be rescheduled. Two days later someone returned my call.

"We cannot push the date back," they said. The reason? "The accused is entitled to a speedy trial."

— JANIS SMITH

When my wife and I showed up at a very popular restaurant, it was crowded. She went up to the hostess and asked, "Will it be long?"

The hostess, ignoring her, kept writing in her book. My wife again asked, "How much of a wait?"

The woman looked up. "About ten minutes."

A short time later we heard an announcement over the loudspeaker: "Willette B. Long, your table is ready."

— HERBERT R. KARP

"He just sits there all day, waiting to chase the email man."

Hoping to learn more about financial matters, I visited a bookstore and grabbed a copy of *Personal Finance for Dummies*. A glance at the book's price sticker, however, revealed just how little credit the store's management gave people like me. It read:

"Publisher's list price: $16.95; our discount price: $17.99."

— NAOMI WELSH

Although I am of Chinese descent, I never really learned to speak Chinese. One evening, I came home boasting about a wonderful meal I'd had in Chinatown. Unfortunately, I couldn't remember the name of the restaurant, but was able to write the Chinese character that was on the door and show it to my mother.

"Do you know what it says?" Mom asked with a smile. "It says 'Pull.'"

— BARBARA MAO

When we take our dog on a car journey, we carry his drinking water in a gin bottle. On one occasion we stopped at a pub for lunch and let him out of the car.

Pouring some water from the bottle into his bowl, I noticed a man watching with fascination. He came over to me and whispered, 'I hope that you're not going to let him drive!'

Early one Saturday morning, the flashing lights of a police car appeared in my rearview mirror. After checking my licence and registration, the officer asked, "Do you know why I pulled you over?"

"No," I responded.

"One of your taillights is out," he said. "I'm going to have to issue a warning."

"Whew," I said, without thinking. "I thought it was because my inspection had expired."

— ANDREA SHIPPER

I was sitting behind an enthusiastic mom at my son's Little League game. Her boy was pitching for the opposing team and she cheered as he threw wild pitch after wild pitch. The poor kid walked every batter. It was only the first inning and the score was 14–0. Then one batter finally smacked the ball.

"Oh no," the mom wailed. "There goes his no-hitter."

— NORMALU COOPER

I called my local utility for help with a minor malfunction in my outdoor gas grill. Their automated phone system put me on hold for over 20 minutes.

As I waited, I was grateful my problem wasn't worse—especially when I heard a pre-recorded message repeatedly advise, "If you smell gas, stay on the line."

— HERB GITLIN

While sitting in the emergency room of our local hospital, I watched as a panicked father-to-be rushed in and told a nurse that his wife had called him at work about 15 minutes earlier. She was going into labour prematurely, he said, and would be arriving at the hospital any minute now.

"How far along is your wife?" the nurse asked calmly.

Glancing down nervously at his watch, the man replied, "Right about now, she should be on Queen Street."

— KAREN MORRIS

When I was in the sixth grade, I lost the sight in my right eye during a playground mishap. Fortunately, the accident had little effect on my life. When I reached my 40s, however, I needed to get glasses.

At the optometrist's office, the doctor's young assistant pointed to an eye chart. "Cover your right eye and read line three," she said.

"I'm blind in my right eye," I told her. "It's a glass eye."

"Okay," she responded. "In that case, cover your left eye."

— BILL SLACK

My flight was delayed in Regina. Since the gate was needed for another flight, our aircraft was backed away from the terminal, and we were directed to a new gate. We all found the new gate, only to discover a third gate had been designated for our plane.

Finally, everyone got on board the right plane, and the flight attendant announced: "We apologize for the gate change. This flight is going to Edmonton. If your destination is not Edmonton, you should deplane at this time."

A moment later a red-faced pilot emerged from the cockpit, carrying his bags. "Sorry," he said, "wrong plane."

— ROY SCHMIDT

While walking through a parking lot, I tripped and fell flat on my face. As I was lying there, a woman stopped and called out,

"Are you hurt?"

"No. I'm fine,"

I said, touched by her concern.

"Oh, good,"

she continued.

"So will you be vacating your parking spot?"

HARIETT WELLING

Frustrated at always being corrected by her husband, my aunt decided the next time it happened she would have a comeback. That moment finally arrived, and she was ready. "You know," she challenged, "even a broken clock is right once a day."

My uncle looked at her and replied, "Twice."

— CINDY COOKSEY

One evening my former boss was getting out of the shower when his wife called, asking him to turn off an iron she had mistakenly left on in the basement before she left for the weekend. Thinking no one would see him, he ran down the stairs into the dark basement without even a towel on.

As he flipped on the light switch, though, he was shocked to hear dozens of people yell "Surprise!" His wife had orchestrated the secret party to celebrate his 40th birthday.

— JENNIFER JASEK

I began viola lessons as an adult. When I started, I called my mother to share my excitement. "Wonderful!" she exclaimed. "But I've never heard a viola. What does it sound like?"

Unable to give an apt description, I phoned my mother a few days later, after buying a CD of viola music. "Listen to this," I said as I placed the telephone receiver next to the stereo speaker, and turned the music on for about 30 seconds of a Schubert sonata. Then I picked up the receiver. "Well, Mom, what do you think?"

A moment of silence followed, then a question: "I'm speechless, Debbie. How many lessons have you had?"

— DEBORAH HAYS

My husband and I stopped at a sporting-goods store famous for its huge once-a-year sale. Seven months pregnant at the time, I caught the attention of a reporter covering the event. When he asked me what we were looking for, I patted my stomach and said we needed a new tent for our growing family.

Then the reporter turned to my distracted husband: "Is this your first?"

"Uh, no," he replied. "We have another tent at home."

— MARY ANN HAEFNER

I frequently receive calls from pollsters asking me to participate in telephone surveys. One woman began with a barrage of questions.

"Wait a moment," I interrupted. "Who are you and whom do you represent?"

She told me and immediately continued asking questions.

"What's the purpose of this survey?" I asked.

"Sir," she replied irritably, "I don't have time to answer your questions." Then she hung up.

— HENRY SHEPPARD

A steak fanatic, my father always picks out cuts that include a bone because he loves to nibble on it. One night Father and I were finishing our dinners at a steakhouse, and I could tell he wanted to start gnawing on the bone. But he couldn't bear to do so in public.

"Excuse me," he said, calling the waitress over, "would you please wrap this bone up for my dog?" Father has never owned a dog in his life, but the white lie seemed a tactful solution to his dilemma.

A few minutes later the waitress returned to our table. "Here's your bone, sir," she said, handing over a large package. "And while I was in the kitchen, I grabbed a few more out of the scrap bucket."

— KAREN FREEMAN

"There's nothing wrong with your eyesight. You're wearing your seat belt too high!"

One afternoon, while touring the Badlands of Alberta, my husband and I pulled into the only hotel in a small town. While signing the register, we asked the young woman behind the desk if our room was air-conditioned.

When she shook her head no, we hesitated, wondering if we should push on to the next town. Sensing our doubt, she brightened as she came up with a solution. "Just turn on the heater," she suggested. "Our customers tell us all that comes out is cold air anyway."

— MARY J. PAYERLE

Flying above Saskatchewan in an airplane, I listened as the captain described points of interest over the loudspeaker. He indicated a giant crater on the ground that was formed by a meteorite thousands of years ago.

A young woman in the row ahead of me looked out the window. She then turned to her companion and exclaimed, "Gee, do you realize that if it had landed a little farther to the right, it would have hit the highway!"

— WALLY COX

The Know-It-All

▶ BY A. J. JACOBS

I had toyed with the notion of reading the Encyclopaedia Britannica for a few years.

I figured it would be a crash course in everything— something I desperately needed. At age 35, about the only thing I could remember from four years of college was that a burrito left on the dorm-room floor is still edible after eight days, as long as you chew really hard. If I read the whole encyclopedia, from A to Z, I might very well become the smartest man in North America. My father, a New York lawyer, had actually tried reading the Britannica years ago. He made it to the mid-B's—I think it was right around Borneo— before he bailed out, blaming his busy schedule.

I called him with the good news. "I'm going to finish what you started," I told him. "I'm going to read the Encyclopaedia Britannica."

There was a pause. "I hear the P's are excellent," he said.

I could tell my wife, Julie, was just as skeptical. "I don't know, honey," she said. "What about eating dinner at every restaurant in New York? You could start with the restaurants with A names and work your way to the Z's." Valiant try. But I was dead serious about Operation Encyclopedia.

I did some research. The Britannica is still the gold standard, the Tiffany's of encyclopedias. Founded in 1768, it's the longest continuously published reference book in history. Over the years contributors have included Einstein, Freud and Harry Houdini. Its current roster includes dozens of academics with Nobels, Pulitzers and other awards with ceremonies that don't feature commentary from Melissa Rivers. During the dot-com craze the Britannica passed through hard times, and it has phased out its door-to-door salesmen. But it keeps chugging.

Yes, there's the Internet. I suppose I could try reading Google from A to Z. But the Internet's hardly what you would call trustworthy, and besides, I prefer books. I don't even want the newfangled CD-ROM for $49.95 or the Britannica's monthly online service. I'll take the leatherette volumes for $1,400—not cheap, but certainly less expensive than grad school.

A couple of days after placing my order, three giant boxes arrive. I rip them open and find a handsome set of books—sleek and black, with gold embossing on the spine. Seeing them in three dimensions not only causes Julie to panic that they'll eat up all our apartment's shelf space, it also drives home the magnitude of my quest. I am looking at 33,000 pages, 65,000 articles, 24,000 illustrations. I have 32 volumes, each weighing 4 pounds. Total word count: 44 million.

I pile all the volumes on the floor in one big stack. It measures four-foot-six—practically a Danny DeVito

44 million words. 33,000 pages. One obsessed guy.

of knowledge. I look at it again. Is this really the best use of my time? Maybe I should try something that's a little easier, like buying a new bathing suit.

I plunk the first volume on my lap. It feels weighty. It feels good. I crack it open. And then I start to read.

A-ak. That's the very first word, followed by this write-up: "Ancient East Asian music. See gagaku."

What a tease this crafty old Britannica is! Now I have a dilemma. Should I flip ahead to Volume 5 and find out what's up with gagaku, or should I stick with the plan and move on to the second word? I decide to stay. Why ruin the suspense? If anyone brings up a-ak in conversation, I'll just bluff. "I love gagaku!" I'll say. Or, "Did you hear that Madonna's recording an a-ak track on her next CD?"

A cappella. A lovely surprise. I know this one. An ex-girlfriend of mine belonged to an a cappella group in college. They sang songs from Def Leppard and called it Rockapella. One for two. Not bad.

Aachen. The next few entries destroy my average. I don't recognize the name of a famous Chinese general or a Buddhist compendium. And I've never heard of Aachen, the German city that's home to Schwertbad-Quelle, the hottest sulphur spring in the country. Oh, well. I try to memorize the information. There can be no discriminating here, not even against obscure Teutonic landmarks.

Aaron. Ah, the brother of Moses. Seems Mom didn't talk about him too much. "Oh, Aaron? He's okay. Still finding his way. But back to Moses: Did you hear about the Red Sea?" This is good stuff. I'm Jewish, but I never got any religious training, though I do have a light lunch on Yom Kippur. So the Britannica will be my saviour.

Abbott, Bud and Costello, Lou. After a bunch of Persian rulers named Abbas, I get to these familiar faces. But any sense of relief fades when I read about their sketchy past. Their partnership began when Costello's regular straight man fell ill during a gig at the Empire Theater in New York. So Abbott—working in the box office—substituted. It went so well, he became Costello's permanent partner. This is not a

▶ The Know-It-All

heart-warming story; it's a cautionary tale. I'm never calling in sick again. I don't want to come back after the 24-hour flu and find out that Robbie from the mail room is now a senior editor. It's a tough world.

Addled Brain Syndrome. Okay, I made this one up. But I'm definitely suffering from something. As I vacuum up facts, I find I'm so overwhelmed I have to take breaks. Walk it off, as my gym teachers used to say. You only sprained that brain; it's not a fracture. Walk it off, son.

Still, the encyclopedia is perfect for someone like me who has the attention span of a gnat on amphetamines. Bored with Abilene, Texas? Here comes abolitionism. Tired of that? The Abominable Snowman's lurking right around the corner (by the way, the mythical Snowman's footprints are probably produced by running bears).

The changes are so abrupt and relentless, you can't help but get mental whiplash. You go from tiny to cosmic, from ancient to modern. There's no segue. Just a little white space and boom! Another fact. But I forge on.

Alcott, Bronson. The father of novelist Louisa May Alcott was famous in his own right. A radical reformer, he opened several schools that had a particularly unusual discipline system: Teachers received punishment from the offending pupils. It was supposed to instill shame in the kids' minds. This is brilliant. I have a long list of teachers I wish I could have disciplined, among them my fourth-grade instructor, who forced us to have a sugar-free bake sale, which earned a humiliating $1.53.

Alger, Horatio. I knew he was the 19th-century author of famous rags-to-riches novels. I didn't know he began writing after being kicked out of a church for allegations of sexual misconduct with boys. The Britannica can be a gossip rag.

Antarctica. One night, when Julie and I go to her friends' house for dinner, I'm prepared to dazzle with all of my newfound knowledge. We arrive at Shannon and David's, exchange kisses and "Great to see you's." Then Julie mentions she's feeling cold.

"Not quite as cold as Antarctica's Vostok Station, which reached a record 128 below zero," I reply.

We sit down and Shannon tells us about an upcoming vacation to St. Barth's. "I can't wait to get some sun," she says. "Look how white I am."

"Albinism affects one in 20,000 North Americans," I say.

Shannon doesn't know quite how to respond. So Julie rescues me by spilling my secret. "A. J.'s decided to read the encyclopedia," she says.

"Wow. That's some light reading," replies David. Pause. So much for social success.

I am constantly being told how absurd this all is. My aunt Marti from Berkeley confronted me in a phone call the other day. "Why are you reading the encyclopedia?" she asked.

"I'm trying to become the smartest man in the world," I replied.

"How are you defining intelligence? The amount of information you have?"

"Yup."

"That's not very intelligent."

"Well," I replied, "I haven't gotten to the letter I." ▲

A. J. Jacobs, a senior editor at Esquire, *did get to the letter "I"—and every other letter. He finished reading the Encyclopaedia Britannica one year and 55 days after he started. He was accepted by Mensa and appeared on "Who Wants to Be a Millionaire," winning $1,000 after narrowly missing $32,000 when he couldn't define erythrocyte, which means red blood cell ("I'll never forget that word for as long as I live," he says).*

It's easy to get a reputation for wisdom. It's only necessary to live long, speak little and do less.

— P. D. JAMES, A Certain Justice (Knopf)

You can't have everything. Where would you put it?

— STEVEN WRIGHT

The one thing that unites all human beings, regardless of age, gender, religion or ethnic background, is that we all believe we are above-average drivers.

— DAVE BARRY, Dave Barry Turns 50 (Crown)

I've come to learn that the best time to debate family members is when they have food in their mouths.

— KENNETH COLE, Footnotes (Simon & Schuster)

When you don't know what you're talking about, it's hard to know when you're finished.

— TOMMY SMOTHERS

Graduation speeches were invented largely in the belief that college students should never be released into the world until they have been properly sedated.

— GARRY TRUDEAU

They say you only go around once, but with a muscle car you can go around two or three times.

— TIM ALLEN on "Home Improvement"

Before you criticize someone, you should walk a mile in their shoes. That way, when you criticize them, you're a mile away and you have their shoes.

— Quoted in The Sisterhood of the Traveling Pants by Ann Brashares (Delacorte Press)

After his wife died, the uncle of one of my friends decided to plan ahead and order a gravesite marker for himself. A week or so later he came home to find a message on his answering machine. It was from a young woman at the company where he'd placed his order.

"I don't know if it's good news or bad," she said, "but your headstone is ready."

— OLIVIA VAZ

On a recent vacation at a resort with my in-laws, we planned to spend an afternoon at the pool with our kids. We wanted to bring our own drinks, but were unsure of the hotel's policy.

My brother-in-law called the front desk, and assuming everyone was familiar with the brand of ice chest he had, asked if it was all right if he brought a Playmate to the pool.

After a pause the clerk asked, "Does she have her own towel?"

— TINA M. DIGIOVANNA

My wife asked me to help one of our neighbours, a young mother whose sailor husband was at sea. Her car had to have something called a freeze plug replaced—a job that took two days. Then I discovered the battery was dead and the starter was shot, so I fixed those too.

Days later I proudly handed the woman her keys saying, "Now your car is good for many more kilometres."

"Thanks," she said. "All I care is that it runs long enough to make it to the dealer. I'm trading it in tomorrow."

— GEORGE T. MARSHALL

We purchased an old home in Quebec from two elderly sisters. Winter was fast approaching, and I was concerned about the house's lack of insulation. "If they could live here all those years, so can we!" my husband confidently declared.

One November night the temperature plunged to well below zero, and we woke up to find interior walls covered with frost. My husband called the sisters to ask how they had kept the house warm. After a brief conversation, he hung up. "For the past 30 years," he muttered, "they've gone to Florida for the winter."

— LINDA DOBSON

When I was a high school senior, I saw an inspirational ad on TV about becoming a teacher. I called the number shown: 800-45TEACH. After a woman answered, I babbled on about how I thought I had found my life's calling and could she send me information. She asked what number I was calling.

After I told her, there was a long pause. Then she said, "You misspelled teach."

— AMY PORTER

I was in line at the souvenir booth of a Renaissance fair when a man asked the clerk, "Do you sell sunglasses?" "Alas, yeoman," she answered in her best fake old English, "coloured bits of glass suspended before the eyes were not invented until after the Renaissance, so those are not goods we purvey."

As he began to turn away, ye olde Renaissance clerk added, "But we do carry baseball caps with our logo on them."

— KATHY SHEEHAN

sign language

At a coffee bar a sign on the staff's tip container said **"Thanks a Latte."**

My sister Susan and her husband, Frank, were entertaining for the first time since the birth of their baby. Everything ran smoothly until one of Frank's buddies arrived with his new girlfriend—a woman Susan did not particularly care for. Susan beckoned her husband upstairs with the excuse that they had to check on the baby. In the privacy of the nursery, she spoke freely of her disdain for the new guest.

When they went downstairs to rejoin the party, they were greeted with an awkward silence—except for the occasional murmurings of the sleeping baby that came from the infant monitor sitting on the table.

— JANE HAWORTH

"Your Honour," began the defence lawyer, "my client has been characterized as an incorrigible bank robber, without a single socially redeeming feature. I intend to disprove that."

"And how will you accomplish this?" the judge inquired.

"By proving beyond a shadow of a doubt," replied the lawyer, "that the note my client handed the teller was on recycled paper."

— R. C. SHEBELSKI

I was having a drink at a local restaurant with my friend Justin when he spotted an attractive woman sitting at the bar. After an hour of gathering his courage, he approached her and asked, "Would you mind if I chatted with you for a while?"

She responded by yelling at the top of her lungs, "No, I won't come over to your place tonight!"

With everyone in the restaurant staring, Justin crept back to our table, puzzled and humiliated.

A few minutes later, the woman walked over to us and apologized.

"I'm sorry if I embarrassed you," she said, "but I'm a graduate student in psychology and I'm studying human reaction to embarrassing situations."

At the top of his lungs Justin responded, "What do you mean, two hundred dollars?"

— J. SMODISH

There was a fire in my neighbourhood, and I arrived just in time to see firefighters carry one of their men out of the burning house and lower him to a sitting position on the lawn. Visibly shaken, he took out a cigarette, lit it and sat there puffing on it to calm his nerves.

"What happened to that poor guy?" I asked a bystander.

"Smoke inhalation," he replied.

— TIM TUINSTRA

My husband and I were touring our friends' new home. Mr. and Mrs. Henry Curtis had put special touches everywhere. In the bathroom my husband leaned over to me and whispered, "They even have monogrammed faucets."

— PAT GNAU

One day I noticed that my sister wasn't wearing a watch. When I asked her about it, she replied, "I don't need a watch. At home there's a clock in every room, and in the car there's a clock on the dashboard."

Knowing my sister's an avid shopper, I inquired, "Well, how do you tell time when you're shopping?"

"That's easy," she replied. "I buy something else, and look at the time printed on the sales receipt."

— MARTITA McGOWAN

I was in line at a restaurant. In front of me was a mother with her college-age son and his girl-friend. It was the middle of the dinner rush, and many customers were restless at the long wait, but the young couple, holding hands and kissing, were oblivious to everything around them. Although clearly not approving, the mother was silent, until one

"'On Dasher, on Dancer, on Prancer and Vixen. On Comet, on Cupid, on Donner and Blitzen...' Wait—this can't be right."

prolonged kiss when the young man had his face and hands buried in his girlfriend's long, curly locks.

"Do you have to do that here?" the embarrassed mother asked.

"I'm not doing anything, Mom," came her son's muffled voice. "My earring's caught in her hair."

— KATHY GASTON

When our dryer broke, my husband set to work. He found the problem quickly and, since he needed to replace the belt, decided to repair a cracked knob and broken hinge too. Upon arrival at the Sears parts counter,

he said he needed a belt, knob, hinge and a crescent-shaped wire he'd found inside the dryer. He didn't know where it belonged, but he confidently assured the clerk that he could figure it out once he got into the job.

"I have the other parts," the clerk said, "but for the wire you have to go to Lingerie. This is an underwire from your wife's bra."

— BARBARA A. YEAGER

When I arrived at school for my daughter's parent-teacher conference, the teacher seemed a bit flustered, especially when she started telling me that my little girl didn't always pay attention in class and was some-times a little flighty.

"For example, she'll do the wrong page in the workbook," the teacher explained, "and I've even found her sitting at the wrong desk."

"I don't understand," I replied defensively. "Where could she have gotten that?"

The teacher went on to reas-sure me that my daughter was still doing fine in school and was sweet and likable. Finally, after a pause, she added, "By the way, Mrs. Gulbrandsen, our appoint-ment was tomorrow."

— J. GULBRANDSEN

Fresh from a visit to the dentist, I decided to stop at my bank. Barely able to enunciate, I told the teller, "I'm sorry about not speaking more clearly. I've just had novocaine."

"You should have used the drive-through," she said.

"Why?"

"Everyone who goes through sounds like that," she explained.

— SUSAN ANDERSON

Dispatching her ten-year-old son to pick up a pizza, my sister handed him money and a two-dollar coupon. Later he came home with the pizza, and the coupon.

When asked to explain, he replied, "Mom, I had enough money. I didn't need the coupon."

— MARGARET E. METZ

I have a cousin who was on a plane that had taken off and was approaching cruising altitude, when one of the flight attendants came on the public-address system. She announced that she was sorry, but the plane's restroom was out of order. The flight attendant went on to apologize to the passengers for any inconvenience.

But then she finished cheerily with: "So, as compensation, free drinks will be served."

— MANJIRI V. OAK

Early in our romance, my fiancé and I were strolling on a beach. He stopped, drew a heart in the sand and inscribed our initials inside the heart. I was thoroughly charmed, and took a photo of his artwork. Later we used that same picture on our wedding invitations.

Seeing the photo, Emily, the preteen daughter of a friend, exclaimed, "Wow! How did you ever find one with your initials on it?"

— CHRISTY G. SMITH

For a late snack, my sisters and I stopped at a diner. Walking in, we smelled cooking gas. When the waitress came to seat us, we urged her to tell someone so they could find the leak. She thanked us, saying she'd look into it right away.

Then she asked us in her most pleasant waitress voice, "Will that be smoking or non-smoking?"

— SHARON SWEENEY

My mother had just finished taking a CPR class at a local college when she and I were in the mall and saw a big crowd gathered around a still body. Suddenly my mother took off running at a speed I didn't know she could muster. "Everyone back," she yelled. "I know CPR!"

Just as she threw herself next to the body and was about to begin the procedure, a pair of strong hands pulled her to her feet.

"Ma'am," barked a police officer standing beside her, "we are trying to arrest this man."

— TALEA TORRES

After an unusually heated argument with what he considered his overbearing parents, my brother announced that the minute he graduated from high school he intended to join the navy. No more was said until a few days later, when he walked proudly into the house and declared that he was to report for duty the following morning.

"Why?" my mother asked tearfully.

"Because," he stormed, "I am sick and tired of taking orders!"

— MRS. A. V. HEIGHES

Because our new refrigerator was taller than our old one, I told my wife I'd have to cut away part of an overhanging cabinet to make it fit. Not wanting to mess it up, I called a local radio home-fix-it program for advice. I was in the middle of getting the instructions when my wife burst into the room. "You won't believe this," she said, "but there's a guy on the radio with the same problem!"

— GARY BRINGHURST

I sold an item through eBay but it got lost in the mail. So I stopped by my local post office and asked them to track it down.

"It's not that simple," the clerk scolded. "You have to fill out a mail-loss form before we can initiate a search."

"Okay," I said. "I'll take one."

He rummaged under his counter, then went to some other clerks who did the same—only to return and confess, "You'll have to come back later. We can't find the forms."

— DOREEN L. ROGERS

As a professor at a technology institute, I taught a series of popular courses on software engineering. The program was highly competitive and difficult to get into, but one prospective student made our decision whether to accept him quite simple.

When asked to fax over his college transcript, the student told me, "Well, I would, but it's the only copy that I've got."

— JIM SKINNER

My husband, who is an auto mechanic, received a repair order that read: "Check for clunking noise when going around corners." Taking the car out for a test drive, he made a right turn, and a moment later heard a clunk. He then made a left turn and again heard a clunk. Back at the shop, he opened the trunk and soon discovered the problem.

Promptly he returned the repair order to the service manager with this notation: "Remove bowling ball from trunk."

— KOREY A. TUTTLE

Which windshield wiper blade always quits first? That's right—the driver's side. This happened to me one day while driving home in the middle of a blinding storm.

Unable to see, I pulled over and tried to figure out a quick fix. I found it in a yellow cotton work glove that was lying on the floor. I wedged the cloth hand under the wiper arm.

It did a great job keeping my windshield clear. Not only that— you'd be surprised at how many people waved back.

— TOM BISCHEL

Aging
Gracelessly

Face it—you're not getting better, you're getting older, and the sooner you come to terms with that, or incorporate Botox injections into your budget, the better.

"That's strange. This suit wasn't a thong last year."

Our dear friend Trudy attended my husband's birthday party. Though she's been through a lot—including a double mastectomy and reconstructive surgery—Trudy was the life of the party as usual. Hugging her goodbye, I couldn't help noticing she had nothing on under her blouse.

"Trudy, you're not wearing a bra!" I whispered.

With a twinkle in her eye she replied, "I may be 70, honey, but they're only 15."

— JUDITH L. KROL

The plane was only half-full. When an attractive young woman asked if the seat next to mine was free, my male ego soared. Soon we were chatting pleasantly, and she told me it was her first flight.

"Mom said to sit next to someone I thought I could trust," she confessed nervously, "and you look just like my dad."

— ROY RAGSDALE

My brother and his wife started their family in their early 40s. One day my sister-in-law and I were commiserating about the effects of time marching on.

"I just got my first pair of glasses," she said, and paused as her two preschool boys thundered past her. "Now, if only my hearing would go."

— IRENE PALM

Rock concerts are a little different now than when I was younger. Recently, I went to a concert with some friends. As the band started to play a ballad, we instinctively raised our cigarette lighters, like all good rock fans I grew up with. But looking around me, I noticed that times had indeed changed.

The mostly under-25 crowd was swaying to the upraised glow of their cellphones.

— ANGELA STIMA

As my 40th birthday approached, my husband, who is a year younger, was doing his best to rub it in. Trying to figure out what all the teasing was about, our young daughter asked me, "How old is Daddy?"

"Thirty-nine," I told her.

"And how old will you be?"

"Forty," I said sadly.

"But Mommy," she exclaimed, "you're winning!"

— KELLEY MARTINEZ

I was hospitalized with an awful sinus infection that caused the entire left side of my face to swell. On the third day, the nurse led me to believe that I was finally recovering when she announced excitedly, "Look, your wrinkles are coming back!"

— FRANCES M. KRUEGER

"Keep making that face and it's going to freeze that way," was what my mother used to say to us as kids. I knew times had changed after she noticed my sister scowling recently and warned, "Keep making that face and you're going to need Botox."

— MARY BOUCK

After working for months to get in shape, my 42-year-old husband and I hiked to the bottom of the Grand Canyon. At the end of two gruelling days, we made it back to the canyon's rim. To celebrate, we each bought an "I hiked the canyon" T-shirt.

About a month later, while my husband was wearing his shirt, a young man approached him. "Did you really hike the canyon?" he asked.

My husband beamed with pride and answered, "Sure did!"

"No kidding!" the fellow said. "What year?"

— CAROL LATKIEWICZ

I was having trouble with the idea of turning thirty and was oversensitive to any signs of advancing age. When I found a prominent grey hair in my bangs, I pointed to my forehead.

"Have you seen this?" I indignantly asked my husband.

"What?" he asked. "The wrinkles?"

— WENDY LILLIE

My 20th high-school class reunion was held at a hotel on the same night that another school's tenth-year reunion was taking place. While my friends and I were in the restroom talking, some unfamiliar women entered.

After their stares became uncomfortable, we turned toward them. One of the women said, "Don't mind us. We just wanted to see how we'd look in another ten years."

— SONDRA OLIVIERI

The summer after college graduation, I was living at home, fishing in the daytime, spending nights with my friends—generally just hanging out. One afternoon my grandfather, who never went to college, stopped by.

Concerned with how I was spending my time, he asked about my future plans. I told him I was in no hurry to tie myself down to a career.

"Well," he replied, "you better start thinking about it. You'll be thirty before you know it."

"But I'm closer to twenty than to thirty," I protested. "I won't be thirty for eight more years."

"I see," he said, smiling. "And when will you be twenty again?"

— MARSHALL K. ESSIG

My sister, Sharon, and I are close, and that allows us to be honest with each other. As I fidgeted in front of the mirror one evening before a date, I remarked, "I'm fat."

"No, you're not," she scolded.

"My hair is awful."

"It's lovely."

"I've never looked worse," I whined.

"Yes, you have," she replied.

— PATRICIA L. SOUZA

On my birthday I got a really funny card from a friend. It joked about how our bodies might be getting older, but our minds were still "tarp as shacks."

I wanted to thank the friend who sent the card, but I couldn't. She forgot to sign it.

— MERIS M. MACK

When a woman I know turned 99 years old, I went to her birthday party and took some photos. A few days later, I brought the whole batch of prints to her so she could choose her favourite.

"Good Lord," she said as she was flipping through them, "I look like I'm a hundred."

— HELEN B. MARROW

"We all do a lot of stupid things when we're young. So, what'll it take to remove that 'Butterball' tattoo?"

Out bicycling one day with my eight-year-old grand-daughter, Carolyn, I got a little wistful. "In ten years," I said, "you'll want to be with your friends and you won't go walking, biking, and swimming with me like you do now."

Carolyn shrugged. "In ten years you'll be too old to do all those things anyway."

— JAMES F. AHEARN

My senior citizens' refresher driving course was almost finished, and the teacher began to drill us. "What do you do when you want to exit from a freeway?" he asked.

"Pull into the exit lane before you slow down," the class chorused.

"Good," replied the instructor. "And what do you do when you want to get off the freeway but miss your exit?"

There was a pause before a woman volunteered, "Ask the post office to forward your mail."

— KATHRYN E. MASON

I had been thinking about colouring my hair. One day while going through a magazine, I came across an ad for a hair-colouring product featuring a beautiful young model with hair a shade that I liked. Wanting a second opinion, I asked my husband,

"I do stay in shape. This is the shape I stay in."

"How do you think this colour would look on a face with a few wrinkles?"

He looked at the picture, crumpled it up, straightened it out and studied it again. "Just great, hon."

— JOAN KEYSER

My grandfather has a knack for looking on the bright side of life. Even after receiving the terrible diagnosis that he had Alzheimer's, he was philosophical.

"There's one good thing that'll come from this," he told my father.

"What's that?" asked Dad.

"Now I can hide my own Easter eggs."

— CHRIS KERN

Both my fiancé and I are in our 40s. I thought it was both amusing and touching when he assumed the classic position to propose to me—down on one bended knee.

"Are you serious?" I asked, laughing.

"Of course I'm serious," he said. "I'm on my bad knee."

— DEBORAH MASSEY

My friend and I were celebrating our 40th birthday the same year. As a gag gift, I gave her a CD by the band UB40.

For my birthday, she retaliated with a CD as well. The group? U2.

— MONA TURRELL

I'm always relieved when someone delivers a eulogy and I realize I'm listening to it.

— GEORGE CARLIN

The last birthday that's any good is 23.

— ANDY ROONEY,
Years of Minutes (PublicAffairs)

Learn to enjoy your own company. You are the one person you can count on living with for the rest of your life.

— ANN RICHARDS in O: The Oprah Magazine

Age is nothing at all...unless you are a cheese.

— ACTRESS BILLIE BURKE ("Glinda, the Good Witch")

Summer is a drag because even normal people become obsessed with their bodies. A bad bathing suit can humiliate you more than anything else in life.

— CONAN O'BRIEN in Details

It's all right letting yourself go, as long as you can let yourself back.

— MICK JAGGER

Retirement is like a long vacation in Vegas. The goal is to enjoy it to the fullest, but not so fully that you run out of money.

— JONATHAN CLEMENTS in The Wall Street Journal

Wrinkles only go where the smiles have been.

— JIMMY BUFFETT,
Barefoot Children in the Rain

My mother always used to say, "The older you get, the better you get. Unless you're a banana."

— BETTY WHITE on "The Golden Girls"
— LIZZY PHAN

During the last days of my mother's life, we discussed many things. One day I raised the topic of her funeral and memorial service.

"Oh, honey," she responded, "I really don't care about the details."

Later she woke from a nap and grasped my hand, clearly wanting to share something with me. As I leaned forward, she said urgently, "Just don't bury me in plaid."

— DIANE WILSON

I was just settling into a barber's chair when I overheard the elderly man next to me say, "I'm not much for pills, but I am taking Ginkgo-Viagra. I want to remember what sex was like."

— BILL WRIGHT

Because they had no reservations at a busy restaurant, my elderly neighbour and his wife were told there would be a 45-minute wait for a table.

"Young man, we're both 90 years old," he told the maitre d'. "We may not have 45 minutes."

They were seated immediately.

— RITA KALISH

I had just moved to an address between Sunset Avenue and Sunrise Boulevard in a pleasant neighbourhood, and was explaining to a clerk where my home was located for billing purposes.

"I live between Sunrise and Sunset," I told her.

"Oh, honey," she knowingly replied, "we all do."

— LINDA McLEAN

For over 40 years my grandfather put in long hours at his job, so I was more than a little curious about the way he filled his days since his retirement.

"How has life changed?" I asked.

A man of few words, he replied, "Well I get up in the morning with nothing to do, and I go to bed at night with it half-done."

— DENNIS LUNDBERG

I was having some chest pains, but my cardiologist assured me nothing was wrong. Then I told him I was planning a cruise to Alaska and asked if he had any suggestions for avoiding the discomfort.

"Have fun," he said with a straight face, "but don't go overboard."

— LES WANDEL

When I was a 20-something college student, I became quite friendly with my study partner, a 64-year-old man, who had returned to school to finish his degree. He confessed he had once thought more than friendship might be a possibility.

"So what changed your mind?" I asked him.

"I went to my doctor and asked if he thought a 40-year age difference between a man and woman was insurmountable. He looked at my chart and said, 'You're interested in someone who's 104?'"

— KELLY MOORE

"I wouldn't raise my hopes too high if I were you."

The Way I Can't See It

This is a story of loss and denial. It begins on the freeway. I am looking for an exit called Drake Way. I notice I am hunched forward, squinting, barely going 40. All around me, drivers beam hate rays into my car. At precisely the moment at which it is too late to veer out of the exit lane, I note that the sign above me does not say Drake Way; it says Homer P. Gravenstein Memorial Highway. This is not good.

I go to my optometrist, who hesitates to up my prescription. She says that with a stronger distance correction, I'm going to start having trouble with what she calls "close work." Apparently she has mistaken me for one of her patients who assemble microchips or tat antimacassars by firelight. I tell her she should go ahead and change the prescription because I don't do close work.

"Do you look things up in phone books?" she asks. "Use maps?" She means, Do I read small print? She means I'm going to have trouble with small print. That I'm suddenly, without warning, old and enfeebled. Nonsense, I insist. She shrugs and gives me a pair of stronger lenses to try. Then she hands me a bottle of lens drops, points to the label and asks me to read it. This puzzles me, for any fool can see there's nothing written on that label, just tiny lines of decorative filigree. I study it harder. It is writing. "Do not use while operating heavy machinery?" I am guessing. "Now with more real fruit? Homer P. Gravenstein Memorial Highway?" I hang my head. It's time to read the handwriting on the wall, which I can most assuredly do—provided it is neatly spaced and billboard-sized. I am old and my eyesight is going. She says to cheer up, that I don't have to get bifocals, "just a pair of reading glasses." In my book, reading glasses are not cause for cheer. They are cause for depression, or regression, or diphtheria, I don't know exactly, because I can no longer read what's in my book.

There was a time when I wanted to wear half-glasses, the way young children want to have crutches or braces until the day they actually need

▶ **BY MARY ROACH**

In my book, reading glasses are not cause for cheer. They are cause for depression, or regression, or diphtheria, I don't know exactly, because I can no longer read what's in my book.

them. Today I do not want to wear reading glasses, not at all. Reluctantly, I wander over to the local drugstore.

The packaging on the reading glasses shows kindly white-haired people in business suits. The eyeglass company has gone out of their way to dress the models like functioning adults, as though people who need reading glasses can still contribute to society, when everyone knows they just sit at home tatting and reading telephone books. I can't go through with it. There has to be another way.

At home, I do an Internet search for "presbyopia." This is a mistake. The websites that turn up have names like SeniorJournal or Friendly4Seniors.com. One site informs me that "presbyopia" comes from the Greek for "elder eye." I don't appreciate this, not one bit. I'm not elderly. I'm 43. Besides, I know some Greek (spanakopita, Onassis, that word you say when the appetizer ignites), and "presbyopia" doesn't sound like any of it. I believe someone made up this "elder eye" business, someone cruel and youthful, with four-point lettering on his business card. I look up the etymology of "presbyopia" in my dictionary, but alas, someone has replaced the words with lines of decorative filigree.

So here's what I'm going to do. I'm not getting bifocals or reading glasses. I'm going to leave my contacts under-corrected and get a pair of distance glasses to wear on top of them, for driving. I figure I've got another five or six years before anyone calls me Elder Eyes. You could say I'm in denial. Or you could write it on a piece of paper, and by God, I'll be able to read it. ▲

I sat there waiting for my new doctor to make his way through the file that contained my very extensive medical history. After he finished all 17 pages, he looked up at me. "You look better in person than you do on paper."

— CAROLYN BLANKENSHIP

Someone recommended a new dentist to me. On my second visit the technician finished cleaning my teeth, and as I prepared to leave, I asked brightly, "And what is your name?"

"Patricia," she answered.

"I can remember that," I commented. "It's my sister's name."

Her reply: "That's what you said last time."

— IRIS CRADDOCK

I was turning 40 and decided to celebrate by fulfilling my long-time dream to go skydiving. Before the jump, my mother and I spent the day at a festival, where we bumped into two of my cousins. They inquired about my upcoming birthday, and when I told them about my jump from 10,000 feet, I could tell they were a bit mystified.

Finally one of them remarked, "Why don't you just get your breasts done like everyone else?"

— BARBARA BIANCO

My husband was bending over to tie my three-year-old's shoes. That's when I noticed my son, Ben, staring at my husband's head.

He gently touched the slightly thinning spot of hair and said in a concerned voice, "Daddy, you have a hole in your head. Does it hurt?"

After a pause, I heard my husband's murmured reply: "Not physically."

— LAURIE GERHARDSTEIN

Just as she was celebrating her 80th birthday, our friend received a jury-duty notice. She called to remind the people at the clerk's office that she was exempt because of her age.

"You need to come in and fill out the exemption forms," they said.

"I've already done that," replied my friend. "I did it last year."

"You have to do it every year," she was told.

"Why?" came the response. "Do you think I'm going to get younger?"

— JONNIE SIVLEY

"You mean the older I get, the older *you* get?"

Checking out of the grocery store, I noticed the bag boy eyeing my two adopted children. They often draw scrutiny, since my son's a blond Russian, while my daughter has shiny black Haitian skin.

The boy continued staring as he carried our groceries to the car. Finally he asked, "Those your kids?"

"They sure are," I said with pride.

"They adopted?"

"Yes," I replied.

"I thought so," he concluded. "I figured you're too old to have kids that small."

— CYNTHIA S. MEYER

I was middle-aged when I went back to college, which meant some of my classmates were 20 years younger. Still, many became my friends.

I ran into one of them recently in a restaurant he manages, and he, my husband and I all had a pleasant chat at the cashier's counter. As we said goodbye, my young friend explained to the couple behind us, "She and I were college classmates." I noticed the confused look on their faces.

Later, I asked my husband, "What do you suppose they were thinking?"

"Either that he's had a very easy life," he replied, "or you've had a very hard one."

— BARBARA OUTLAW LEE

Fans of '60s music, my 14-year-old daughter and her best friend got front-row tickets to a Peter, Paul and Mary concert. When they returned home, my daughter said, "During the show, we looked back and saw hundreds of little lights swaying to the music. At first we thought the people were holding up cigarette lighters. Then we realized that the lights were the reflections off all the eyeglasses in the audience."

— TRACY FLACHSBARTH

Back at my high school for the tenth reunion, I met my old coach. Walking through the gym, we came upon a plaque on which I was still listed as the record holder for the longest softball throw.

Noticing my surprise, the coach said, "That record will stand forever."

I was about to make some modest disclaimer that records exist to be broken, when he added, "We stopped holding that event years ago."

— GENE HEAD

"Higher."

Recently visiting my hometown, I ran into Bev, a classmate I had not seen in years. We updated each other on careers, marriages, children, and found common ground discussing the joys and hardships of being the single parent of a teenager.

She admitted the decisions she made and advice she gave as a mother were based on hope and instinct rather than any certainty of what was best. I agreed, but said our parents probably felt the same way—and we hadn't turned out too badly.

"Yeah," she replied. "But we had real parents. Our kids just have us."

I understood exactly what she meant.

— JOHN R. GRIFFIN

As a university professor, I taught during the day and did research at night. I would usually take a break around nine, however, calling up the strategy game Warcraft on the Internet and playing with an online team.

One night I was paired with a veteran of the game who was a master strategist. With him at the helm, our troops crushed opponent after opponent, and after six games we were undefeated. Suddenly, my fearless leader informed me his mom wanted him to go to bed.

"How old are you?" I typed.

"Twelve," he replied. "How old are you?"

Feeling my face redden, I answered, "Eight."

— TODD SAYRE, PH.D.

My hearing had gotten worse, and ultimately I was faced with a decision: buy a pontoon boat, which I could enjoy all summer, or get a hearing aid. The choice was obvious—to me at least. However, my sisters did not approve of the boat.

One day during lunch with them, I was having trouble following the conversation. Finally I leaned over to one of my sisters and asked what had just been said.

"Giving up on the diet, Lenny?"

"You should have brought along your pontoon boat," she replied.

— BETTY JO HENDRICK

One of the English classes I taught at a high school consisted of a particularly well-motivated group of juniors. Students felt free to ask questions on any subject that concerned them.

One afternoon a girl raised her hand and asked me to explain all the talk about a woman's "biological clock." After I'd finished, there was a moment of silence, and then another hand shot up.

"Mrs. Woodard," a student asked, "is your clock still ticking, or has the alarm gone off?"

— LINDA R. WOODARD

We had our ten-year-old daughter late in life, long after our two boys were born. She is the joy of my husband's life, but he is self-conscious about being an older father. He likes to jokingly tell people that by the time she graduates from high school, he'll be in a nursing home.

One day she asked, "Mom, you know how Dad always says he'll be in a home when I graduate?" I nodded, expecting some sad question about mortality.

"Can I have the car then?"

— TERRI GRAY

As an assistant high-school track coach, I recorded the results of each home meet and made copies for all the coaches. But because our track shed did not have electricity, I had to use carbon paper. A freshman team member offered to help, and I showed her how to place the carbon paper shiny side down so that the image would transfer to the sheet beneath it.

"What will they think of next?" she said in astonishment. "Pretty soon we won't need copy machines anymore."

— BARBARA LOOMIS

Korey, my granddaughter, came to spend a few weeks with me, and I decided to teach her how to sew. After I had gone through a lengthy demonstration of how to thread the machine, Korey stepped back and put her hands on her hips. "You mean you can do all that," she said in disbelief, "but you can't operate my Game Boy?"

— NELL BARON

While my friend Emily was visiting her mother, they went for a walk and bumped into an old family acquaintance. "Is this your daughter?" the woman asked. "Oh, I remember her when she was this high. How old is she now?"

Without pausing, Emily's mother said, "Twenty-four." Emily, 35, nearly fainted on the spot.

After everyone had said their goodbyes, Emily asked her mother why she'd told such a whopper.

"Well," she replied, "I've been lying about my age for so long, it suddenly dawned on me that I'd have to start lying about yours too."

— ROBERT LEE WHITMIRE

I've been considering a facelift, but it's very expensive, so I've seesawed back and forth. One day my husband and I discussed it yet again when I asked, "What if I drop dead three months later? Then what would you do?"

After a moment of reflection he offered, "I guess we'd have an open casket."

— CAROL FUGERE

During a visit with a friend at an assisted living centre, I was invited to stay for lunch. As we entered the cafeteria, she leaned toward me and whispered, "They have two lines here. We call them cane and able."

— MARTHA LEONARD

At his 103rd birthday party, my grandfather was asked if he thought that he'd be around for his 104th.

"I certainly do," he replied. "Statistics show that very few people die between the ages of 103 and 104."

— HARRY P. COLEMAN

Most of my boarding school students are more computer literate than I. So I was surprised to find one sophomore writing a term paper on an electric typewriter.

In a reminiscent mood I said, "When I was in school my typewriter wasn't even electric."

She looked at me in shock and asked, "Do you mean it was battery-operated?"

— AMY D. FOSTER

"Not those! At our age, we need all the preservatives we can get."

143

Facing My Midlife Crisis

▶ BY CATHERINE GILDINER

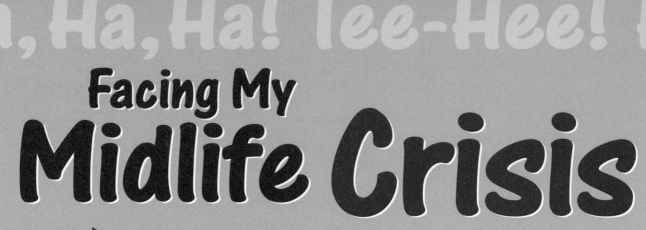

Not long ago I hit the high-water mark, the big 5-0. I was having breakfast with my rowing team at 6:30 a.m. after a tough workout on the lake. We were sprawled in our booth, in unflattering spandex uniforms that were designed for 18-year-olds, when an old friend sauntered by looking like Miss Universe on the runway. Naturally we grilled Nicole* about her spa, her masseuse, her skin cream. She dismissed all with a flick of her acrylic nails. "I had my eyes done," she whispered.

Impressed, I booked an appointment with Nicole's plastic surgeon. I had to wait three months for the appointment, but as Nicole said, I'd need it more by then, anyway.

On a summer's day when everything except me was in bloom, I trooped off to Toronto's tony Yorkville district, which should have been my first financial tip-off, and there, appro-

* Not her real name

priately located near an antique store, was a door that simply said Cosmetic Surgery.

I figured if I was at my worst, the good doctor might be more sympathetic and give me an extra stitch or two, so I arrived in my rowing uniform, a hideous hat and tube socks. Out of breath, I approached the desk at 9 a.m. to announce my wrinkled arrival and was told the doctor was already running an hour late. I had no idea you could be "done" at dawn.

I was greeted by four very thin assistants in taupe Armani outfits. One of them asked if I needed water, another brought Swiss water-washed decaf from a gold carafe, and one handed over a clipboard that asked my age and "how I wanted to see myself." The last one told me I had to pay $160 for the consultation before I saw the doctor.

The office was decorated entirely in taupe. In fact the taupe assistants were detectable only when they moved. As a woman next to me placed her pedicured feet upon a Ralph Lauren ottoman, she advised, "It's always best to elevate." Every one of the other clients looked about 35, yet somehow exhausted. All had deep tans, small black T-shirts and sandals with huge platform soles. Their hair was tousled, looking as though they had just stepped out of a Mercedes convertible, and highlighted with various shades of

blonde. Most wore a size 4, and no one was larger than a 6. I felt like a sumo wrestler in my size 8.

Later when I told Nicole about these 30-something, fatigued and wasted women in the waiting room, she looked at me as though I was too stupid to be believed and said, "They looked strained because they're in their 50s and they've been done—stretched to the limit." I was facing an aesthetic dilemma. Was it better to look 35, tired and anorexic, or 50, happy and rested? To put this in some perspective: I could still look really young and spry at a seniors' yoga class.

I was soon called in to meet The Doctor. Deposited in one of a labyrinth of consulting rooms, I gazed around at walls covered in gold-filigreed mirrors.

The light was unflattering; I found wrinkles I'd never noticed, even in sunlight. Naturally I did what any woman my age would do: I pulled back my skin at the hairline to see how a facelift would help.

Finally the doctor entered, jauntily. He was trim and wore a sports jacket in raw-silk pastel, the kind men wear to early-bird dinners in Miami. "I don't think I really need to be here—I just came for a consult," I said.

He glanced at my chart and looked intently at my face. He then uttered his first bit of insight in what turned out to be a seven-minute consult: "Mrs. Gildiner," he said, "let me assure you—you look every one of your 51 years." (For this I'm paying $23 a minute!) Trying to scrape my face off the floor, I replied with suitable understatement, "I thought I might just get my eyes done—very subtly of course."

"Look in the mirror." He held up a magnifying mirror, the kind they used on Snow White's stepmother, and asked, "What could be improved?" As I gazed, the mirror began announcing, actually screaming, all kinds of new imperfections.

I hesitated, mesmerized by the Medusa before me, and the doctor leaped into the pause.

"I'll tell you what I see. The eyes are a given. I won't even go there. What about the bags underneath, and the puffiness? Of course, the brow would have to be tightened." He tapped my chin and all along my jawbone. "What are we to do with this Elizabethan collar? This all needs tightening." Staring at my face dead-on, he said: "Then, of course, there are the jowls. I'd get a jump on it."

I managed to whimper, "Nicole only had her eyes done."

"Well," he said, "you're not Nicole." He pulled my cheeks out until they almost hit the opposite walls, and said, "Nicole doesn't have that kind of elasticity."

Concluding his seven-minute consultation, he announced, "Whatever you have done will have to be repeated in five years."

▶ Facing My Midlife Crisis

As he breezed out the door, he called: "I'm off! The girls will tell you all you need to know."

One of the taupe four came in and took me to a wood-panelled room, dimly lit by a green-shaded desk lamp. In this light, she showed me a scrapbook of miracle lifts. A few of the women really looked a lot younger, but most looked like Zsa Zsa Gabor before and after.

No one had mentioned price. At the risk of sounding crass, I asked what the cost would be for eyes and the tiniest of tucks, say two or three stitches. She slid an envelope that said Personal and Confidential in tiny taupe letters across the table.

I opened it. In my head I heard the ka-ching! of a cash register. The tab was more than $20,000, payable by certified check.

"Gee, $20,000 seems like a lot of money," I squeaked. The assistant replied: "It beats the $37,500 you'd pay for the work that was suggested. Remember, it's an investment. Do you ever take your car in for a tune-up and an oil change?" I nodded my corrugated face in the affirmative. "Well, that's only a car."

Later that day I went for my annual dermatologist's appointment, to find out if any of my thousands of freckles had turned into melanomas. When I told the doctor about my morning sojourn, he asked one question: the price. When I told him, he chirped like a bird on speed: "Cheap, cheap, cheap. Go for it!" Looking closely at my forehead, he added: "But for God's sake, don't let them inject Botox into those worry lines in your forehead. Tell them to just cut that muscle or they'll grow back."

Once you realize that the fear of death is the hub of the midlife crisis and deal with that, the rest is just details.

"What's Botox?"

"It's a poison from the same family as botulism toxin. The plastic surgeon injects Botox to paralyze your muscles so you can't pull your eyes together or furrow your brow and make those lines again."

I wondered aloud, "If you can't furrow your brow, does that mean you aren't worried anymore?"

The dermatologist rolled his eyes.

When I finally staggered home, walking up my street feeling like the Elephant Man, my neighbour Helen, who is over 70 and still looks beautiful and vibrant in every light, was out tending her nasturtiums. As I regaled her with the day's events, she furrowed her non-Botoxed brow and said, "I'll give you a free bibliographic consult." She went into the house and reappeared with a book—*The Denial of Death* by philosopher Ernest Becker. Handing it to me, she said, "I'll bet that doctor doesn't have this in his waiting room." Samuel Johnson was right when he suggested that the prospect of death wonderfully concentrates the mind. Once you realize that the fear of death is the hub of the midlife crisis and deal with that, the rest is just details.

I now tuck my Elizabethan collar into my turtleneck and fold my jowls under my balaclava in winter. I have begun to realize that I earned these lines. And on the odd day when I want to deny the inevitability of death, I simply wear a tight hair band. ▲

"No gel—I mixed Rogaine and Viagra."

Shortly after my father's death, my 90-year-old grandmother insisted that my mother have a complete physical. After some debate, my mother reluctantly made an appointment. The doctor not only gave her a clean bill of health, but remarked that she'd probably live to be 110.

To our surprise, my grandmother did not seem entirely pleased by the good report. She sat quietly for a few minutes, then said with a sigh, "And just what am I going to do with a 110-year-old daughter?"

— B.L.M.

When my husband worked at a prison, we had only one car, so I used to roll out of bed at 5 a.m., drive him to work, then come home and go back to sleep. One day while talking to some co-workers, my husband took out his wallet and showed them pictures of me and my daughter. One of the photos of me was a "glamour shot" that I had posed for at the mall.

"Wow," a colleague remarked. "Who's that?"

"My wife," my husband proudly replied.

"Oh," his friend responded, looking puzzled. "Then who's that woman who drops you off in the mornings?"

— LISA J. PROCTOR

My grandfather's aunt passed away, and he went to pay his respects. At the funeral home, he overheard two women as they peered into the open casket.

"She looks wonderful," said one. "I've never seen her look so good. Why, she looks better than I do!"

"You're right," the other replied. "But remember, you have the flu."

— SARAH SHORT

A friend spent more than two hours in the salon getting her hair coloured, cut and blow-dried. After all that, was it too much to ask to be treated like Cinderella entering the ball?

Yet when she went to the desk to pay, the receptionist said to her, "Hello, who is your appointment with today?"

— PETER CROMPTON

Heading off to college at the age of 40, I was a bit self-conscious about my advancing years. One morning I complained to my husband that I was the oldest student in my class.

"Even the teacher is younger than I am," I said.

"Yeah, but look at it from my point of view," he said optimistically. "I thought my days of fooling around with college girls were over."

— BRENDA McMILLEN

"It's definitely hereditary. It's called aging."

A few years ago, I opened the invitation to my cousin's 100th birthday party. On the front—in bold letters—it screamed, "If he's heard it once, he's heard it a hundred times. Happy Birthday, Sam!"

— LOUIS GLICKMAN

My four-year-old nephew, Brett, had drawn a picture for his grandmother, and was anxious to show it to her. Finding the door to her bathroom unlocked, he burst inside just as she was stepping out of the shower, soaking wet and without a towel.

He looked her up and down for a moment, then stated quite matter-of-factly, "Grandma, you look better with your glasses on."

A student in my college math course developed a severe case of tendinitis. Since she couldn't write, she brought a video camera to tape my lectures. After three or four classes, I asked her if she found the method satisfactory. She said it was working quite well, even better than note-taking.

"Actually," she confessed, "I have another reason for doing this. When I told my mother you were a widower, she wanted to see what you look like."

— GERSHON WHEELER

I had laryngitis and finally decided to go to the doctor. After the nurse called for me, she asked my age. "Forty-nine," I whispered.

"Don't worry," she whispered back. "I won't tell anyone."

Lola P. Bell

Turning 50 two years ago, I took a lot of good-natured ribbing from family and friends. So as my wife's 50th birthday approached, I decided to get in some needling of my own. I sat her down, looked deep into her eyes, then said I had never made love to anyone who was over 50 years old.

"Oh, well, I have," she deadpanned. "It's not that great."

— BOB MORELAND

Approaching 40, my frugal husband yearned for a boat. Frugality won out until the day he came across the obituary of an old high-school classmate, Ted. Certain this was a sign that life was too short, my husband purchased a boat that weekend.

Days later, a former classmate called. "Sure was a sad thing, wasn't it?" he said. "You know, Ted's boating accident and all."

— CHRISTINE CRAIG

I was having lunch with several thirty-something friends when talk turned to the dismal prospect of our growing older.

"Well, judging by my mother," I said, "at least my hearing will improve. My mother can hear my biological clock ticking from 200 kilometres away."

— SHERRY YATES

I had just had my 50th birthday and found the decade marker traumatic. When I went to get my driver's licence renewed, a matter-of-fact woman typed out the information, tested my vision, snapped the camera and handed me a laminated card with my picture on it.

"You mean I have to look at this for the next four years?" I jokingly said to her.

"Don't worry about it," she replied. "In four years it'll look good to you."

— NANCY FIRESTONE

We invited some old friends to help celebrate my 40th birthday. My husband went out to buy a gift, and he saw some cute little music boxes. A blue one was playing "Happy Birthday to You." Thinking they were all the same, he picked up a red one and asked the clerk to have it gift-wrapped.

When we sat down to dinner, he gave it to me, asked me to open it and—surprise—out came the tune to "The old gray mare, she ain't what she used to be."

— MRS. EARL DAVENPORT

Now that I'm over 40, younger teammates have begun to tease me about my declining abilities as a softball player. During one game, I was playing third base when a batter ripped a shot over my head. I leapt as high as I could, but the ball tipped off the end of my glove and fell safely for a hit.

At the end of the inning, I was heading for the dugout when our left fielder caught up with me. "That much!" he called, holding his thumb and forefinger a few centimetres apart.

"I know," I replied. "I almost had it."

"No," he said. "I mean that's how far you got off the ground."

— RANDY HAWKINS

"Dad?!"

After a shopping expedition, my friend Gina and I stopped in a local bar for a drink. We hadn't been seated long when she leaned over and said that four young men at the next table were watching us. Since we're both thirty-something, married with children, we found the situation flattering. We sat a little straighter and tried to look slimmer and younger.

In a few minutes, one of the men got up and came toward our table. "Excuse me," he said. Then he reached over our heads to turn up the volume on the televised ball game.

— SANDRA LYONS

While on maternity leave, a woman from our office brought in her new bundle of joy. She also had her seven-year-old son with her. Everyone gathered around the baby, and the little boy asked, "Mommy, can I have some money to buy a soda?"

"What do you say?" she said.

Respectfully, the boy replied, "You're thin and beautiful."

The woman reached in her purse and gave her son the money.

— MERCURY NICKSE

You can get old pretty young if you don't take care of yourself.

— YOGI BERRA,
What Time Is It? You Mean Now? (Simon & Schuster)

I wear glasses, so I can look for things I keep losing.

— BILL COSBY, Time Flies (Bantam Books)

Hair is the first thing. And teeth the second. A man's got those two things, he's got it all.

— JAMES BROWN

Wisdom comes with age, but keep it to yourself.

— MARY ROACH in Health

I'm at the age where my back goes out more than I do.

— PHYLLIS DILLER

One of the best parts of growing older? You can flirt all you like since you've become harmless.

— LIZ SMITH
in The Older the Fiddle, the Better the Tune by Willard Scott (Hyperion)

Let the wind blow through your hair while you still have some.

— DAVE WEINBAUM

What I've learned is that life is too short and movies are too long.

— DENIS LEARY in GQ

The key to successful aging is to pay as little attention to it as possible.

— JUDITH REGAN in More

The Naked Truth

▶ BY MARY ROACH

Once you hit 40, it is time to think twice about miniskirts. Also, string bikinis, midriff-baring tops, skintight or low-rise jeans that have been sanded white the length of the thighs, as though the wearer had been tied to a bumper and dragged facedown around the block a few times. These are clothes for young people.

Alas, this is what the stores are selling. Today's popular clothing chains appeal strictly to teenagers, who can be counted upon to change their tastes every 30 days, as the latest *Cosmo Girl* or *Teen Vogue* arrives in the mail. Customers like me cannot possibly afford new clothing more than once a decade, owing to the financial strain of paying for teenage children's rapidly shifting fashion needs. So no one bothers to make clothing for us.

This is a dangerous situation. Expose a middle-aged woman to nothing but miniskirts and abbreviated tops for long enough, and she's bound to cave. One day, when her self-esteem is dangerously high and the dressing room lights dangerously low, she'll try on something designed for her daughter and say to herself, "Oh, why not?" If she happens to be shopping with her children, the answer to this question will be provided for her. But middle-aged husbands offer no such reality check. They live in a candyland of denial and residual carnality. They still, bless them, like to see a little flesh.

My husband recently made me try on a bikini. A bikini is not so much a garment as a cloth-based reminder that your parts have been migrating all these years. My waist, I realized that day in the dressing room, has completely disappeared beneath my rib cage, which now rests directly on my hips. I'm exhibiting continental drift in reverse.

The buttocks, too, have overrun their boundaries, infringing on territory that rightly belongs to the thighs. I have encouraged my thighs to do something about this—restraining order, guard dog—but they have not. Your thighs are rarely there for you.

"Cute!" says Ed dementedly. "Turn around."

"You turn around first."

Ed does not understand what all women my age understand. The mature lady's buttock does not wish to come out and take a bow. Designers of mature ladies' swimwear know this. They've built little curtains into their designs,

> A bikini is not so much a garment as a cloth-based reminder that your parts have been migrating all these years.

God help me, I've entered the Age of Skirted Swimwear.

enabling the sagging buttock to keep hidden, and/or cast votes in privacy. God help me, I've entered the Age of Skirted Swimwear. This is the age right after Accessorizing with Reading Glasses and a few years before Can't Name Anyone on the Radio.

Even the knees are in on the betrayal. I recently saw a tabloid photograph of a 40-something Demi Moore with her knees circled in red, highlighting the fact that they were disappearing under the shifting shoals of her thighs. Ha-ha, I said to myself. Just deserts for having a face and breasts (and a boyfriend) that look 25. Then I looked at my own knees, which I plan never to do again.

The foot is more or less the one body part that time leaves alone. Well into your 70s, you can wear whatever style shoes you feel like wearing. Positioned, as they are, at the bottom of the heap, gravity is not an issue. Or so I thought. Shortly after the swimsuit debacle, I tried on a pair of pointy-toed black pumps, the sort that actresses on "Sex and the City" were wearing for 30 days back in spring.

"How do those work for you?" the salesgirl asked. I told her they were pinching me, and not in an appreciative, you-look-just-like-that-gal-on-"Sex and the City" way.

"You know," she said brightly, "your feet flatten as you age."

I went to find Ed, and I told him about my flattening instep. He smiled and put his arm around me. That still fits, and for this I'm happy. ▲

My father, at age 93, had only the most basic needs and very few wants. Last fall, my sister-in-law, hoping to get a little help in choosing a suitable birthday gift for him, asked, "Pa, what would you like for your birthday this year?"

"Nothing," he replied.

"But, Pa," she kidded, "that's what we gave you last year."

"Well," he answered, "I'm still using it."

— L.M. COUILLARD

I was with my husband at a baseball game when I decided to go get myself a hot dog. As I stood up my husband asked me to buy him a beer. The young clerk at the concession stand asked to see verification of age.

"You've got to be kidding," I said. "I'm almost 40 years old." He apologized, but said he had to insist. When I showed him my licence, the clerk served me the beer. "That will be $4.25."

I gave him $5 and told him to keep the change. "The tip's for carding me," I said.

He put the change in the tip cup. "Thanks," he said. "Works every time."

— ANGIE DEWHURST

Venus and Mars

Speaking of war and laughter—put together, it's called marriage. Despite thousands of years of practice, men and women still don't connect well. But it's fun to watch 'em try.

"My son's into extreme sports, my daughter's into extreme makeover, and my husband's into extreme denial."

Our Lamaze class included a tour of the pediatric wing at the hospital. When a new baby was brought into the nursery, all the women tried to guess its weight, but the guy standing next to me was the only male to venture a number. "Looks like 9½ pounds," he offered confidently.

"This must not be your first," I said.

"Oh, yes, it's my first."

"Then how would you know the weight of a baby?"

He shrugged. "I'm a fisherman."

— TIM LOVERSKY

Heavy snow had buried my van in our driveway. My husband, Scott, dug around the wheels, rocked the van back and forth and finally pushed me free. I was on the road when I heard an odd noise. I got on my cell and called home.

"Thank God you answered," I said when Scott picked up. "There's this alarming sound coming under the van. For a moment I thought I was dragging you down the highway."

"And you didn't stop?"

— PAIGE FAIRFIELD

My husband and I, married 13 years, were dressing for a party. I'd spent all day getting a haircut and permanent, then as we were leaving, we met in the hall and he said nothing. I complained that he had not even noticed my hair. "You used to pay attention to every little thing, and now you don't notice anything! You take me for granted!"

My husband stood there rubbing his face as he let me rant and rave. Then it hit me: He'd shaved off his six-month-old beard.

— MELONY ANDERSON

My sister's lack of sports knowledge recently became evident when we attended a hockey game. After one of the home players scored, the crowd screamed and the monitors around the rink flashed: "G O A L."

After cheering wildly, my sister turned and asked, "Who's Al?"

— KAREN KELLY

As part of our regular service, members of the congregation are permitted to make announcements or requests for prayers. One man, Bob, mentioned his upcoming 37th wedding anniversary. At the obvious nudging of his wife, he quickly corrected that to 38.

As the chuckling died down, heard from the back of the church was, "I'd like to offer a prayer for Bob."

— JUDITH L. LENSINK

My sister went shopping for blue jeans with her husband, Steve. She chose a few pairs to try on and went into the fitting room, while Steve waited outside. A minute later he heard her crying softly. Concerned, Steve said through the door, "Honey, really, it doesn't matter if you've gone up a size or two."

Soon she came out, limping slightly and pretty upset. The problem wasn't the size of her pants; she had stubbed her toe in the dressing room.

— JULIE LAW

Timeless Humour from the '50s

A husband-and-wife photography team we know shoot their pictures together, do their developing and printing together—in fact, they're together 24 hours of the day. We wondered how they managed to keep up such good working relations.

"Well, frankly," the wife said, "it wouldn't work out if one of us didn't have a good disposition."

"Which one?" we asked.

"Oh," she laughed, "we take turns."

— ELIZABETH JETER

After my husband and I had a huge argument, we ended up not talking to each other for days. Finally, on the third day, he asked where one of his shirts was. "Oh," I said, "now you're speaking to me."

He looked confused. "What are you talking about?"

"Haven't you noticed I haven't spoken to you for three days?" I challenged.

"No," he said. "I just thought we were getting along."

— BETH DORIA

After the birth of my son, a woman from the records department stopped by my hospital room to get information for his birth certificate. "Father's date of birth?" she asked. When I told her, she said, "Do you realize that his birthday is exactly nine months before your son's birth?"

"No, I hadn't thought about it," I responded, "but now that you mention it, I have a daughter who turned two a couple days before the same date."

After she finished taking down all the data, she patted my hand and said, "Maybe you should start buying your husband a tie for his birthday."

— M. K. PIGOTT

"Romance has nothing to do with it. Dan and I are renewing our marriage vows because he has forgotten them."

When my parents run the dishwasher, they let each other know the dishes are clean by placing the box of detergent on the counter. When Mom got home from work one day, she was surprised to find the detergent on the counter, since she had emptied the dishwasher the night before. She couldn't understand why my dad would run the dishwasher again—until she opened it and found the top tray full of golf balls.

— MICHELE FERGUSON

My daughter had absentmindedly left her sneakers on our kitchen table. "That's disgusting," my husband grumbled. "Doesn't she realize we eat off that table?" Then he went out back to work on the car.

I cleaned the table and left to do my grocery shopping. When I came home I couldn't set my bags down anywhere. Sitting in the middle of the kitchen table was a car muffler.

— KATHERINE HORGAN

It seemed that all our appliances had broken in the same week, and repairs were straining our budget. So when I picked up the kids from school and our Jeep started making rattling sounds, I decided that rather than burden my husband, I'd deal with it. I hadn't reckoned on my little tattletales, however. They rushed into the house with the news: "Daddy, the Jeep was breaking down, but Mom made the noise stop!"

Impressed, my husband asked, "How did you fix it?"

"I turned up the volume on the radio," I confessed.

— RUTH TEN VEEN

Curious when I found two black-and-white negatives in a drawer, I had them made into prints. I was pleasantly surprised to see they were of a younger, slimmer me taken on one of my first dates with my husband.

When I showed him the photographs, his face lit up. "Wow! It's my old Plymouth."

— DONNA MARTIN

During my brother's wedding, my mother had managed to keep from crying—until she glanced at my grandparents. My grandmother had reached over to my grandfather's wheelchair and gently touched his hand. That was all it took to start my mother's tears flowing. After the wedding, Mom went over to my grandmother and told her how that tender gesture triggered her outburst.

"Well, I'm sorry to ruin your moment," Grandmother replied. "But I was just checking to see if he was awake."

— MARK SAMPLE

Every December it was the same excruciating tradition. Our family would get up at the crack of dawn, go to a Christmas tree farm and tromp across acres of snow in search of the perfect tree. Hours later our feet would be freezing, but Mom would press on, convinced the tree of her dreams was "just up ahead."

One year I snapped. "Mom, face it. The perfect tree doesn't exist. It's like looking for a man. Just be satisfied if you can find one that isn't dead, doesn't have too many bald spots and is straight."

— CHRISTY MARTIN

Standing in line at the clothing store's counter, I watched as the woman ahead of me handed the clerk her credit card. The customer waited for a long time while the saleswoman went to verify the account. When she finally returned, the clerk said, "I'm sorry, but this card is in your husband's name, and we can't accept it because the records show he is deceased."

With that, the woman turned to her spouse, who was standing next to her, and asked, "Does this mean I don't have to fix lunch for you today?"

— MARILYN ARNOPOL

"You realize, of course, there's a five-day cooling-off period on sports car loans."

161

While I was dining out with my children, a man came over to our table and we started talking. He asked where my kids go to school. I told him we home-school them. With a raised eyebrow he asked if my husband is the sole breadwinner for our family. I said no, I also work—out of our home. Then, noticing our two-month-old son, he mentioned that his daughter had just had a baby, and he wondered what hospital our son was born in.

"He was born at home," I answered.

The man looked at me, then said, "Wow, you don't get out much, do you?"

— LAURA HANSER

After his marriage broke up, my manager became very philosophical. "I guess it was in our stars," he sighed.

"What do you mean?" I asked.

"Her astrological sign is the one for earth. Mine is the one for water. Together we made mud."

— LORI PHILLIPS

The first time I met my wife, she was an intense aerobics instructor at my health club and I was an out-of-shape new member. After one gruelling workout, I gasped, "This is really helping me get toned."

She looked me up and down. Feeling self-conscious, I added, "Big men run in my family."

She raised an eyebrow. "Apparently not enough."

— JOHN PARKER

My mom had always wanted to learn to play the piano, so Dad bought her one for her birthday. A few weeks later, I called and asked how she was doing. "We returned the piano," said Dad. "I persuaded her to switch to a clarinet."

"Why?" I asked.

"Because," he explained, "with a clarinet, she can't sing along."

— DON FOSTER

His aching back made it impossible for my friend's husband to get a decent night's rest on their lumpy mattress. "Until I feel better, I'm going to sleep on the couch," he announced.

Ordinarily, a spouse moving out of the bedroom isn't a good sign for the marriage. So his wife couldn't resist: "Okay, but as soon as we have an argument you're back in our bed."

— ANNA GUTHRIE

When my friend got a job, her husband agreed to share the housework. He was stunned by the amount of effort involved in keeping a house clean with small boys to pick up after, and insisted that he and his wife shop for a new vacuum cleaner.

The salesman gave them a demonstration of the latest model. "It comes equipped with all the newest features," he assured them.

The husband was not convinced. "Don't you have a riding one?" he asked.

— PAT MONTGOMERY

"God may have forgiven you, George, but I haven't."

Mobile phones are the only subject on which men boast about who's got the smallest.

— NEIL KINNOCK, British politician

The remarkable thing about my mother is that for 30 years she served us nothing but leftovers. The original meal has never been found.

— CALVIN TRILLIN

Weddings have less to do with being married than with the fact that it is best to begin the most arduous journeys surrounded by friends and wearing nice clothes.

— TONY EARLEY, Somehow Form a Family (Algonquin)

Behind every great man is a woman rolling her eyes.

— JIM CARREY in "Bruce Almighty"

Men want the same thing from their underwear that they want from women: a little bit of support, and a little bit of freedom.

— JERRY SEINFELD

When you're in love, it's the most glorious two-and-a-half minutes of your life.

— RICHARD LEWIS

Here's the secret to a happy marriage: Do what your wife tells you.

— DENZEL WASHINGTON

She's Got Game

▶ BY MARY ROACH

On any given night for the 14 or so months of the year corresponding to baseball season, our TV is likely to be tuned to a sports channel. In order to maintain some semblance of personal contact with my husband, Ed, during these months, I often sit beside him on the couch with a book. I don't mind the chatter of the sportscasters, for my brain processes sports talk in the same way it processes paid political announcements and the cellphone conversations of strangers.

A man in a navy blazer will say, "No atta-babies in that at-bat!" and his companion will chime in with, "It was right there, in the whack-me zone!" and it's as though they're not there.

Sometimes I find myself staring at the game anyway. I watch sports the way a dog will watch TV: I'm attracted by the motion and colour, but no actual comprehension is taking place. Ed forgets that this is the case. He'll see me looking at the screen and assume I'm following the game and expect me to keep track of what happens while he goes to the kitchen for a refreshing beverage. Sometimes I'm able to bluff my way through it ("He had it right there in the whack-me zone, honey!"), but more often I am forced to confess that I have not grasped the significance of anything I have seen.

This is where it gets ugly. This is where Ed tries to turn his wife into—as the men in the blazers like to say—a serious student of the game. Plainly put, this cannot be done. You'd have more luck getting a pug to understand "Jeopardy." Take, for instance, the Infield Fly Rule, which begins, in the breezy parlance of the Official Baseball Rules, like this: "The batter is out when it is declared, and the ball does not have to be caught. Because the batter is declared out, the runners are no longer forced to run, but they can run if they wish, at the risk of being put out..."

"What?" Ed will ask. "What don't you get?" Apparently this language speaks to him in a way that it does not speak to me. One night I decided to try putting it to work. It was seven o'clock and cutlets were growing cold. I cleared my throat. "The wife is declared put out when it is dinnertime and the game is still running. The husband's attention has to be caught and because the wife is put out, the husband may wish to run..."

Ed begged leniency on the grounds that it was "the top of the ninth." Here again, communication breaks down. For me, there can be no understanding of a sport where the "top" of an inning is the first half. "Think of ladders," I said, as Marvin Benard stepped up to the plate. "You start at the bottom and go to the top." But Ed wasn't listening.

This is where it gets ugly.

Benard struck out, and Ed said hurtful things about him. This is my other qualm with pro sports. I feel bad for the players when they mess up. The ball Benard missed was going 90 m.p.h., and it went all crooked. If I were the umpire, I would have laid a

Sometimes I'm able to bluff my way through it ("He had it right there in the whack-me zone, honey!").

hand on the man's shoulder and said, "Take your base, Marv. You were really close."

Last October my tolerance for Ed's devotion to sports, already threadbare, began to unravel. The baseball season was winding down, leading me to think that we could resume our normal adult activities, if only we had any. I came into the living room one Sunday to find Ed, a man who dismisses football as "a bore," engrossed in a Broncos game. He wore a guilty grin. "Third and long, sweetie!"

It was around that time that I came across a book about sports "addiction." It said that for many men, their relationship with their team fulfills a need for intimacy. This got me right there in the whack-me zone. Was J. T. Snow doing more for my husband than I was?

I confronted Ed. There was an NFL game on that day, but he wasn't watching. He was making banana bread. Though he denied the charges, he wouldn't rule out the possibility that J. T. Snow could make him happy. Then he asked if I wanted to go for a bike ride. I decided to drop the sports addiction thing, because truly, Ed doesn't deserve the hassle. He's the winningest guy I know, and I mean that from the bottom of my heart, which is the part that comes before the top. ▲

In the frozen-foods department of our local grocery store, I noticed a man grocery shopping with his son. As I walked by, he checked something off his list, and I heard him whisper conspiratorially to the child, "You know, if we really mess this up, we'll never have to do it again."

— JANET CAMPBELL

During the hectic time after our son was born, my husband and I went weeks without being romantic, and it was taking its toll. As he helped me fold the laundry one day, I pointed to a pile of socks. "Those haven't been mated," I said.

"I know the feeling," my husband muttered under his breath.

— ROBBIN CEDERBLOM

After I completed a frantic afternoon of chores, I walked into the living room to find my husband reclining in his chair. He was looking bemusedly at our new puppy, who was napping. "If I wanted to look at something lying around sleeping all day," he complained, "I would have bought a cat."

"Or you could have just bought a mirror," I said.

— TRACEY SMITH

My husband is a big Blue Jays fan. When I saw an ad on television for a baseball autographed by one of his favourite players that cost $42, I rushed out and bought it for him as a gift.

That evening as we were watching television, the same commercial came on. Slyly I glanced over at my husband just as he commented, "What kind of idiot would pay $42 for a baseball?"

— JANICE ADAMS

Every year on their wedding anniversary my boss, Woody, and his wife celebrated by staying at the same resort hotel. On their 25th anniversary they booked their usual room. But when the hotel's bell captain escorted them upstairs, they were in for a big surprise.

"There must be some mistake," Woody said. "This looks like the bridal suite."

"It's okay," the bell captain reassured him. "If I put you in the ballroom, that doesn't mean you have to dance."

— CONNIE L. SELLERS

One morning a customer entered my flower shop and ordered a bouquet for his wife. "No card is necessary," he instructed us. "She'll know who sent them."

The delivery truck hadn't even returned to the store when the phone rang. It was the customer's wife. "Who sent the flowers?" she asked.

After explaining that the customer had requested that no card be included, I considered the matter closed—but not so. A bit later, she came rushing in the front door. "You've got to tell me who sent the flowers," she demanded, "before my husband gets home."

— LINDA O. COUCH

"Our credit card was stolen, but I've decided not to report it. The thief is spending less than you did!"

Pregnant with my third child, I was stricken with a bout of morning sickness and lay down on the living-room couch to rest. Just then one of the workmen who was doing repairs in my house walked by and gave me a curious look. "Taking a little break," I explained. "I'm in my first trimester."

"Really?" he said. "What's your major?"

— CARA ANDERSON

When, by means of an at-home early pregnancy test, my wife discovered she was pregnant, she tried to get in touch with me at work. I was out, so she left a message. Later, I found a note on my desk: "E. P. T. —phone home."

— JON RISING

Our dentist recently hired a beautiful young blonde as a dental hygienist. We exchanged small talk for half an hour as she cleaned my teeth and I gazed into her pale-blue eyes. When she finished, she smiled and said, "You have the most perfect mouth." My heart skipped a beat.

Then she continued: "Usually I have a lot of trouble reaching people's wisdom teeth. But your mouth is so big, I can get both hands in easily!"

— PHILLIP B. MURRAY

As a paper salesman, I have a habit of turning over containers and looking for trademarks. This really annoys my wife. After dinner at a pizzeria, we were handed a box for leftovers. I craned my neck to get a better look under it. When she rolled her eyes, I said, "I'm just trying to see who made that box."

"I know," she sighed. "You used to look at me that way."

— CHRIS J. RATTAN

My husband, Mike, and I had several stressful months of financial difficulties. So one evening I was touched to see him gazing at the diamond wedding ring that symbolized our marriage.

"With this ring…" I began romantically.

"We could pay off Visa," he responded.

— DAWN HILL

I realized that the ups and downs of the stock market had become too big a part of our life one night as my husband and I prepared for bed. As we slid beneath the covers, I snuggled up to him and told him I loved him.

Drifting off to sleep, he drowsily whispered back, "Your dividend growth fund went up three days this week."

— SHIRLEY S. DILLON

While in the checkout line at my local hardware store I overheard one man say to another, "My wife has been after me to paint our shed. But I let it go for so long she got mad and did it herself."

His friend nodded. "I like women who get mad like that."

— C. V. MAYNARD

When a woman in my office became engaged, a colleague offered her some advice. "The first ten years are the hardest," she said.

"How long have you been married?" I asked.

"Ten years," she replied.

— TONYA WINTER

When my younger brother and his wife celebrated their first anniversary, they invited the rest of the family to join them for dinner. The conversation focused on the newlyweds and how they happened to meet. Caught up in the romance of the story, one by one the men related how we had met our wives. Eventually everyone had told his story except for my youngest brother.

All eyes were on him when he said, "Oh, Cindy and I met in college. We were matched up by a computer according to compatibility."

"That's the whole story?" my wife asked incredulously.

"Oh, no," he replied with a grin. "They've fixed the computer since then."

— JOHN MORRISSEY

The family was viewing old slides and one flashed on the screen that caught everyone's attention. My father, wearing his favourite golf shirt, was holding me at the tender age of three weeks.

The look on his face told all. "There's my prize possession," my father said.

Touched, I smiled at him as he continued, "I wonder whatever happened to that golf shirt?"

— JEANNE GRAVES

> My wife-to-be and I were at the client service centre for our marriage licence. After recording the vital information—names, dates of birth, etc.—the clerk handed me our licence and deadpanned, "No refunds, no exchanges, no warranties."
>
> **Albert J. Campbell**

My husband, an exercise enthusiast who spends an hour and a half at an athletic club every morning before work, encouraged a middle-aged and quite overweight friend to join him for his morning sessions. The co-worker decided not to tell his wife about his new project until after he had lost some weight, and he faithfully began meeting my husband at 6 a.m. every day.

At the end of the first week, the friend's wife rolled over in bed and offered this parting advice: "I don't know where you're going, dear, or what you are doing. But just remember: You aren't used to it."

— DEBBIE BEAUCHAMP

Some newly married friends were visiting us when the topic of children came up. The bride said she wanted three children, while the young husband demurred, saying two would be enough for him. They discussed this discrepancy for a few minutes until the husband thought he'd put an end to things, saying boldly, "After our second child, I'll just have a vasectomy."

Without a moment's hesitation, the bride retorted, "Well, I hope you'll love the third one like it's your own!"

— LISA MONGAN

While waiting for a flight, I glanced over at a nearby couple. He was reading a sailing association's book, *Basic Cruising*. She was reading *Adrift: 76 Days Lost at Sea*.

— BRUCE NEAL

My husband is wonderful with our baby daughter, but often turns to me for advice. Recently I was in the shower when he poked his head in to ask, "What should I feed Lily for lunch?"

"That's up to you," I replied. "There's all kinds of food. Why don't you pretend I'm not home?"

A few minutes later, my cellphone rang. I answered it to hear my husband saying, "Yeah, hi, honey. Uh…what should I feed Lily for lunch?"

— JULIE BALL

Rushing to a bridge tournament, I was pulled over for going 63 in a 50 k.p.h. zone. "What'll I tell my husband?" I worried, explaining to the police officer that he was a self-described "perfect" driver.

The cop took a second look at the name and address on my licence. "Did your husband go duck hunting this morning?" he asked.

Baffled, I answered, "Yes."

"I stopped him for going 65."

— ANN ALENE DUNN

Once my divorce was final, I went to the local Department of Motor Vehicles and asked to have my maiden name reinstated on my driver's licence. "Will there be any change of address?" the clerk inquired. "No," I replied.

"Oh, good," she said, clearly delighted. "You got the house."

— POLLY BAUGHMAN

To our shock and horror, my sister-in-law and I realized we had each been married nearly 50 years. "That's a long time," I observed.

"A long, long time," she agreed. Then she smiled. "Something just occurred to me."

"What's that?"

"If I had killed your brother the first time I felt like it, I'd be out of jail by now."

— BARBARA MASON

Timeless Humour from the '60s

My friend's husband is always telling her that housekeeping would be a snap if only she would organize her time better. Recently he had a chance to put his theory into practice while his wife was away.

When I popped in one evening to see how he was managing, he crowed, "I made a cake, frosted it, washed the kitchen windows, cleaned all the cupboards, scrubbed the kitchen floor, walls and ceiling and even had a bath."

I was about to concede that perhaps he was a better manager than his wife, when he added sheepishly, "When I was making the chocolate frosting, I forgot to turn off the mixer before taking the beaters out of the bowl, so I had to do all the rest."

— MARY L. COSTAIN

"I'm going to Venus. He's going to Mars."

Ha, Ha, Ha! Tee-Hee! Ho

What Women Want

▶ BY DAVE BARRY

The other day my son and I were talking about women and I realized that it was time he and I had a Serious Talk, the kind every father should have with his son yet avoids because it's so awkward.

The subject? Buying gifts for women.

This is an area where many men do not have a clue. Exhibit A: my father, a thoughtful man who once gave my mother—on their anniversary—an electric blanket.

He honestly could not understand why, when she opened the box, she gave him That Look. (You veteran men know the one I mean.) After all, this was the deluxe model electric blanket. With automatic thermostat! What more could any woman want?

The mistake that my dad made, and that many guys make, was in thinking that when you choose a gift for a woman, it should do something useful. Wrong! The first rule of buying a gift for a woman is: The gift should not do anything, or if it does, it should do it badly.

Let's consider two possible gifts,

both of which, theoretically, perform the same function:

Gift 1: A state-of-the-art gasoline-powered lantern, with electronic ignition and dual mantles, capable of generating 1,200 lumens of light for ten hours on a single tank of fuel.

Gift 2: A scented beeswax candle containing visible particles of bee poop and providing roughly the same illumination as a lukewarm corn dog.

To a guy, Gift 1 is clearly superior because you could use it to see in the dark. To a woman, Gift 2 is much better, because women love to sit around in the gloom with reeking, sputtering candles. Don't ask me why.

All I'm saying is that this is the kind of thing a woman wants. That's why the ultimate gift is jewelry: It's totally useless.

The second rule of buying gifts for women is: You are never finished.

This is the scary part, the part that my son is just discovering. If you have a girlfriend, she will give you, at minimum, a birthday gift, an anniversary gift, a Christmas Hanukkah Kwanzaa gift and a Valentine's Day gift.

Every one of these gifts will be nice-

ly wrapped and accompanied by a thoughtful card. And when she gives you this gift, you have to give her one back. You can't just open your wallet and say, "Here's, let's see . . . $17!"

And, as I told my son, it only gets worse. Looming ahead are bridal showers, weddings, baby showers, Mother's Day and other Mandatory Gift Occasions that would not even exist if men—as is alleged—really ran the world. Women observe all of these occasions, and more.

My wife will buy gifts for no reason. She'll go into one of those gift stores at the mall that men never enter, she'll find something—maybe a tiny cute box that couldn't hold anything larger than a molecule and is therefore useless—and she'll buy it, plus a thoughtful card.

And she doesn't even know who the recipient is yet!

Millions of other women are out doing the same thing, getting further and further ahead, while we guys are home watching instant replays. We have no chance of winning this war.

That's what I told my son. It was time he knew the truth. ▲

"They said he has a real fear of intimacy."

One night my friend John and I were sitting at a bar where he used to work, when an attractive woman, a former co-worker, came in and sat next to him. She told him she had just had a fight with her husband, a police officer, and needed to get out of the house for a while.

They had been talking for a few minutes when, as a joke, I leaned over to John. "Don't look now," I whispered, "but a guy about six-five just walked in. And he's got a gun."

Without hesitating, John turned to me. "Quick, Ed," he said, "kiss me on the lips."

— E. J. KRAMER

I had taken a rare day off from work and, having shed the corporate uniform, was dressed scruffily, with my hair in rollers. Glancing out my window, I saw a van blocking my driveway.

Incensed, I flew to the door and told the driver to move it immediately.

About an hour later, all dressed up to go shopping, I was backing my car out of the driveway and noticed the driver standing on the sidewalk. A little embarrassed, I smiled and nodded hello.

"Ma'am," he said to me, "I hope your grandmother is only visiting. She is one tough old cookie."

— JEAN HENRY

Driving my friend Steve and his girlfriend to the airport, we passed a billboard showing a bikini-clad beauty holding a can of beer. Steve's girlfriend glanced up at it and announced, "I suppose if I drank a six-pack of that brand, I'd look like her."

"No," Steve corrected. "If I drank a six-pack, you'd look like her."

— JOHN D. BOYD

My boyfriend and I were taking his 19-year-old niece to a weekend festival. When we arrived at her house to pick her up, she appeared in tasteful but very short shorts, and a tank top with spaghetti straps. A debate began immediately about appropriate dress. I took the girl's side, recalling that when we began dating, I dressed the same way.

"Yes," said my boyfriend sternly, "and I said something about it, didn't I?"

Everyone looked at me. "Yeah," I replied. "You said, 'What's your phone number?'"

— CHARNELL WALLS WATSON

For our 20th anniversary my husband and I vacationed in Hawaii, where we went snorkelling. After an hour in the water everyone got back on the boat, except for me and one handsome young man. As I continued my underwater exploring, I noticed that everywhere I swam, he swam. I snorkelled for another 40 minutes. So did he. I climbed back in the boat; so did he.

I felt very flattered and, as I took off my fins, asked him coyly why he had stayed in the water for so long. "I'm the lifeguard," he replied matter-of-factly. "I couldn't get out until you did."

— SHARON FORGUE

One morning I found a beautiful long-stemmed rose lying by the kitchen sink. Even though the flower was plastic, I was thinking how, after all the years we had been married, my husband could still make such a wonderful romantic gesture. Then I noticed a love note lying next to it. "Dear Sue," it read. "Don't touch the rose. I'm using the stem to unclog the drain."

— SUZAN L. WIENER

A woman friend looked at my chest and said, "Of course."

That's when I realized I was wearing a T-shirt I had picked up at an annual biker rally. It read "If a man says something in the woods where no woman can hear, is he still wrong?"

— RUSS HARGREAVES

My wife and her friend Karen were talking about their labour-saving devices as they pulled into our driveway. Karen said, "I love my new garage-door opener."

"I love mine too," my wife replied, and honked the horn three times. That was the signal for me to come out and open the garage.

— GENE WARD

My husband knows the pitfalls of trying to communicate with the opposite sex—especially me. For instance, I recently tried on a pair of pants and needed a second opinion about how they looked. "Do I look too fat in these pants?" I asked.

"No," he said, pausing, obviously worried about his response. "You look…just fat enough."

— KATHY SEUFERT

For years my sister's husband tried unsuccessfully to persuade her to get a hearing aid. "How much do they cost?" she asked one day after he had pitched the idea to her again.

"They're usually about $3,000," he said.

"Okay, well, if you say something worth $3,000," she replied, "I'll get one."

— EDWIN A. REINAGEL

Timeless Humour from the '50s

A Manitoba chap, an incorrigible practical joker, often makes his long-suffering wife the butt of his painful pranks. But last fall she finally got her chance to even the score. The couple were spending the weekend in a Chicago hotel. It was a hot night, and when they got back to their room after the theatre, the husband peeled off his clothes and stretched out on the bed to cool off. By the time his wife was ready for bed, he was fast asleep and she decided not to disturb him.

Some hours later, he woke up and groped his way in the dark toward the bathroom. By mistake he opened the outside door and, still groggy, was halfway down the hall before he became aware of his predicament. He turned back hastily. Then, to his horror, he realized that he was not only locked out but had forgotten his room number.

Frantic, he rushed to the elevator bank, pressed the button and hid around the corner. When the elevator arrived, he thrust out his arm and beckoned wildly. The operator took one look, slammed the elevator door and went for the house detective.

When the detective arrived, he found the unfortunate guest cowering in a corner. He gave him a sheet from the linen closet, called the desk to check his assertion that he was registered at the hotel with his wife and escorted him to his room.

Pounding on the door until the wife opened it, the detective said, "This man claims to be your husband. Is he?"

For a moment she stared at the sheet-draped figure; then she said icily, "I've never seen him before in my life."

— A. E. TATHAM

One evening my husband's golfing buddy drove his secretary home after she had imbibed a little too much at an office reception. Although this was an innocent gesture, he decided not to mention it to his wife, who tended to get jealous easily.

Later that night my husband's friend and his wife were driving to a restaurant. Suddenly he looked down and spotted a high-heel shoe half hidden under the passenger seat. Not wanting to be conspicuous, he waited until his wife was looking out her window before he scooped up the shoe and tossed it out of the car. With a sigh of relief, he pulled into the restaurant parking lot. That's when he noticed his wife squirming around in her seat.

"Honey," she asked, "have you seen my other shoe?"

— JOAN FELDMAN

I spent an afternoon helping my boyfriend move into a new home. In one carton I found a crockpot, with an odd-looking and very dirty metal lid. Later I ushered my boyfriend into the kitchen and asked why he hadn't mentioned this perfectly good pot.

He stared at it, then replied, "Well, after I broke the lid I never thought of replacing it with a hubcap."

— CAROLINE C. JONES

Soon after we were married, my husband, Paul, stopped wearing his wedding band.

"Why don't you ever wear your ring?" I asked.

"It cuts off my circulation," Paul replied.

"I know," I said. "It's supposed to."

MARILYN WARE

After I had taken on a few too many projects, my responsibilities began piling up on me. To keep my forgetfulness to a minimum, I started a daily reminder list, scratching off items as I completed them. Some two weeks later I bragged to my husband, Clarence, "Thanks to that list I have never once overlooked a single important detail."

Not long afterward I returned home from a late-night meeting and picked up my list to check on the next day's activities. There, in my husband's handwriting, wedged between "1:30 hair appointment" and "Clean the linen closet," was the notation: "Seduce Clarence."

— MARY E. HOWELL

For a while my husband and I had opposite schedules. He worked during the day and I worked at night. One morning I noticed he left a note to himself on the kitchen counter that said "STAMPS" in large letters. As a helpful surprise, I bought him some at the post office and put them on the counter before going to work.

The next morning I found the same note. "STAMPS" was crossed out. Underneath he had written, "ONE MILLION DOLLARS."

— STEPHANIE SHELLEY

"I guess I thought if we came to France, you wouldn't still be **you know, you!**"

Night Light Fight

▶ BY MARY ROACH

If my husband, Ed, had his way, you could pop by our place any given night and see me sitting in bed, struggling to hold my head up under the weight of a night-vision headset. Ed is an early-to-sleep sort of chap, who'll announce around 8 p.m., "Just going to change into my pj's and read for a while." Once he becomes horizontal, however, it's pretty much over.

This makes it difficult for yours truly, for I really do read in bed, including the part where you turn the page and read a second one and then a third one. Ed would like for me to do this in a quiet, motionless, pitch-dark manner. Instead, I do it in a chip-crunching, light-on, getting-in-and-out-of-bed-for-more-chips manner. In the spirit of compromise, I bought Ed earplugs and a black satin sleep mask. "It's dashing,"

I said of the mask. "You look like Antonio Banderas in *Zorro*." This was a lie. He looked like Arlene Francis in "What's My Line?"

"Zorro didn't wear a sleep mask," countered Ed. "His had eyeholes cut out."

"It was a special fencer's sleep mask. Come on," I said. "That movie is all about sleep. Why do you think he writes Z's everywhere?"

Ed's argument was that as the awake person, I should have to wear the uncomfortable head wear.

We were inching toward the marriage counselor's couch when in the nick of time, I found a product called Light Wedge: "The only personal reading light that has the ability to save the 50 percent of marriages that end in divorce." It's a thin, glowing slice of acrylic that lies on the page, enabling one to read "in the dark without keeping his or her partner awake with an irksome reflection."

I settled in with my Light Wedge and a bowl of chips. "Happy now?"

"No," said Ed. "You get crumbs in the bed and steal the blankets. I'm still going to want that divorce."

A married couple can best be defined as a unit of people whose sleep habits are carefully engineered to keep each other awake.

A married couple can best be defined as a unit of people whose sleep habits are carefully engineered to keep each other awake.

I offered to stop eating in bed if Ed would agree to wean himself from his need for multiple pillows. I roll over in the middle of the night and find myself suffocating against a towering mound of goose down.

We call it Pillow Mountain.

Ed has fallen for the great marketing ploy of the decade: the decorative pillow ploy. It is no longer enough to buy one pillow per head. There must be a decorative pillow behind one's normal head-resting variety, and a spray of bolsters and scatter pillows in front. Each of these must be of a unique size and shape, so as to require the purchase of a specially fitted pillowcase.

Ed corrected me. "It's called a sham."

No argument here. It's a total sham. To outfit the modern bed with its indulgence of pillows and their little pillow outfits costs hundreds of dollars. Beds now contain entire pillow families, six or seven of them, all nestled together against the headboard, as though watching Leno. "That's okay," I tell them, backing out of the room. "I'll go sleep on the couch."

As we were arguing over the pillow issue, Ed got out of bed to open the bedroom door, which I'd closed so as not to hear the odd poppings and clickings of our refrigerator. Our refrigerator is unique among large appliances, in that it appears to suffer from insomnia. Every night around 4 a.m., it begins shifting, fidgeting and cracking its joints. No doubt it wants some warm milk, which, for a refrigerator, is an existential crisis of considerable weight.

Ed claims not to hear these sounds. He says he needs to have the bedroom door open; otherwise it gets so stuffy he can't sleep. I can't tell him to open a window, because then it'll be too cold. There'll be an all-night struggle for blanket superiority, and no one, to quote Zorro, will catch any Z's. We'll end up out in the kitchen at 4:30, playing cards with the refrigerator.

I know a lot of other couples have similar bedtime issues, and I hope this column has been helpful. I hope this column has the ability to save the 50 percent of marriages that end in divorce. Or that, at the very least, it helps put one of you to sleep. ▲

I was examining cantaloupes at the grocery store and turned to the produce clerk, who was refilling the bins. "Choosing a cantaloupe is a bit like picking a mate for marriage," I observed casually. "A person has no idea what he's getting until it's too late."

He said nothing at first, but as I walked to the next aisle, he called after me, "I know. I've had three cantaloupes."

— GLORIA WEGENER

As a single, never-married woman in my 40s, I have been questioned endlessly about my status by friends, relatives and co-workers. Over the years I've noticed a subtle change in the nature of their inquiries.

In my teens, friends would ask, "Who are you going out with this weekend?"

In my 20s, relatives would say, "Who are you dating?"

In my 30s, co-workers might inquire, "So, are you dating anyone?"

Now people ask, "Where did you get that adorable purse?"

— MARY A. ELDER

"No one's winning. It's ballet."

Timeless Humour from the '70s

Neighbours of ours had a terrible disagreement over a patio they wanted for their backyard. The wife had rather grand ideas, while the husband wanted costs kept to a minimum. The wife won out, and the construction bill climbed higher and higher.

I dropped by one day, when the patio was near completion, and was surprised to find the husband smiling from ear to ear as the workmen smoothed over the surface. I remarked how nice it was to see a grin replace the frown he had been wearing lately.

"You see where they're smoothing that cement?" he replied. "I just threw my wife's credit cards in there."

— R. HORN

My wife, a registered nurse, once fussed over every pain or mishap that came my way. Recently, however, I got an indication that the honeymoon is over.

I was about to fix the attic fan, and as I lifted myself from the ladder into the attic, I scratched my forehead on a crossbeam. Crawling along, I picked up splinters in both hands, and I cut one hand replacing the fan belt. On the way down the ladder, I missed the last two rungs and turned my ankle.

When I limped into the kitchen, my wife took one look and said, "Are those your good pants?"

— RICHARD J. SCHWIETERMAN

Birdwatching is a passion of mine, and my wife has always been impressed by my ability to identify each species solely by its song. To help her learn a little bit about birds, I bought a novelty kitchen clock that sounds a different bird call for each hour. We were relaxing in our yard when a cardinal started singing. "What's that?" I challenged.

She listened closely. "It's three o'clock."

— RICH L. PERSHEY

A woman in my office, recently divorced after years of marriage, had signed up for a refresher CPR course. "Is it hard to learn?" someone asked.

"Not at all," she replied. "Basically you're asked to breathe life into a dummy. I don't expect to have any problem. I did that for 32 years."

— PAULETTE BROOKS

After ten years of widowhood, I remarried. Leaving work one wintry evening, I told a colleague that it was very gratifying to once again have someone worry about me if the roads were icy. My new husband would be awaiting my arrival, I said, and would hurry out to meet me at the car.

I couldn't have been more right. As I pulled into the driveway, my husband burst out the door and came up to me. Rubbing our new car, he anxiously queried, "Did you get salt on it?"

— L. CATHERINE FERGUSON

Recently engaged, my brother-in-law Jeff brought his fiancée home to meet the family. When asked if she was enjoying herself, she politely replied yes. "She would say that," Jeff interjected. "She's not the type to say no."

"I see," my husband said after a brief silence. "And that explains the engagement."

— ALLISON BEVANS

When my wife had to rush to the hospital unexpectedly, she asked me to bring her a few items from home. One item on the list was "comfortable underwear." Worried I'd make the wrong choice, I asked, "How will I know which ones to pick?"

"Hold them up and imagine them on me," she said. "If you smile, put them back."

— ROBERT KERCHER

On my way home from a long and stressful day at the office, the phone rang. It was my husband. "Will you be joining me in the whirlpool bath tonight?" he asked.

What a lovely way to spend an evening, I thought. I was about to tell him how considerate he was when he continued, "Because if you're not, I need to start adding more water to the tub."

— SUSAN NELSON

"Don't ask questions, Ralph. Just tell me who you'd rather look like—Sean Connery or Robert Redford."

No matter what kind of backgrounds two men are from, if you go, "Hey, man, women are crazy," you've got a friend.

— CHRIS ROCK in Us Weekly

Why leave the nut you got for one you don't know?

— LORETTA LYNN in Esquire

My husband is so confident that when he watches sports on television, he thinks that if he concentrates he can help his team. If the team is in trouble, he coaches the players from our living room, and if they're really in trouble, I have to get off the phone in case they call him.

— RITA RUDNER

Love is the answer, but while you're waiting for the answer, sex raises some pretty good questions.

— WOODY ALLEN

Three words strike fear into the hearts of men: Pop the question.

— ROXANNE HAWN
in The Denver Post

Instead of getting married again, I'm going to find a woman I don't like and just give her a house.

— ROD STEWART

According to *Modern Bride* magazine, the average bride spends 150 hours planning her wedding. The average groom spends 150 hours going, "Yeah, sounds good."

— JAY LENO

My wife and I were comparing notes the other day. "I have a higher IQ, did better at university and make more money than you," she pointed out.

"Yeah, but when you step back and look at the big picture, I'm still ahead," I said.

She looked mystified. "How do you figure?"

"I married better," I replied.

— LOUIS RODOLICO

A friend and her husband were participating in a blood drive, and as part of the pre-screening process, an elderly volunteer was asking some questions. "Have you ever paid for sex?" the woman asked my friend's husband sweetly.

Glancing wearily over at his wife, trying to calm a new baby and tend to several other children milling around her, he sighed, "Every time."

— WENDI WOOLF

While in the men's room at a beach park in British Columbia, I noticed they had a plastic baby-changing table installed on the wall. Apparently, some sportsmen had co-opted this politically correct amenity for their own use. Above the table was a sign saying: "It is unlawful to clean fish on this table."

— CLIFF REVELL

While at a marine-supply store stocking up on equipment for my boat, I also purchased an inflatable life preserver. "It was my wife's idea," I explained to the grizzled salesman at the counter. "She's buying it for me as a gift."

"Lucky you," he said as he started to write up the order. "My wife got me a length of chain and a cement block."

— THOMAS FRONCEK

My friend's mother is a proper Southern lady and a passionate gardener who spends hours outside with her plants. In her neighbourhood, where she has lived most of her life, no one has fences and every yard is open to the next. Recently one of her longtime neighbours, an elderly man, moved away. "Are you going to miss him?" my friend asked.

"Actually I'm relieved," her mother replied. "Now I can bend over."

— RENEE WALKER PRITZKER

Timeless Humour from the '70s

In Alberta, my husband and I attended the wedding of a man and woman of different faiths. A Protestant minister and a Catholic priest performed an ecumenical marriage ceremony. In unison they proclaimed the couple husband and wife.

Afterward, a man was overheard congratulating the father of the bride. "Fifty years ago this could not have happened."

"No," replied the father. "Religion has come a long way."

"Religion! Who's talking about religion? I mean a cattleman's daughter marrying a sheepman's son."

— MRS. RICHMOND PARKER

"There! Now we're getting somewhere."

The Guys & Dolls Syndrome

▶ BY DAVE BARRY

1 You're on a tight deadline for developing a big sales proposal, but you've hit a snag. You want to go one way; a co-worker named Bob strongly disagrees.

To break the deadlock, you:

(a) Present your position, listen to the other side, then fashion a compromise.

(b) Punch Bob.

2 Your favourite team is about to win the championship, but at the last second the victory is stolen away by a terrible referee's call. You:

(a) Remind yourself that it's just a game, that there are far more important things in life.

(b) Punch Bob.

How to Score: If you answered "b" to both questions, then you are

a male. I base this statement on an article in *The New York Times* about the way animals, including humans, respond to stress. According to the article, a group of psychology researchers have made the breakthrough discovery that—prepare to be astounded—males and females are different.

The researchers discovered this by studying both humans and rats, which are very similar to humans except that they are not stupid enough to purchase lottery tickets. The studies show that when males are under stress, they respond by either fighting or running away—the so-called "fight or flight" syndrome. Females respond by nurturing others and making friends—the so-called "tend and befriend" syndrome.

This finding is big news in the psychology community, which is apparently located on a distant planet. Here on Earth, we've been aware for some time that males and females respond differently to stress. We know that if two males bump into each other, they'll respond like this:

First Male: Hey, watch it!

Second Male: No, YOU watch it!

First Male: Oh, yeah?

(They deliberately bump into each other again.)

Two females in an identical situation will respond like this:

When men go ape, women go shopping.
And that's all you need to know about gender.

First Female: I'm sorry!
Second Female: No, it's my fault!
First Female: Say, those are cute shoes!
(They go shopping.)

If the psychology community needs further proof of the difference between the sexes, I invite it to attend the party held in my neighbourhood each Halloween.

This party is attended by several hundred small children who are experiencing stress because their bloodstreams—as a result of the so-called "trick or treat" syndrome—contain roughly the same sugar content as Cuba. Here's how the sexes respond:

- The females, 97 percent of whom are dressed as either a ballerina or a princess, sit in little social groups and exchange candy.
- The males, 97 percent of whom are dressed as either Batman or a Power Ranger, run around making martial-arts noises and bouncing violently off one another like crazed subatomic particles.

Here are some other gender-based syndromes that the psychology community might want to look into:

- The "laundry refolding" syndrome: This has been widely noted by both me and my friend Jeff. The male will attempt to fold a piece of laundry. When he is done, the female, with a look of disapproval, will immediately pick it up and refold it so that it is much neater and smaller. "My wife can make an entire bedsheet virtually disappear," Jeff reports.
- The "inflatable pool toy" syndrome: From the dawn of civilization, the task of inflating inflatable pool toys has fallen to the male. It is often the female who comes home with an inflatable pool toy the size of the Hindenburg, causing the youngsters to become very excited. But it is inevitably the male who spends two hours blowing the toy up, after which he keels over, while the kids, who have been helping out by whining impatiently, leap joyfully onto the toy, puncturing it immediately.

I think psychology researchers should find out if these syndromes exist in other species. They could put some rats into a cage with tiny pool toys and miniature pieces of laundry, then watch to see what happens. My guess is that there would be fighting. Among the male researchers, I mean. It's a shame, this male tendency toward aggression, which has caused so many horrible problems such as war and hockey.

It frankly makes me ashamed of my gender.
I'm going to punch Bob. ▲

At the airport check-in counter, I overheard a woman ask for window seats for her and her husband. The clerk pointed out that this would prevent them from sitting together.

"Sweetie," the woman replied. "I just spent ten days of quality time in a compact rental car with this man. I know what I'm requesting."

— CAROL GORES

I was about to leave the house on an errand, and my husband was getting ready for a dental appointment. "I wish we could trade places," I said, knowing how much he dreaded the coming ordeal.

He watched as I gathered our newborn onto my left arm and picked up a package with that hand. I flung a diaper bag and my purse over my right shoulder, grabbed our two-year-old with my free hand and wrestled the car keys from him.

My husband shook his head. "No, thanks," he said. "At least where I'm going they give you anaesthesia."

— LINDA CHIARA

My mother and I were having a mother-daughter talk about the qualities to look for in a husband. She stressed that husband and wife should be as much alike as possible in interests and backgrounds. I brought up the point that opposites often attract.

"Diane," she said emphatically, "just being man and woman is opposite enough."

— DIANE RENZI

"We're still at that stage where she loves me more than I annoy her."

Canadian Follies

Let's face it, nationalism without humour is like a cause without the célèbre! So what is it that makes Canadians Canadian?

On Being Canadian:
An Inventory

▷ BY WILL FERGUSON

Pierre Berton once defined a Canadian as "someone who knows how to make love in a canoe." But John Robert Colombo was quick to correct him: "A Canadian is someone who thinks he knows how to make love in a canoe."

What are some of the larger delusions and fixations that define us—what do we have?

1. **Oh. Those Americans! They make me so mad.**
2. **The Queen rah, rah.**
3. **French on our Cheerio boxes.**
4. **_____ (in reference to Native Canadians.)**

This is, of course, only the short list. We could also add Mounties, Moose and Molson's. Hockey brawls. Using steroids. Being really smug about the fact that the Red Rose Tea is available in Canada. And getting heart palpitations by drinking thirty-seven cups of Tim Hortons coffee a day (plus doughnuts). We can also add Kraft Dinner, baby pablum and frozen food to our list of Canadian accomplishments. Our symbols are equally as varied: Maple Leaves. Maple Trees. Maple Sap. Maple Syrup. Maple Sugar. Maple Pie. Maple Soup. Maple Cheese. And just all-round Mapleness.

Consider the following a test of nationality then, a check list to see how Canadian you truly are. There is the Group of Seven. Cirque du Soleil. Lacross. Harlequin Romance. Anne of Green Gables. Sunshine Girls (Canada's chaste version of Britain's Page Three Girls). Totem poles. Bonhomme Carnaval. The Calgary Stampede. The Big Owe. Casa Loma. The Confederation Bridge. The Centennial Everything. Mainstream "fringe" festivals. Inuit art. Trivial Pursuit. Pissing off the French. Maria Chapdelaine. Stompin' Tom. And Marc Garneau (who brought a hockey puck with him into outer space; is that Canadian or what?).

There is also Screech. Poutine. Saying "eh?" a lot. Mumbling the words to "O Canada" (but in a proud way). Harbouring Nazi war criminals. Pretending to enjoy Cape Breton fiddle music. Going over Niagara Falls in a barrel. Showing up at the U.S. border in December wearing Bermuda shorts and shades, asking "Where is all the sun?" Being baffled by Marshall McLuhan. Being baffled by Leonard Cohen. Being baffled by Red Green. Being generally baffled. Hating Toronto. Moving to Toronto. Wishing you could move to Vancouver. Staying in Toronto. Hating Vancouver.

You know you are Canadian when someone says "Elvis" and you think "figure skating." If you get most of your current events by watching *This Hour Has 22 Minutes* (remove the punch lines and you have a pretty good news broadcast), you are a Canadian. And that's not all.

There is also clubbing baby seals. Discovering insulin. Drinking Canada Dry. Knowing how to spell Gzowski. Knowing how to *pronounce* Gzowski. Knowing who the hell Gzowski is in the first place. Worshipping Donovan Bailey. Taking credit for

How's it goin', eh?

absolutely everything: the telephone, basketball, the airplane, the wheel, Big Bird, *Saturday Night Live*. Wearing toques at a jaunty angle. Being really proud of the CN Tower. Understanding Celsius. Using the loonie. Being secretly fascinated by the toonie. Having a passionate but doomed crush on Dini Petty. Having an equally doomed crush on Valerie Pringle (the Mary Tyler Moore of Canadian broadcast journalism). Attending Royal Commissions. Wearing wool socks during sex—not because it's cold but just because it's chic. Getting all sentimental over Robert Munsch. Missing *The Beachcombers*. Knowing almost all the words to the *King of Kensington* theme song. Feeling a deep affinity with snow. Owning at least one book by Pierre Berton. Riding toboggans. Sharpening skates. Freezing pucks. And more: The Sasquatch. The Ogopogo. The Canadarm. The Guess Who.

   As you can see, the list of Canadian cultural touchstones is endless. Why, you would need a book, an entire book, just to skim the surface of the vast and fascinating field of Things Canadian. What follows then is the meagrest of sampling, a cross-section of Canadian icons and delusions, from Beavers to Superheros. ▲

- **50°F** (10°C): Americans turn on the heat; Canadians plant gardens.
- **40°F** (4.5°C): Californians shiver uncontrollably; Canadians sunbathe.
- **35°F** (1.5°C): Italian cars won't start; Canadians drive with the windows down.
- **32°F** (0°C): Distilled water freezes; Canadian water gets just a little thicker.
- **0°F** (–18°C): New York City landlords finally turn on the heat; Canadians have the last cookout of the season.
- **–40°F** (–40°C): Hollywood disintegrates; Canadians rent some videos.
- **–60°F** (–51°C): Mt. St. Helen's freezes; Canadian Girl Guides sell cookies door-to-door.
- **–100°F** (–73°C): Santa Claus abandons the North Pole; Canadians pull down their earflaps.
- **–173°F** (–114°C): Ethyl alcohol freezes; Canadians get frustrated when they can't thaw the keg.
- **–459.4°F** (–273°C): Absolute zero—all atomic motion stops; Canadians start saying "cold, eh?"
- **–500°F** (–295°C): Hell freezes over; The Leafs win the Stanley Cup.

Q: Why did the Canadian cross the road?
A: Because that's the direction his car was sliding.

A doctor informed a Newfoundland couch potato that it was imperative for him to lose weight. The doctor recommended that the Newfoundlander run five kilometres a day for 300 days and this would result in a weight loss of up to 75 pounds. At the end of the 300 days, the Newfie called the doctor to report he had lost the excess weight, but he had a problem. "What's the problem?" asked the doctor. "Well," responded the now-svelte Newfie, "I'm 1,500 kilometres from home!"

One evening in the pub a bartender offered a free round to anyone who could order a drink he hadn't heard of. Everyone began requesting the most outlandish beverages, from Singapore slings and Manhattans to pina coladas. But each time the bartender knew exactly how to make them. Business was now booming and nobody was even coming close to winning the bartender's challenge, when somebody said: "I'd like a Halifax, please." The bartender had to admit defeat and invited the customer behind the bar to show him what he had in mind. "It's really very simple," said the customer, taking a bottle from the shelf. "It's a large port."

"That's right, Ma'am... Two red bars representing the end zones and a maple leaf at centre ice."

It was a young woman's first time on a plane. She boarded an Air Canada jet at a small airport in Northern Ontario and found herself a window seat at the front of the plane. After she settled in, a man came over and insisted that she was in his seat. She ignored him. Again, the man insisted that she was in his seat, so she told him to go away. "OK," replied the man, "if that's the way you want it, you fly the plane!"

A Canadian man left the snowy streets of Winnipeg for a vacation in Florida. His wife had to work, but would be meeting him there the next day. When he reached his hotel, he decided to send his wife a quick email. However, he couldn't find the scrap of paper on which he had written her email address, so he decided to try to type it in from memory. Unfortunately, he missed one letter, and his note was directed instead to an elderly woman whose husband had just passed away only the day before. When the grieving widow checked her email, she took one look at the monitor, let out a piercing scream, and fainted. At the sound her family rushed into the room and saw this note on the screen:

Dearest Wife,
Just checked in. Everything is ready for your arrival tomorrow.
Your Loving Husband.
P.S. Sure is hot down here!

A Canadian gets drunk and decides to go ice fishing. He takes his pole and tackle and goes out on the ice and starts to chop a hole in it. Suddenly he hears a great booming voice coming from above him. "THERE'S NO FISH THERE." Startled, the Canadian looks around but can't see where the voice came from. So he staggers a few metres away to a different spot, and again starts chopping a hole in the ice. And AGAIN, the voice booms out. "THERE'S NO FISH THERE." The Canadian is spooked, but we're a stubborn people. So he gathers up his gear and staggers to a third spot on the ice. He raises his ice axe, but before he can even start chopping he hears the voice again. "THERE'S NO FISH THERE EITHER!" The Canadian looks up and shouts, "God? Is that you?" "NO. THIS IS THE ARENA MANAGER."

"Showoff."

"I'd much rather work in Toronto than Vancouver. For a start, you get paid three hours earlier."

Canada: Land of the Freeze

▶ BY JOSH FREED

When the world media recently declared Canada a "cool country," we knew just how accurate they were. Because in the coldest months of winter, Canada becomes the wind-chill factory of the planet, the closest thing human beings have experienced to a landing on Mars.

We are living in a country so cold flesh freezes faster than you can get your keys out of your pocket and into your door. A place parents scream: "No! You can't go outside and play! Just get back to the TV where you belong!"

At times like this it's only natural to become philosophical about our native land. Why are we Canadians here? Why do we live in a place where noses go numb, lips frost over and eyelids freeze shut? Let me answer your queries with a brief history of Canada: Land of the Freeze.

Question 1: Why did people first come to Canada?

They were lost. The first humans arrived here 13,000 years ago, after crossing the frozen Bering Strait from Asia.

According to primitive ice-cave drawings, they were seeking a route to a mythical land of the gods they called "My Amee," where you could play golf and drive convertibles all year.

Unfortunately, Canadian road signs were as bad ten millennia ago as they are now, and those leading the expedition were men, who refused to ask for directions. It was only after several centuries of trudging through arctic snow that they finally admitted they had no clue where they were.

They gave up and turned back toward home. But by then, the passage over the Bering Strait was covered in water—and they were trapped on this continent, with no way back. They named their new homeland Canada: an ancient native word for "Big Mistake."

Question 2: Why did people keep coming?

In the 1500s, the first French explorers crossed the Atlantic looking for Asia, but found the way blocked by a large island. They figured China was just on the other side, which is how we got the name of the "Lachine" Rapids.

By the time the explorers figured out where they were, winter had arrived and they were freezing their boats off. So they went charging out to hunt for furry animals to wrap themselves in.

These brave hunters soon became known as "coureurs de bois," which literally means "Running To Keep Warm."

Back in Europe, hat manufacturers somehow convinced fashionable Europeans it was cool to wear a dead beaver on your head. Thus, the Canadian fur trade was born and thrived for two centuries, selling fur to furreigners.

Over time, Canadians chased the furry rodents farther and farther inland in search of warm clothing, and accidentally explored a country. Mexico was colonized in a quest for Aztec gold; Canada in a quest to escape the cold.

Question 3: Why didn't everyone just leave?

Many French "woods-runners" did try to return home those early winters, or find a ship south to the mythical land of "Mon-ami." But winter boats were hopelessly crowded.

Most explorers had saved up huge amounts of Fur Miles, and it was impossible to get through to a reservation agent at Canoe Canada, which was hopelessly overbooked and going bankrupt. Thus, was Canada born, a nation of trapped fur trappers.

Gradually, those who stayed got acclimatized and became Canadian in their attitudes. Early visitors like Voltaire dismissed Canada as "a few acres of snow without a decent French restaurant for 3,000 miles." But later settlers like Champlain said: "Nah, this was just a bad winter. It will never happen again. Besides, I hear we're getting global warming next century."

And so it's continued ever since, with visitors to Canada divided into two groups. One type arrives, stays a night like Voltaire and flees to someplace warmer the next day. The other type stays, grumbles all winter and then gets amnesia when summer arrives.

Complicating matters was the fact Canada used the Fahrenheit system, where water freezes at a balmy 32°. This made our country sound much warmer than it was and lured many innocent immigrants, fooled by 30-degree temperatures as well as government of Canada photos of Banff in July.

In the 1970s, Canada finally adopted an honest advertising policy and switched over to Celsius. Suddenly, millions of Canadians were shocked to learn they had come to a country where the temperature was actually below zero most of the year.

Adding to their shock was the discovery of "wind chill" in the 1980s, which made it horribly apparent we live on a frozen glacier somewhere between the Atlantic and Pacific oceans.

But it was too late to undo history, or move everyone to "My Amee."

Over 30 million people were stranded on a desolate iceberg with friends, family and colleagues, living under the mass delusion that they lived in a perfectly normal country. Even worse, they thought they were cool. Extremely cool. ▲

Canadian Humour:
A Retrospective

Some humour pundits argue that Canadian humour began one day at Harbord Collegiate in Toronto when young Johnny Wayne and Frank Shuster looked at each other in English class as Shakespeare's *Julius Caesar* was being discussed. Thus was born the "I told him, Julie don't go!" comedy sketch beloved by all Canadians over 50. It's ironic that the one Wayne and Shuster line people can remember was spoken by neither Wayne nor Shuster.

It's difficult today to convey to younger Canadians the importance of Wayne and Shuster in Canadian comedy. They were practically regulars—along with Topo Gigio and Señor Wences—on *The Ed Sullivan Show.* (For younger readers, Topo Gigio was sort of a mouse and Señor Wences was a ventriloquist, and Ed Sullivan—oh, never mind. And a ventriloquist—do I have to explain everything? Did they teach you nothing in school?)

But this wasn't the beginning of Canadian humour. We'd been laughing for, well, several years. Early Canadian history was not exactly a laff-riot, you understand. As your mother might have warned you, there's nothing funny about scurvy, ice, snow, bears, blackflies, mosquitoes, millions of acres of rock, occasional hostility from people who had already been living here for centuries—none of these factors contributed in the short term to a national sense of humour.

That said, adversity has a long-term beneficial effect on comedy. Good-looking rich kids don't become comedians. They don't need to. They have better ways of impressing girls and they don't need defence mechanisms to avoid being beaten up. This is why Americans have had to import so many Canadian comics, from Marie Dressler to John Candy to Mike Myers...

Very possibly the earliest Canadian joke involves British explorers coming upon some Portuguese fishermen. "What is this place called?" asked the Brits. The Portuguese, not understanding the question, replied "¡Aqui nada!", which is their way of saying "There's nothing here!" Which the Brits heard as "Canada!" Not everyone believes this to be a true story. Some people say Canada is an old Iroquois word meaning "Roll up the rim to win." I prefer the Portuguese story.

Canadian humour hit it big with Stephen Leacock, an economics professor who wrote short comic pieces in his spare time but is now best known as the name of a literary prize awarded annually to a book that is at least somewhat funny

▶ BY NICK PASHLEY

…there's nothing funny about scurvy, ice, snow, bears, blackflies, mosquitoes…

or could be perceived as somewhat funny. Well, you can't be too careful. Canadians are suspicious of funny books. What we like in a Canadian novel is plenty of suffering, not much sex (only enough to have awful consequences), and no jokes. Here's the question that bedevils us: is Canadian humour different from American? Well, I guess so, eh? We spell it differently, for starters. How can you take "humor" seriously? Or comedically? Like our spelling, Canadian culture tends to be a mix of British and American influences. We were enjoying *Monty Python* long before the Americans. We got irony years before the Americans had heard of it. Many Americans still think it has something to do with laundry.

What makes Canadian humour different from other people's humour is that we have something they don't have: Newfies. I say that in the best possible sense. Don't think the noble Newfoundlander occupies the same place in our humour as, say, Poles once did in American jokes. Those jokes were offensive. The Newfie joke is completely different because, well, because I say so.

But don't take my word for it, judge for yourself: A couple of guys from Toronto go to Newfoundland for a fishing holiday, booking a local guide for two weeks. The weather is cold and wet and, after only a week, the guys from Toronto are getting bored and uncomfortable. Just then one of them feels pressure on his line and reels it in to find a rusty old lamp on the hook. Predictably he gives the lamp a rub and out pops the predictable genie. "You know the rules," says the genie. "Three wishes. One apiece. How about you, buster?"

The first guy from Toronto thinks a bit. "Jeez," he says, "I like being here and all but it's kinda cold and the Leafs are on TV tonight and I wouldn't mind being back in my condo in Mississauga watching the game." An instant later he was gone.

The second guy from Toronto says, "Yeah, this is nice here, don't get me wrong, but the forecast is pretty lousy, and the Argos are at home tonight to the Ticats and I'd love to be there." Poof, he vanishes.

The genie looks at the Newfie guide. "Step on it, pal," he says, "I was in that water a long time. I got places to go, people to see." The Newfie guide thinks for a moment. "I dunno," he says, "I guess I'm used to the weather and we were catching some fish. I liked them guys from Toronto. I was having a good time. I kinda wish they were back here." ▲

How many MPs does it take to screw in a light bulb? 21! One to change it and 20 to form a fact-finding committee to learn more about how it's done!

A man in a Montreal bar was boasting to a friend. "I have an excellent memory," he said. "In fact, I can recite from memory all of the names on several pages of the Montreal phone book."

His friend was skeptical and bet him $10 he couldn't do it.

The man accepted the bet, then began to recite, "Richard, Richard, Richard, Richard…"

Q: What's the difference between a United States senator and a Canadian senator?

A: In America, you must win an election to become a senator. In Canada, you have to lose one.

A Ukrainian from Winnipeg goes to the Motor Vehicle branch to apply for a driver's licence. He has to take an eye test. The clerk shows him a card with the letters:

C Z W I X N O S T A C Z

"Can you read this?" the clerk asks.

"Read it?" the Ukrainian replies, "I know the guy."

Three hockey fans go mountain climbing. One climber is a devoted Canucks fan, one is a Maple Leafs fan, and one is a fan of the Canadiens. As they climb higher, they get into a heated argument about which of them is the most loyal to their particular team. Finally, as they reach the summit, the Vancouver climber takes a running leap and throws himself off the mountain, yelling, "This is for the Canucks." Not wanting to be outdone, the Toronto fan walks to the edge of the precipice and yells, "This is for the Toronto Maple Leafs," then pushes the Montreal Canadiens fan off the cliff.

Q: How do you stop Canadian bacon from curling in the frying pan?

A: Take away its broom!

It's game seven of the Stanley Cup Final, and a man makes his way to his seat right at centre ice. He sits down, noticing that the seat next to him is empty. He leans over and asks his neighbour if someone will be sitting there.

"No," says the neighbour. "The seat will stay empty."

"This is incredible," said the man. "Who in their right mind would have a seat like this for the Stanley Cup and not use it?"

The neighbour says, "Well, actually, the seat belongs to my wife. She was supposed to come with me, but she passed away. This is the first Stanley Cup we haven't been together at since we got married over 30 years ago."

"Oh, I'm sorry to hear that. That's terrible. But couldn't you find someone else, a relative or friend, to take the seat?"

The man shakes his head. "No, they're all still at the funeral."

Canadian Cuisine
(And How to Avoid It...)

Canadians have made great contributions to world cuisine. The two most celebrated being (this is true) baby pablum and frozen peas. The chefs of France are sick with envy over this. Granted, some critics have had the audacity to suggest Canadian food is bland, over processed and sort of mushy. But we at the HOW TO BE A CANADIAN INSTITUTE say pshaw! Pshaw, we say.

Sure, if you let a Canadian get anywhere near a piece of food they are sure to fling it into a deep fryer. Or cover it with sugar. Or fling it into a deep fat fryer and then cover it with sugar.

Admit it; you could go for something deep-fried and sugar-coated right about now, couldn't you?

This is why Tim Hortons (a.k.a. CoffeeTime) represents the peak and the epitome, the acme and the apex of Canadian cuisine. Everything in a Tim Hortons—including the countertops (completely), the staff (inevitably) and the customers (eventually)—is covered with a layer of warm grease and dusted with icing sugar. The chain itself was named in memory of a hockey player who died because he was driving dangerously in a sports car. This makes him a hero.

Question: Why?

Answer: Who knows?

Sadly, Tim Hortons has, of late, priced itself out of the market. That is, their prices are too damn low. Who wants to buy a coffee for less than $3.50? A coffee and a doughnut for a toonie—with change back? Who needs that? Into this gap have stepped several proud chains not afraid of charging more—much more—for their coffee. The leader in Charging More for Coffee has been the U.S.-based Starbucks chain, also known as Second Cup, also known as A.L. Van Houtte.* It remains to be seen whether Tim Hortons will be able to withstand this assault.

*Who was, sadly, the passenger in the car that Tim Horton drove off the road.

▶ BY WILL FERGUSON AND IAN FERGUSON

Still, there is more to Canadian cuisine than Tim Hortons Not much more mind you, but it's still worth exploring, if only to better understand the lesser-known, non-doughnut aspect of the Canadian diet.

Behold the Breathtaking Glory that is Canadian Cuisine!

One has only to go to that Glorious Forum of Canadian Cuisine to see the splendour, the variety and—yes—the magnificent bounty of the Canadian approach to food. We are speaking, of course, of … the FOOD COURT. (*Cue:* Hallelujah chorus and parting clouds.) Hermetically sealed and climate-controlled, where many varied cultures of the world are reduced to fast food: Is there anything more Canadian than a shopping mall Food Court? What a splendid cornucopia awaits the Food Court denizen! What a dizzying array of choices. Greek! Chinese! Italian! Vietnamese! American! Mexican! Japanese! The glory of the Canadian Food Court is unparalleled.

The greatest cultures on earth have flourished at the crossroads, and the bazaar of modern Canadian life is exemplified by the bustling excitement of the Food Court. The culinary offerings of the world, luke-warm and crusted, sit tantalizingly in their heat trays. All you have to do is grab your own tray and line up!

Now, you may be asking yourself, what about French cuisine? Well, what about it? You want French cuisine, go to France. In Quebec, they don't eat snails and frou-frou entrees. In Quebec, they guzzle spruce beer and wolf down steamed hot dogs. Indeed, *steamés*, as these hot dogs are known, are the National Food of Quebec. If the Quebec School of Culinary Arts ever chose an emblem, it would be a hand holding a steamed hot dog proudly in the air, like a beacon, like a sword. The people in Quebec eat at fast-food emporiums such as Burger King and La Belle Province more often than they ever dine on *pâté* and *aubergines*. When the Québécois go to France, they ask for ketchup. When they are served Belgian waffles, they ask for syrup. When they go to the beach, they eat corn dogs.

In Quebec, something that is perfect is described as *c'est chocolat,* and they have a point. After all, other than Molson Ex, what could possibly be better than chocolate? The Québécois slang for "first class"—this is true, too—*ketchup,* proving once again that they are as much North American as they are French.

Yes, the Québécois are hosers just like the rest of us, and any claims to the contrary can be dismissed with a single word: *Florida*. If you want to find out how elevated and sophisticated French Canadians are compared to their uncouth English-Canadian cousins, take a trip to sunny Florida. The inhabitants there know first-hand how urbane and suave, how

▶ Canadian Cuisine (And How to Avoid It...)

refined and worldly Canada's French-speaking population is: Speedos? *Oui!* Svelte bodies? *Non.* Toques, beer, hockey and maple syrup: French or English, we're all still Canadians at heart.

We now present, for your delectation, a handy guide to Canadian cuisine.

Poutine: Quebec's contribution to fine cuisine, French fries covered with cheese curds and gravy. Only 12,486 calories a serving. (Also true: In Quebec, something that's a lot of nonsense is described as *"C'est de la poutine!"*)

Prairie oysters: Western Canada's contribution to fine cuisine. Fried testicle of young bull, consumed mainly in anecdote. (Reportedly tastes like chicken.)

Pemmican: Native Candian contribution to fine cuisine. Leathery food prepared by Native guides for Hudson's Bay Company traders. Made from pounded buffalo meat, raw fat and cranberries. Tough to chew and hard to swallow, it has a half-life longer than plutonium. Rumoured to be a pratical joke played on the whites.

Dulse: Maritimer's contribution to fine cuisine. Tastes like iodine and smells like fish secretions, with the texture and allure of boiled licorice. Rumoured to be a practical joke played on Upper Canadians. "Why, I bet they're so gullible they'd eat these smelly wet weeds I found along the docks." These are the same folks, remember, who routinely try to get people to eat fronds (otherwise known as *fiddleheads*).

Maple syrup: Ketchup may be Canada's Official Condiment, but the sentimental favourite is still *sucre du pays.* Give a Canadian a jug o' maple syrup and they are in hoser heaven, splashing it over anything within striking distance: pancakes, waffles, ice cream, small pets, patio furniture, in-laws, etc. Maple syrup is the great Candian foodstuff. (The term "foodstuff" being particularly apt when describing Canadian cuisine. "What'cha eatin'?" "Food stuff.")

Canada produces more than 80% of the world's supply of maple syrup, and most of it comes from Quebec, where the people are basically sugar junkies. They're addicted to incredibly sweet foods. Examples includes *tarte au sucre* (sugar pie), *trempette* (a piece of bread soaked in maple sugar) and *tire sur la neige* (maple taffy on snow). And let's not forget the very popular and oh-so-disgusting *sucre à la crème*, which is essentially sweetened condensed milk. With sugar added. *"Menum, menum!"*

There are even—this is true—maple syrup "connoisseurs," who act like wine tasters, only stickier and (we imagine) chubbier. These connoisseurs sniff, taste and grade maple syrup, ranking it as "sweet," "spicy," "nutty," "flowery" and so on.

"Ah yes, a medium amber—from the lower St. Lawrence, Canada No. 2, B Grade if I'm not mistaken. A fine bouquet and impeccable vintage, insouciant yet subtle, cloyingly sweet yet horribly syrupy."

Other contributions that Canada has made to world cuisine include Coffee Crisp ("It's chocolate—and caffeine!"), Catelli ("It's spaghetti sauce—in a can!"), Habitant Pea Soup ("It's pea soup—in a can!") and, of course, Red Rose tea ("It's tea—but only in Canada!").

And you've got to love a country that gave us Coffee Crisp. "Do you know what this chocolate bar needs? A good shot of caffeine." That pretty much sums up the Canadian approach to cuisine. Canadian food will rot your teeth and make you fat. Pass the cheese curds—and mind the dulse! ▲

We are in the extreme centre, the radical middle. That is our position.

— PIERRE TRUDEAU

Your majesty, I thank you from the bottom of my heart, and Madame Houde thanks you from her bottom too.

— MONTREAL MAYOR CAMILLIEN HOUDE
(in 1939 to King George VI)

...if some countries have too much history, we have too much geography.

— WILLIAM LYON MACKENZIE KING

Canada has never been a melting-pot; more like a tossed salad.

— ARNOLD EDINBOROUGH

If the national mental illness of the United States is megalomania, that of Canada is paranoid schizophrenia.

— MARGARET ATWOOD

In any world menu, Canada must be considered the vichyssoise of nations, it's cold, half-French, and difficult to stir.

— STUART KEATE

Canada is like an old cow. The West feeds it. Ontario and Quebec milk it. And you can well imagine what it's doing in the Maritimes.

— TOMMY DOUGLAS

The U.S. is our trading partner, our neighbour, our ally and our friend...and sometimes we'd like to give them such a smack!

— RICK MERCER

SOME RELIGIOUS SYMBOLS FROM AROUND THE WORLD....

CHRISTIANITY
(EUROPE)

HINDUISM
(INDIA)

TAOISM
(CHINA)

ISLAM
(MIDDLE EAST)

JUDAISM
(ISRAEL)

BUDDHISM
(FAR EAST)

SHINTOISM
(JAPAN)

MEDICARE
(CANADA)

AISLIN 02
MONTREAL
THE GAZETTE

How do Europeans think of Canadians:
As unarmed Americans with a free health care plan!

At an international symposium on elephants, each nation had to deliver a report on the animal.

France's report: "The Love Life of an Elephant."

America saw the economic values in: "Raising Elephants for Fun and Profit."

Great Britain expressed a unique view: "The Elephant and the British Empire."

The Canadian report was, of course, typically Canadian: "The Elephant: A Federal or Provincial Responsibility?"

A Saskatchewan RCMP officer found a perfect spot to catch speeders, but wasn't getting many. Then he discovered the problem—a 10-year-old boy was standing up the road with a hand-painted sign, which read "RADAR TRAP AHEAD." The officer then found a young accomplice down the road with a sign reading "TIPS" and a bucket full of money.

An Englishman, a Canadian, and an American were kidnapped. The kidnapper said "Before I shoot you, you will be allowed to say last words."

The Englishman replied, "I wish to speak of my loyalty and service to the crown."

The Canadian replied, "Since you are involved in a question of national purpose, national identity, and secession, I wish to talk about the history of constitutional process in Canada, special status, distinct society and uniqueness within diversity."

The American replied, "Just shoot me before the Canadian starts talking."

WINTER FORECASTING FOLKLORE:

MILD WINTER

COLD WINTER

HEATING OIL

MISERABLE WINTER

On the sixth day, God turned to the angel Gabriel and said, "Today I am going to create a land called Canada. It will be a land of outstanding natural beauty, snow-capped mountains, beautiful blue lakes, forests of elk and moose, silver rivers full of salmon. With pure, clear air. I will make the country rich in oil and the people there shall prosper. They will be called Canadians, and become known as the friendliest people on earth." "Don't you think," asked Gabriel, "that you're being a bit overly generous to one country?" "Wait," said God. "You haven't yet seen the neighbours I'm going to land them with."

I was meeting a friend in a bar in Flin Flon, and as I went in I noticed two pretty girls looking at me. "Nine," I heard one whisper as I passed. Feeling pleased with myself, I swaggered over to my buddy and told him a girl had just rated me a nine out of ten.

"I don't want to ruin it for you," he said, "but when I walked in, they were speaking German."

How to Drink Like a Canadian

Why beer? Beer was not invented in Canada. It was not perfected in Canada. Canadian beer is *not* world famous, and Canadians, unlike the Germans, have not distinguished themselves by the great quantities they quaff. In fact, when it comes to per capita beer consumption, Canada is not even in the Top 10 among Western nations. As beer drinkers, Canadians are wimps. And yet, in spite of this, beer is a point of eternal pride among Canadians and is, in fact, an essential item in the Standard Canadian Identi-Kit.

A sociologist—particularly an incompetent one—might explain the Canadian affinity for beer something like this: For all its tourist-brochure-encoded imagery of majestic mountains and rugged malamutes, Canada is a hopelessly middle-class, suburban nation whose average citizens couldn't pick a moose out of a police lineup. If Canadian society were an actor, it would be described as having "bland good looks." The Kevin Costner of nations, that's us.

Understandably, most Canadians would rather cling to an outdated stereotype: that of the rough-and-ready, frontier-bred Canadian, big of heart and blue of collar—an outdoorsy, affable, individualistic yet law-abiding, broad-chested guy. Beer, then, is a psychological prop in this national lumberjack role-playing game. A totemistic touchstone, if you will. So you can see just how incompetent a sociologist would have to be to come up with such a theory. (We're sure glad *we* didn't suggest it.)

No. The Canadian fetish for beer goes deeper than mere role-playing. Much deeper. It springs from the dark, musty, mildewed corners of the national psyche. It strikes at the very heart of the great Canadian Inferiority Complex vis-à-vis (who else?) the Americans. Simply put, brewing beer is one of the few things that Canadians do better than Americans. Which may also explain the irresistible attraction between beer and curling.

Sure, the average Englishman may sniff with disdain at the mild brown lager that is our National Drink, but what do Canadians care? It is not the Brits that we want to beat. Hell, they drink their beer *warm*, for Chrissake! A Canadian wouldn't drink a warm beer if they had just been pulled out of a snowbank in Saskatoon. I'm sorry, but "Give me a warm one!" just doesn't scan.

Pop Quiz

Canadian beer is stronger than American beer. True or false? True—but just barely. The numbers on the beer labels lie. The average Canadian beer is a mere 0.5% stronger than the average American beer. You see, Americans use a different method of measuring

BY WILL FERGUSON AND IAN FERGUSON

Had Descartes been Canadian his first principle
of philosophical certainty would be the fact that
Canadian beer is superior to American…

alcohol percentage than do Canadians, so a 5%
Canadian beer is actually *equal* to a 4% American.
Not a big difference. Negligible, in fact. We know, we
know. It goes against everything Canadians have
been taught to believe. Canadian beer really *isn't* that
much stronger than American. (Check out Jackson's
Pocket Guide to Beer if you don't believe us.)

Nope. Canadian beer is not strong. The Swiss
mock it. The Germans use it to gargle. And the
Irish? Ah yes. Try quaffing a "meal in itself" Guinness if you want strong. You can float small change
on the surface of real Guinness stout. Patrons
regularly get Guinness stuck between their teeth.
Seabirds often tragically get caught in Guinness
slicks and have to be rescued by conservationists.

It isn't the amount of alcohol per bottle that gives
Canadian beer its charm. It is, quite simply: *the
taste*. Canadian beer tastes better than American
beer. Period. This is the one indisputable, self-
evident fact of which Canadians are certain. Had
Descartes been Canadian instead of whatever he
was (French or Belgian or something), he would
have started with beer when he formulated his first
principle of philosophical certainty, and the fact that
Canadian beer is superior to American would now
be the foundation of modern Western thought.

Instead of "I think, therefore I am," Descartes's
maxim would have been something like "I think I
need another beer, therefore I am—going to have
one, that is."

So why does Canadian beer taste better? The
answer, as always, lies rooted deep in our collective past. The history of Canadian
beer reveals early cultural influences, and indeed, one could
argue that to know beer
is to know Canada,
although one
would proba-
bly have to
be drunk
at the
time.

Beer first
took hold in
Canada in the
eighteenth centu-
ry, when it was
introduced by Irish,
English and Scottish
settlers who set up
small breweries that

produced *ale*. Ale is made by fermenting the yeast at the top of the brew, a method that produces the heavy and bitter drink still preferred in Britain today.

In America, however, it was the Slavic and German immigrants who first mass-produced beer, and they preferred *lager*—a pale, light drink made with *bottom*-fermenting yeast. (*Stout*, meanwhile, is whatever guck they can scrape off the bottom of the barrel after everything else has been taken.)

These two cultural backgrounds, one British and the other German, are reflected today in the names of the leading North American breweries: Molson and Carling O'Keefe on one side of the border; Schlitz, Pabst and Anheuser-Busch on the other. Labatt, the other major brewery in Canada, was also founded by an Englishman, despite the French-sounding name.

In time, tastes changed. Canadians may have begun with ale, and the Americans with lager, but over the years the American lager grew more and more anemic until it finally became the pale *eau d'bier* they now call "lite," which greatly confuses Canadian visitors, who see it as a redundancy. ("*Lite* American beer? Is there any other kind?")

Meanwhile, in the Great White North, Canadian tastes changed as well. Breweries here gradually abandoned ale and began producing lager instead. But the early preference for ale lingers on in the darker, tangier quality of Canadian beer. Hence the present difference in taste between American and Canadian beer (i.e., Canadian beer *has* taste). With current trends, Canadians have been drifting toward draft beer and the Americans toward beige water.

American beer, as they say, is like making love in a canoe. If you already know it, chances are you yourself are Canadian. So, grab a cold one and pull up a seat.

SCREECH (AND OTHER POISON)

We would be remiss in discussing the refined tastes of Canadians with regard to alcoholic beverages (meaning: beer) without mentioning a few regional variations. Quebecers, for one, make *le caveau du dépanneur* their wine cellar of choice.

In the West, the famed drink is the Calgary Red Eye: beer and an egg—or tomato juice or something. Calgary was also the city where the Caesar was invented. It happened at a local hotel, when an enterprising bartender said, "You know what would make for a really refreshing beverage? Clamato, Tabasco sauce and salt."

But the real triumph of regional beverages is Newfoundland's drink of choice—the bane of every weak-kneed, tender-footed tourist ever to stumble into Newfoundland. Screech! The elemental fire, the sound of fingernails on blackboard, the cry of the Valkyries, the cackle of witch-fire, the—well, you get the idea.

Screech, for those of you fortunate enough to have avoided it until now, is the national drink of Newfoundland. Cheap rum. Wrathful, fire-breathing, eyeball-bleeding, sear-yer-gut and melt-yer-eyebrows Jamaican rotgut. One of the great pastimes of Newfoundlanders (who are, let's face it, a particularly sadistic people) is to torment visitors with screech.

Centuries ago, Newfoundlanders began trading salt fish to Jamaica in return for rum, and the arrangement was so mutually beneficial that the bilateral "rum for salt fish" trade has more or less continued to this day. Jamaican rum is now the mainstay of Newfoundlanders everywhere, and salt fish is now the national dish of Jamaica. The Jamaicans got the better part of the deal.

Summary: Canadians like beer. In Quebec they like cheap wine, and in Newfoundland they like cheap rum. ▲

A teacher asked her class to name an animal that has eyes but cannot see, that has legs but cannot run, and that can jump as high as the CN Tower.

The kids thought about it but could not come up with an answer.

Finally, the teacher said, "A wooden horse. It has eyes but cannot see, and legs but cannot run."

One of the kids, "But a wooden horse can't jump."

The teacher replied, "Neither can the CN Tower."

A fellow left Montreal heading toward Quebec City and decided to pull in at a rest stop. The first stall in the bathroom was occupied, so he went into the second one. He was no sooner seated than he heard a voice from the next stall say, "Hi, how are you doing?"

Though he wasn't the type to chat with strangers in highway restrooms, he answered anyway. "Not bad."

The guy in the first stall said, "And what are you up to?"

"Well, I'm driving east."

Then he heard the stranger say: "Look, I'll have to call you back. There's some idiot in the next stall answering all the questions I'm asking you."

— JACK COOPER

A blonde calls Air Canada and asks, "Can you tell me how long it'll take to fly from Toronto to Vancouver?" The agent replies, "Just a minute…" "Thank you," the blonde says, and hangs up.

A fisherman was boasting to a fellow fisherman about a 20-pound salmon he had caught in Campbell River. "Twenty pounds, huh?" remarked the other guy, with skepticism. "Were there any witnesses?"

"Of course" said Willis. "Otherwise it would have weighed thirty pounds."

Jim and Dave were both big hockey fans. They made an agreement that whichever one of them died first would try to come back from the dead and tell the other whether or not hockey was played in Heaven.

Well, Dave passed away first, and Jim began going to mediums, trying to get in touch with his old pal. Finally, about two years after Dave's death, Jim found a powerful medium, who reached Dave's spirit.

Dave said, "I've got good news and bad news for you. The good news is, yes, we play great hockey in Heaven. The bad news is, you're starting in goal next week."

An Italian couple immigrated to Canada. After three years they successfully applied for citizenship. Proudly holding the papers, the husband said, "Maria, we're Canadian now." She shoved an apron at him and said, "Good. Now you do the dishes."

A motorist was mailed a picture of his car speeding through an automated radar post on an Alberta highway. An $80 speeding ticket was included. Being cute, he sent the police department a picture of $80. The RCMP responded with another mailed photo of handcuffs.

A Canadian hunter had been hunting all day. He fell asleep but was awakened in the middle of the night by a large grizzly bear. The bear ripped off the front of his tent and stood on its hind legs and roared. The hunter dropped to his knees, closed his eyes, and prayed, "Lord, please let this be a Christian bear." When the hunter opened his eyes, he saw that the bear had dropped to its knees, praying: "Lord, thank you for this meal which I am about to receive…"

I worked as a demonstrator at the Saskatchewan Science Centre, where we recently had a display called Animal Sounds. It showed how different cultures imitate the same animal sounds differently, depending on their language. For instance, we say woof, woof for a dog, whereas Russians say gahf, gahf. Visitors could press a button to listen to the actual animal sound.

I walked up to one small girl who was frowning at the display. "This machine isn't working," she complained, pressing a button. As the sound of a barking dog came out loud and clear, she said, "See, he only speaks English!"

— JENNIFER ROTHECKER

Two lions escaped from a circus visiting Ottawa. They went their separate ways, but after a week they met in a downtown park. One lion said, "I'm having a hard time finding food, and people are always trying to catch me." The other lion said, "I found a great hiding place in the Senate. I eat a senator every day, and nobody even notices anyone missing."

The British Columbia department of natural resources issued an advisory, warning people going into the woods to watch out for grizzlies. The advisory urged hikers and campers to wear little bells to alert bears to their presence, and to carry pepper spray for self-defence. The warning also advised people to look for telltale signs of bear presence in the area where they are hiking or camping. It explained that people should look for evidence such as bear droppings. The notice went on to explain that bear droppings can be identified by stool contents and odour—it frequently contains undigested berries, the fur of small animals like squirrels or raccoons, as well as little bells— and oh, it often smells like pepper spray.

Welcome to the Canadian Psychiatric Hotline. "Please choose from the following options: If you are obsessive-compulsive, press 1 repeatedly. If you are co-dependant, ask someone to press 2. If you have multiple personalities, press 3, 4, 5 and 6. If you are paranoid-delusional, we know who you are and what you want. Just stay on the line until we can trace the call. If you are schizophrenic, listen carefully and a little voice will tell you which number to press. If you are manic-depressive, it really doesn't matter which number you press. No one will answer."

How Boring Is Canada

▶ BY NICK PASHLEY

To begin with, is Canada, in fact, boring? Oh, you must be kidding. Of course Canada's boring. The question is, how boring? How do we stack up internationally? The answer: Pretty well, actually. Certainly, all the surveys put us in the top ten. Well, all right, the top five. So have it your way, the top three.

Forty or fifty years ago we wouldn't have cracked the top ten, not with tedium powerhouses like Belgium and New Zealand out there. In fact, we were too dull by half. No one even knew we were here. Sometimes you can be too boring for your own good.

In recent years, however, the depth of our dullness has been acknowledged globally and we have slowly edged past competitors as varied as Latvia, Ecuador, and Oman. In some cases formerly boring countries have turned interesting, if only briefly, through natural disasters, accusations of genocide, or by being invaded by the Americans. It's difficult to believe today, for example, that we once thought Iran boring. (The whiff of possible nuclear weapons automatically makes a country less boring. The Americans, on many levels, are more boring than anybody—think Barry Manilow, reality television, Kenny G, and so much more—but they could blow us all to bits in a second, which carries a certain frisson of interestingness.)

Canada's rise to the top three on the planet has not been without its glitches. In the sixties we actually had a sex scandal that starred a German sexpot named Gerda Munsinger, a Soviet "diplomat," and a federal cabinet minister. It didn't last, of course, and we haven't had a sex scandal since, unless you count Belinda Stronach dumping poor Peter MacKay. Admittedly, back when Pierre Trudeau was dating Barbra Streisand, Canada seemed for a moment almost interesting. Leonard Cohen might have blown it altogether for Canada had he not moved away all those years ago. Joe Clark was prime minister for only a few hours in 1979–1980 but he single-handedly put us right back into the thick of things, boredom-wise, and we've never looked back. Who's our greatest living icon? Wayne Gretzky. Heck of a hockey player, but not someone who exactly lights up a room. Even his restaurant in Toronto is boring.

First place seems to be out of the question. Even a country that boasts something called "the notwith-standing clause" can't realistically expect to contend with Switzerland. The Swiss have been at the top of the standings since 1658 when they crept past Denmark on the strength of the mildly interesting Siege of Copenhagen. (The Danes really blew their chances in 2006 with the Mohammed cartoon fracas; we won't see them back in the top ten of the snooze stats for years to come.)

There has long been controversy about the Japanese holding on to second place as long as they have. Critics point out the lasting appeal of samurai

Underwhelming! Dull!

Canadians dream that one day they may hold their heads high and proudly proclaim: "We're number one! We're top dog—or . . . er . . . beaver—in the snooze stats."

warriors, Mount Fuji, and the popularity of sushi. They even have an emperor, which is kind of interesting, but there's no avoiding the fact that the Japanese as a nation live to work. They require legislation to take a day off. They even have a word—"karoshi"—for working yourself to death, which is a bad sign. Even the Swiss—who have several dozen official languages—don't have an equivalent in any of them.

Canadians aren't obsessed with working, except in Toronto. Our strength, our ace in the hole, when it comes to boring the pants off the wider world, lies in our eternal constitutional issues. Boredom experts argue that we should have passed Japan long ago in the Sominex stakes simply on the strength of the Rowell-Sirois Commission alone. Don't remember exactly what that was? Nor does anybody else. Not even Rowell or Sirois, whoever they are. And the very idea of Meech Lake makes our eyelids feel a trifle heavy—I'm already sorry I mentioned it.

Years of hard slogging have taken us past the likes of Suriname and Equatorial Guinea but we can still do better. We can be even more boring if we make the effort. What we need is a Royal Commission. Let's straighten out the big question of whether boredom is a federal or provincial jurisdiction, then we can show the Swiss and the Japanese a thing or two. ▲

How Suzanne Remembered It

Well, that was odd, she thought after he'd left. She'd gone out after work for a drink with some other people from Accounting and they'd wound up in some bar that has just opened, called "Sky" and she'd met him. Leonard. Leonard something. A Jewish name. He wasn't really her type, shorter than she usually liked, but there was a quiet intensity to him. When he looked at you, you stayed looked at, she thought. He had told her he was a poet. Suzanne had heard that line before.

He recited a poem to her. She wasn't much one for poetry, so she'd said in that breezy style guys seemed to like, "Well don't give up your day job!" It turned out it was his day job. Suzanne felt a bit stupid, but he didn't seem to mind.

He suggested they leave the bar, and she took him down to her place by the river. He commented on the garbage and the flowers, which she hadn't really noticed before. She wished she'd done some shopping. She had almost nothing in the fridge and he seemed hungry. She made him some tea and gave him a couple of oranges she'd bought at the little Chinese grocery store at the corner. He seemed to think the oranges had actually come all the way from China, which was nuts. She gave up trying to explain. He had looked at her as if she were half crazy. Then he said, "That's why I want to be here." Like, as if, that explained anything.

He noticed everything. He saw the little crucifix on her wall, which her mother had insisted on, and he said, in that matter-of-fact, gravelly voiced way of his, that Jesus was a sailor. She started to point out that, in fact, Jesus had been a carpenter—she thought that, being Jewish, Leonard was getting Jesus confused with somebody else—but she let it go. It was kind of cute that he was taking an interest.

At one point he said, apropos of absolutely nothing at all, "You can hear the boats go by."

"That's rivers for you," Suzanne replied.

He'd been pretty good in the sack, she had to admit. Mind you, she'd had some kinky requests from guys in the past, but Leonard outdid them all. What was it? Something about touching his perfect body with her mind. Or was it the other way round? How the heck do you do that? She'd been a bit woozy at the time and wasn't entirely sure what she was supposed to do. He seemed to like it, anyway. He had a pretty good body, but she wouldn't have used the word "perfect!" That seemed a bit conceited.

In the morning she made more tea. Leonard had the last of the oranges, though he seemed to have forgotten about the China stuff, which was just as well. Maybe he'd been drunk too. Looking out her window the night before, he had pointed out heroes in the seaweed, but she hadn't been able to see them. She couldn't see them now either, though there

Canada's Most Famous Romance

▶ **BY NICK PASHLEY**

were still children—children in the morning, he had said. Big deal. There were a lot of kids in the neighbourhood, frequently leaning out of their windows at any time of day. But it seemed unlikely they would lean that way "forever," as Leonard ludicrously claimed. They would grow up and move away and not be children any more. Some of the things he said really didn't stand up in daylight. He can't be much of a poet, she mused.

Suzanne wondered if she'd see him again. She wondered if he'd call. He seemed to like her. He had said something about her getting him on her wavelength, also something about wanting to travel with her. That was promising. Though she could imagine her dad's reaction if she told him she was dating a poet. Anyway, it didn't seem likely. Leonard was one of those guys with a lot of big talk. He'd probably forgotten all about her already. No, she thought, nothing will come of this. ▲

An American was writing a book about churches of the world. On his first day of research, in a New York church, he noticed a golden telephone with a sign stating "$10,000 per call." The scholar asked a priest what the phone was for. The priest said that it was a direct line to heaven and for $10,000 you could talk to God.

Next stop, in a Boston cathedral, he saw the same phone with the same sign. Again, to his inquiry, he received the same reply. He visited churches across America and in every church he saw the same golden phone with the same sign.

The scholar began his research in Canada inside a Toronto cathedral where he saw the same phone, but this time the sign read "10 cents per call." The American was shocked so he said to the priest: "Father, I've travelled all over America and I've seen this same golden phone in many churches. I'm told that it is a direct line to Heaven, but in every state the price was $10,000 per call. Why is it so cheap here?"

The priest smiled and answered, "You're in Canada now son, it's a local call."

Q: What does a Canadian say when you step on his foot?
A: "Sorry."

A Canadian magazine held a contest to come up with a Canadian analogue to "as American as apple pie." The winner was "as Canadian as possible under the circumstances."

Q: How do you get a Canadian to apologize to you?
A: Step on his foot.

A couple of small-town Australians stop at a pub after work. They're enjoying their pints when they notice a couple of out-of-towners come into the bar. Being a friendly fellow, one of the Aussies decides to go see who these guys are. He says "Excuse me, guys. You aren't from around here, are you? Where you from?"

"Saskatoon, Saskatchewan," comes the reply.

The Aussie turns around and heads back to his buddy at the table.

"So? Where are they from?"

"I don't know, but they don't speak any English."

Q: How do you get 20 teenage Canadian boys to get out of a swimming pool?
A: Stand by the edge of the pool and say, "Time to get out of the pool, boys."

Q: How do you get 20 drunk Canadians out of a swimming pool?
A: You say, "Excuse me, could you please get out of the pool?"

What's Up, Doc?

Humour's an easy pill to swallow, especially when it's aimed at our doctors, our bodies and our doomed attempts to get healthy. These will keep you in stitches!

"The other foot, too, Mrs. Zipsky."

A fellow walked into a drug-store and headed to the back to speak with the pharmacist. "Do you have anything for hiccups?" he asked.

Without warning, the pharmacist reached over and smacked the man on the shoulder. "Did that help?" he asked.

"I don't know," the startled man replied. "I'll have to ask my wife. She's waiting in the car."

— NANCY MACMILLAN

During my uncle's physical exam, his doctor mentioned that he was slightly overweight. "Do you get any exercise?" the physician asked.

"Well, I used to have an exercise bike in the TV room," my uncle began.

"Used to!" the doctor said. "Where is it now?"

"I had to store it in the basement," my uncle confessed, "because it got in the way of my snack trays."

— WAYNE R. REIF

The patient who came to my radiology office for abdominal X-rays was already heavily sedated. But I still had to ask her a lot of questions, the last one being, "Ma'am, where is your pain right now?"

Through her medicated fog, she answered, "He's at work."

— JEFF DOTY

My husband was going on a diet, but when we pulled into a fast-food restaurant, he ordered a milkshake. I pointed out that a shake isn't exactly the best snack for someone who wants to lose weight. He agreed but didn't change his order.

The long line must have given him time to make the connection between his order and his waistline. As the woman handed him his shake, she said, "Sorry about the wait."

"That's okay," he replied self-consciously. "I'm going to lose it."

— KAREN NAZARENUS

"I think my wife's going deaf," Joe told their doctor.

"Try to test her hearing at home and let me know how severe her problem is before you bring her in for treatment," the doctor said.

So that evening, when his wife was preparing dinner, Joe stood three metres behind her and said, "What's for dinner, honey?"

No response.

He moved to two metres behind her and asked again.

No response.

Then he stood one metre in back of her and tried again but still got no answer. Finally, he stood directly behind her and asked, "Honey, what's for supper?"

She turned around. "For the fourth time—I said chicken!"

— GORDON BAYLISS

During a CPR training class, we were paired up to practise the Heimlich manoeuvre. The instructor set the scene by saying, "Imagine you're at a dinner party with your spouse and he or she starts choking."

He then reminded us not to do anything to people who were coughing, because they'd probably dislodge the obstruction on their own. We were to calm such victims with quiet talk and encourage them to continue coughing.

When the role playing began, one woman moved close to her coughing "husband." She placed a hand on his shoulder and whispered, "Honey, did you remember to mail your life insurance premium cheque last week?"

— TOM CLEVELAND

Timeless Humour from the '50s

I was waiting in the office of our lone, overworked doctor when a local repairman, father of seven children, dashed in looking worried and distraught.

To the nurse he explained, "My kids are all sick with some kind of bug. I know that Doc is too busy for me to bring 'em all in here, but I wondered if I could bring in one for a sample?"

— NANCY CURRY

Walking to work one day, my husband was hit by a car. It was a minor accident and the driver apologized, adding, "You certainly are lucky. We're right next to a doctor's office."

"I don't know how lucky that is," my husband replied. "I'm the doctor."

— SANDRA MARCHAND

In the Lamaze childbirth classes I teach, the first hour is a lecture. During the second hour, the couples get on the floor to practise breathing and relaxation techniques. The lecture one evening was "Sex During Pregnancy."

When I finished presenting the material, I asked if there were any questions. After waiting a moment, I tried to proceed—only to be interrupted when the class burst out laughing. It took me a few seconds to realize what I'd said: "Okay, if there are no questions about sex during pregnancy, let's get down on the floor and practise."

— NANCY ROMANS

A hairdressing client of mine told me of her husband's recovery after having double bypass heart surgery. She had recounted the doctor's orders to her husband, saying, "In six weeks you'll be able to walk up two flights of stairs, lift ten kilos, and you can resume normal sexual activity."

Her husband responded, "If I'd known about the sex, I would've had the surgery a long time ago!"

— PAMELA L. HOUSTON

This couple was heading to the hospital with their 16-year-old daughter, who was scheduled to undergo a tonsillectomy. During the ride they talked about the procedure.

"Dad," the teenager asked, "how are they going to keep my mouth open during surgery?"

Without hesitation her father quipped, "They're going to give you a phone."

— KINGSLEY COLACO

Our house is on the route of a triathlon. Every year my parents invite friends over to sit on our deck and cheer the athletes.

Last year one older runner impressed my father. The man ran by and Dad called out, "I admire your courage!"

Glancing at Dad sitting comfortably on the porch, the man shouted back, "I admire your wisdom!"

— JUDY A. HALL

"It sounds like a power struggle between the B.B.Q. chicken and the poutine."

An 80-year-old man goes to a doctor for a checkup. The doctor is amazed at his shape. "To what do you attribute your good health?"

"I'm a turkey hunter and that's why I'm in good shape. Get up before daylight, chase turkeys up and down mountains."

The doctor says, "Well, I'm sure it helps, but there have to be genetic factors. How old was your dad when he died?"

"Who says my dad's dead?"

"You're 80 years old and your dad's alive? How old is he?"

"Dad's 100. In fact, he turkey hunted with me this morning."

"What about your dad's dad— how old was he when he died?"

"Who says my grandpa's dead?"

"You're 80 years old and your grandfather's still living? How old is he?"

"118."

"I suppose you're going to tell me he went turkey hunting this morning?"

"No. He got married."

The doctor looks at the man in amazement. "Got married? Why would a 118-year-old guy want to get married?"

The old-timer answers, "Who says he wanted to?"

— ARDELL WIECZOREK

"I'm prescribing a low-carb diet for your diabetes, a high-carb diet for your colon, a low-fat diet for your heart and a high-fat diet for your nerves."

With today's focus on exercising, I've been trying to talk my husband into joining me in a 20-minute walk each night. One evening after reading an article called "Brighten Your Sex Life," I felt I had a new argument to present.

I told my husband that, according to what I read, if he just walked 20 minutes a day it would improve his sex life.

He replied, "Who do I know that lives 20 minutes away?"

— BONNIE SHORTT

sign language

Spotted in a newspaper:

"Fitness Club Closes, Going Belly Up."

For several years, my job was to answer all viewer phone calls and mail concerning the daytime television soap operas our company produced. One day a woman called wanting medical advice from an actor who portrayed a doctor on one of our shows. I explained that the man wasn't a real doctor and couldn't help her.

After a moment of shocked silence, the woman replied indignantly, "Well, no wonder it takes his patients months to recover!"

— SANDY GRANT

A friend of mine had resisted efforts to get him to run with our jogging group until his doctor told him he had to exercise. Soon thereafter, he reluctantly joined us for our 5:30 a.m. jogs on Mondays, Wednesdays, and Fridays.

After a month of running, we decided that my friend might be hooked, especially when he said he had discovered what "runner's euphoria" was. "Runner's euphoria," he explained, "is what I feel at 5:30 on Tuesdays, Thursdays, and Saturdays."

— NEIL P. BUDGE

I was watching a new workout video to prepare myself for an exercise session the next morning.

My husband stuck his head in the room, looked around, and said, "That would probably work a lot better if you actually did the exercises."

— JAY SARAH ASHLYNN

When one of my patients came to me complaining of ear trouble, I looked around for the appropriate instrument with which to examine him. Unable to find it, I buzzed my receptionist and asked, "Have you seen my auroscope?"

"No," came the reply. "What sign do you come under?"

— J. G. MANN, M.D.

As a dental hygienist, I try to relieve my patients' anxiety by going over the procedures before starting. After talking to one patient, a police officer, I asked him if he had any questions.

I must have been a little too graphic in my description, because he replied, "I have just one. I've never given you a ticket, have I?"

— WANDA E. CRUMPLER

The orthopaedic surgeon I work for was moving to a new office, and his staff was helping transport many of the items. I sat the display skeleton in the front of my car, his bony arm across the back of my seat. I hadn't considered the drive across town.

At one traffic light, the stares of the people in the car beside me became obvious, and I looked across and explained, "I'm delivering him to my doctor's office."

The other driver leaned out of his window. "I hate to tell you, lady," he said, "but I think it's too late!"

— TRUDY Y. VINEYARD

When an increased patient load began to overwhelm our hospital's emergency room, we initiated a triage system to ensure that the most critical people were treated first. However, some of the less seriously ill patients occasionally had to wait as long as several hours before they could be seen. Complaints were common.

One day, trauma cases abounded, and the wait was particularly long. A police officer came in and approached the unit clerk. "I hate to tell you this," he said apologetically, "but we just got a 911 call from your waiting room."

— JINA KARGER

"I'm going to prescribe something that works like Aspirin but costs much, much more."

221

QUOTABLE QUOTES

There is no rejection in life quite like a cancelled shrink appointment.

— BILL SCHENK

"Vegetarian" is an old Indian word for "doesn't hunt well."

— PAUL HARVEY

In California virtually everyone has had their teeth whitened. If they all smiled at once, they would give us a headache.

— GARRISON KEILLOR

I think I have a disease called spontaneous disclosure. I need to tell everyone my life story instantaneously.

— KELLY RIPA

One good thing about living in America is that there is no neurosis too insignificant to merit its own paperback.

— DEBORAH SOLOMON

Be careful about reading health books. You may die of a misprint.

— MARK TWAIN

"Exercise" is such a dirty word in my household that whenever I even think of it, I wash my mouth out with chocolate.

— LEONORE FLEISCHER

Carol was pregnant with her first child, and her husband was about to leave on a two-week business trip. When Carol went to her doctor appointment, she had some questions.

"My husband wants me to ask you something—" Carol began.

The doctor interrupted her. "I get asked that question all the time," he said in a reassuring tone. "Sex is fine until late in the pregnancy."

"No, that's not it!" an embarrassed Carol confessed. "My husband wants to know if I can still mow the lawn."

— ANN CATES

I have become very cholesterol-conscious and am trying to change the family's eating habits. We are now consuming lots of oat bran, and I've substituted turkey for most of the meats we used to enjoy. I use ground turkey in spaghetti sauce and we eat turkey hot dogs.

My 18-year-old daughter was getting tired of all the turkey and cholesterol talk. One day she came home from school and asked the usual, "What's for dinner?"

"Chicken," I replied.

With a tired sigh she inquired, "Real chicken or turkey chicken?"

— PATRICIA SCHAFER

My sister and I were out on the town one night when we ran into a man I knew. "You're sisters?" he asked incredulously. "You look nothing alike."

Pointing to her nose and my chin, my sister said, "Different plastic surgeons."

— CAROL LENNOX

A colleague was planning a trip to my business office and asked if I could find him a hotel with exercise facilities. I called several hotels, with no luck.

Finally I thought I had found one. I asked the receptionist if the hotel had a weight room.

"No," she replied, "but we have a lobby and you can wait there."

— SUE GIBSON

┌─────────────────────────────────────┐

Timeless Humour from the **'50s**

A group of Yukon housewives had gotten together for morning coffee and, since several of us were pregnant, the talk drifted to babies and doctors.

One of the women announced that she was now going to a woman doctor. "At least," she said, "I'll be able to depend on my doctor being around during moose season!"

— NANCY P. DONNER
└─────────────────────────────────────┘

One rainy morning, my mother went for her daily run. As she returned to the house, she slipped and fell, hitting her head on the driveway.

I called the paramedics. When they arrived, they asked my mom some questions to determine her coherency. "What is today?" inquired one man.

Without hesitation, Mom replied, "Trash day."

— JAIME SWART

Suffering with a herniated disk in his back, my husband told his cousin that a well-respected doctor was treating him. His cousin asked the name of the doctor, and on hearing it, he replied, "I never heard of him—that's a good sign." The cousin is a medical-malpractice attorney.

— BARBARA ROSENBLATT

My friend Kimberly announced that she had started a diet to lose some weight she had put on recently.

"Good!" I exclaimed. "I'm ready to start a diet too. We can be dieting buddies and help each other out. When I feel the urge to drive out and get a burger and fries, I'll call you first."

"Great!" she replied. "I'll ride with you."

— KATINA FISHER

Immediately after my husband's company built a weightlifting facility for its employees, he and a colleague of his named Jamie joined the program. Although Jamie dropped out of the program, my husband continued faithfully.

Several months later, a co-worker came up to him and expressed interest in weight training. My husband was flattered that someone had noticed the results of his dedicated effort, until the man exclaimed, "Yeah, I just saw Jamie—and he looks great."

— KARLA HANSEN

About to have a blood test, I nervously waited while the nurse tightened a tourniquet around my arm. "I understand you're from Edmonton," she said. "Are you an Eskimos fan?"

"Absolutely!" I replied.

"Well," she continued as she raised the needle, "this may hurt a little. I'm from Calgary."

— JANET THOMPSON

I'm never very comfortable with any kind of physical test or procedure, but when I was referred to a doctor for a breast exam, I agreed to see him. I don't know the doctor, and he doesn't know me, I told myself. It is no big deal.

On the day of the appointment, I was a little nervous. But the exam went smoothly, and I breathed a sigh of relief when the doctor told me he was finished.

Just as I was about to step out of the office, however, his voice stopped me in my tracks. "By the way," said the doctor, "I really enjoyed your performance at the symphony concert last week!"

— MARY A. KEEZER

My husband met me at the doctor's office for my routine checkup, and from there we decided to go out to eat. Since we had driven in separate cars, I arrived at the restaurant first.

"One for dinner?" asked the hostess.

"No," I replied. "There will be two of us in just a minute."

When I saw the panicky look on the hostess's face, I realized I had forgotten about my appearance. Anybody could see that I was at least $8\frac{1}{2}$ months pregnant.

— LOANN K. BURKE

Recovering from knee surgery and the extraction of impacted wisdom teeth, I was lying on the couch with an ice bag on my leg and hot-water bottles against both cheeks.

From the kitchen I heard my mother cry out in pain. Through a mouth stuffed with gauze I asked her what had happened.

"You know," she replied, "there's nothing worse than a paper cut."

— LISA APPLEBAUM

sign language

Advertisement spotted in the classifieds:

"Nordic Track for sale. New, hardly used, now $250. Ask for Chubby."

"I'm sorry, I thought I could **save him,** but there was too much paperwork."

After I warned the nurse taking blood that it would be very hard to find a vein on me, she said, "Don't worry. We've seen worse. Last year we had a girl come in to get a blood test for her marriage licence and we had to stick her six times in four places before we got anything."

"Yes, I know," I said. "That was me!"

— CONNIE DOWN

While walking through the Prince Albert airport, my dentist ran into a group from his hometown. Among them was one of his patients. When he said hello, she gave him a curious look, saying he looked familiar but she could not quite place him.

"Lean back and look up at me," he suggested. She did. "Oh! Dr. Harrison!"

— GEORGE JUST

When my wife called a friend on our touch-tone phone, the line was busy. She tried several more times, but without success. Watching her, I asked why she wasn't using the redial button.

"Honey," she answered, "I need the exercise."

— HENRY H. POLITZER

I was lying on my couch, burning up with a fever, when my husband said I should go to bed. At three o'clock the next morning, I woke up soaked from head to toe. When my husband heard me stirring, he said that my fever must have broken.

I decided to spend the rest of the night back on the couch so as not to disturb him any further. But then, three hours later, he appeared in the living room soaking wet. "Your fever didn't break," he said, still dripping. "The water bed did."

— SUSAN BARR

There is a woman at my health club who always begins her workout with sit-ups and leg-lifts. One afternoon she entered the exercise room and, as usual, lay down on the slant board as if she were about to do sit-ups. This time, though, she did none. Instead, she turned around on the board and positioned herself for leg-lifts.

Again she stayed there for several moments without doing a single exercise. Finally she got up and headed out of the room. As she walked past me, she said, "Thinking about it was enough for today."

— STEPHEN R. CAUBLE

Throughout her pregnancy, my sister Joanne insisted that she wanted no medication during labour. When the big day came, though, she wondered if she had made the right decision.

Knowing my sister's stance on drugs, the midwife did everything else to ease Joanne's pain. "You look uncomfortable," she said at one point. "Would you like to change positions?"

"Yes," Joanne replied. "I want to be the midwife!"

— REBECCA WOODWORTH

Not all chemicals are bad. Without hydrogen and oxygen, for example, there would be no way to make water, a vital ingredient in beer.

— DAVE BARRY in The Miami Herald

The problem with the gene pool is there's no lifeguard.

— STEVEN WRIGHT

You've got bad eating habits if you use a grocery cart in a 7-Eleven, OK?

— DENNIS MILLER, Ranting Again (Doubleday)

The only way to keep your health is to eat what you don't want, drink what you don't like, and do what you'd druther not.

— MARK TWAIN

Being in therapy is great. I spend an hour just talking about myself. It's kinda like being the guy on a date.

— CAROLINE RHEA

For sleep, riches and health to be truly enjoyed, they must be interrupted.

— JEAN PAUL RICHTER

When my generation was your age, we took crazy risks. The wildest thing was— prepare to be shocked—we deliberately ingested carbohydrates!

— DAVE BARRY

Ha, Ha, Ha! Tee-Hee! Ho

How I Caught Every
Disease
on the Web

▶ BY MARY ROACH

The Internet is a boon for hypochondriacs like me. Right now, for instance, I'm feeling a shooting pain on the side of my neck. A Web search produces five matches, the first three for a condition called Arnold-Chiari Malformation.

This is the wonderful thing about looking up your symptoms on the Internet. Very quickly you find yourself distracted from your aches and pains. The symptom list for Arnold-Chiari Malformation is three pages long. Noting the four out of 71 symptoms that match, I conclude that I have this condition. A good hypochondriac can make a diagnosis on the basis of one matching symptom.

While my husband, Ed, reads over my shoulder, I recite symptoms from the list. " 'General clumsiness' and 'general imbalance,' " I say, as though announcing arrivals at the Army Ball. " 'Difficulty driving,' 'lack of taste,' 'difficulty feeling feet on ground.' "

"Those aren't symptoms," says Ed. "Those are your character flaws."

Ha, ha. But I know how to get back at him. "Hey, what's this thickening, or nodule, on the back of your neck?" Ed is more of a hypochondriac than I am. "Looks like it could be Antley-Bixler Syndrome," I say. I got this one from the National Organization for Rare Disorders Web site, which has an index of rare diseases that I've pretty much memorized. I move in for the kill. "Ever feel any fatigue?"

Ed gets on the computer to see if there's a self-test for Antley-Bixler Syndrome. We're big fans of self-tests, and the Internet is full of them. I once happily passed the afternoon self-testing for macular degeneration, emotional eating, hypochondria, bad breath. Ed found me taking the Self-Test for Swine Farm Operators. ("I conduct manure nutrient analysis: Annually. Every five years. Never.") It's probably fair to say that I'm addicted to self-tests, but until there's a self-test for self-test addiction, I can't be sure.

The dangerous thing about Internet diagnosis is that most hypochondriacs will attempt it late at night, when everyone else is asleep and no one is around to reassure them that they're nuts. This is what happened to me on October 2, sometime past midnight, when I entered the words "red spots on my face" into

Ha, Ha, Ha! Tee-Hee! Ho

A good hypochondriac can make a diagnosis on the basis of one matching symptom.

the Google search page. I'd noticed the spots while scanning my face for star-like speckles, an early symptom of Ebola virus.

I ignored the 20 or 30 entries for broken capillaries and zeroed in on the following: "Leprosy…begins with red spots on the face…. Bones are affected and fingers drop off." I began to feel panicky and short of breath. I added those symptoms to my search and found this: "I developed little red spots on my face and arms. Then last spring I started becoming short of breath…." Bottom line, I had interstitial lung disease.

I tried to keep calm. I tried to focus on entry No. 18: "Spicy pork rinds cause me to break out in red spots on my face." I couldn't recall eating spicy pork rinds, but perhaps I'd ordered a dish that was made with them but failed to state this on the menu. From now on, I'd be sure to ask, "Waiter, is the flan made with spicy pork rinds?"

In the end, it was no use. I was up all night, fretting over interstitial lung disease. For a hypochondriac, simply running the name of a new disease through your mind once or twice is enough to convince you that you've got it. I frequently remind myself of my step-daughter Phoebe, who, some years ago, heard someone talking about mad cow disease. The next day when a friend of the family said, "Hi, Phoebe, how are you?" she stated calmly, "I have mad cow disease." But Phoebe was a child. I am an adult. I should know better. Perhaps there's something wrong with me. ▲

My friend Esther told me about her son's fifth-grade career day, where the children were asked, "Who knows what a psychiatrist does?"

Esther's son replied, "That's someone who asks you to lie down on a couch and then blames everything on your mother."

— CARLA GATES

Last New Year's Eve found me in the hospital scheduled for an operation to remove hemorrhoids. So while others donned party hats and sipped champagne, I wore a hospital gown and swigged painkillers. That's not to say the holiday spirit was completely absent.

The next day, January 1, I woke up to a banner on my bedroom wall. It screamed "Happy New Rear!"

— MARILYNN BELLMANN

Following a major hurricane, my husband worked long hours clearing the jumble of trees that littered our property. The longer he worked, however, the more painful it became for him to move his right arm.

CENTRE FOR THE STUDY OF WHY EVERYTHING YOU THOUGHT WAS GOOD FOR YOU, IS NOW BAD FOR YOU

He ignored my pleas to see the doctor until one night he yelped, "Ow! This is getting serious." As I turned to him in concern, he added, "Now it hurts to push buttons on the remote control!"

— WENDY CLAY

Everyone vows to join a gym and go three days a week. Yeah, right. A woman once called me at the health club where I used to work. "I got a note saying it was time for me to renew my membership," she said. "As much as I love to work out, I don't think I'll renew."

"Fine," I said, "but you'll have to come down here to fill out forms."

After a long pause—"Umm, where are you located?"

— JENNIFER HUGHES

During a visit with my mother, who was in the hospital, I popped into the cafeteria for breakfast. I set a piece of bread on the moving toaster rack and waited for it to return golden brown. Instead, it got stuck all the way in the back. When I couldn't reach it, the woman in line next to me took control of the situation. Seizing a pair of tongs, she reached in and deftly fished out the piece of toast. "You must be an emergency-room worker," I joked.

"No," she said, "an obstetrician."

— DONALD GEISER

A doctor and his wife were having a big argument at breakfast. "You aren't so good in bed either!" he shouted and stormed off to work. By mid-morning, he decided he'd better make amends and phoned home. After many rings, his wife picked up the phone.

"What took so long to answer?"

"I was in bed."

"What were you doing in bed this late?"

"Getting a second opinion."

— EDWARD B. WORBY

Since maternity patients at the small hospital where I work must travel 30 km to another hospital for the actual delivery, they often check with us first to verify that they are, indeed, in labour.

One morning, a pregnant woman walked in, and we confirmed that delivery was definitely imminent. So a nurse called her husband at home, getting him out of bed. "Your wife's about to give birth," she told him. "You need to go to the hospital."

"Okay," he said groggily. "I'll wake her up and tell her."

— ROSALIE DEAN

Employed as a dental receptionist, I was on duty when an extremely nervous patient came for root-canal surgery. He was brought into the examining room and made comfortable in the reclining dental chair. The dentist then injected a numbing agent around the patient's tooth, and left the room for a few minutes while the medication took hold.

When the dentist returned, the patient was standing next to a tray of dental equipment. "What are you doing by the surgical instruments?" asked the surprised dentist.

Focused on his task, the patient replied, "I'm taking out the ones I don't like."

— PAULA FONTAINE

As we left the gym after our first real workout in years, my husband and I both felt energized. "Let's renew our commitment to do it three times a week," I said.

"Absolutely," my husband agreed, "three times as a minimum."

"And no whining," I said. "No excuses."

"No, we'll do it with energy and enthusiasm."

"And on my late night, we can just meet here at the gym."

"The gym?" my husband said, crestfallen. "I thought we were talking about sex!"

— LINDA JOHNSON

A friend of mine was working as a nurse in a West Australian coastal town when a tourist came into the medical centre with a fishhook lodged deep in his hand. Since it was the weekend, my friend had to summon the doctor from home.

The tourist was dismayed to see that the doctor was young, had long hair and wore sandals and a very casual shirt. "You don't look much like a doctor to me," he said dubiously.

The doctor examined the hook in the tourist's hand and responded, "And you don't look much like a fish to me."

— MARION O'LEARY

"You are in a deep, deep sleep.
When you awaken you will feel sweaty and exhausted."

**"I'm afraid you have...
Oh, what's that thing called when you can't remember stuff..."**

A member of a diet club bemoaned her lack of willpower. She'd made her family's favourite cake over the weekend, she explained, and they'd eaten half of it. The next day, however, the uneaten half beckoned. She cut herself a slice. Then another, and another. By the time she'd polished off the cake, she knew her husband would be disappointed.

"What did he say when he found out?" one club member asked.

"He never found out," she said. "I made another cake and ate half."

— HUSAIN ALI

Butch, our boxer, hated taking his medicine. After a lot of trial and error my father eventually figured out the simplest way to get it into him: blow it down Butch's throat with something called a pill tube. So Dad put the large tablet in one end of the tube, forced the reluctant dog's jaws open, and poked the other end into his mouth.

Then, just as my father inhaled to blow, Butch coughed. A startled look appeared on Dad's face. He opened his eyes wide and swallowed hard. "I think I've just been de-wormed," he gasped.

— JOHN ROBERTSON

Bob, age 92, and Mary, age 89, are all excited about their decision to get married. While out for a stroll to discuss the wedding they pass a drugstore. Bob suggests they go in.

Bob asks to speak to the pharmacist. He explains they're about to get married, and asks, "Do you sell heart medication?"

"Of course we do," the pharmacist replies.

"Medicine for rheumatism?"

"Definitely," he says.

"How about Viagra?"

"Of course."

"Medicine for memory problems, arthritis, jaundice?"

"Yes, the works."

"What about vitamins, sleeping pills, Geritol, antacids?"

"Absolutely."

"Do you sell wheelchairs and walkers?"

"All speeds and sizes."

"Good," Bob says to the pharmacist. "We'd like to register for our wedding gifts here, please."

— RUMESA KHALID

I called a video store to order the war movie *Battle of the Bulge.* "Hold on," said the clerk. "I'll check our aerobics tapes."

— M. HOLLAND

Hypochondriac that I am, I constantly log on to the Internet to self-diagnose my latest ailment. But even I knew it was time to lighten up the day I typed in the keywords "liver disorders." That led me to a medical site. With growing alarm I realized I had each of the first seven symptoms.

Then I came to No. 8 and suddenly felt much better: "Feeling of lethargy. No longer enjoys romping and wagging tail."

— DEBORA DAWSON

Although I was only a little overweight, my wife was harping on me to diet. One evening we took a brisk walk downtown, and I surprised her by jumping over a parking meter, leapfrog style.

Pleased with myself, I said, "How many fat men do you know who can do that?"

"One," she retorted.

— R. T. McLAURY

Hoping to lose some weight, my wife told me she wanted to get an exercise bicycle. I reminded her that she had a very nice and rather expensive bike in the garage. She explained that she wanted a stationary one.

"Your bicycle has been stationary," I remarked. "That's why you need to lose weight."

— JIM WHITE

It had been a long time—seven years to be exact—since my friend Brian had been to see his doctor. So the nurse told him that if he wanted to make an appointment, he would have to be reprocessed as a new patient.

"Okay," said Brian, "reprocess me."

"I'm sorry," she told him. "We're not accepting any new patients."

— BARBARA SAMPSON

A veterinarian sent one of his employees to get a flat tire repaired in the tire store that I own. When I asked which tire needed to be fixed, he replied, "Hind left."

— GLENN RYE

Timeless Humour from the '60s

Resting in the hospital after the birth of our third child, I thought I would finally get a chance to finish reading Boris Pasternak's famous novel, *Doctor Zhivago*, and had it handy on my bedside table.

When the student nurse came in, it caught her eye and she looked at it skeptically. "If you want the real low-down on baby care," she said confidentially, "you can't beat Doctor Spock."

— MRS. DAVID LYCHE

"Well, the drug's no good, but the side effects are bitchin'."

233

Standing on the sidelines, during a game being played by my school's football team, I saw one of the players take a hard hit. He tumbled to the ground and didn't move.

We grabbed our first-aid gear and rushed out onto the field. The coach picked up the young man's hand and urged, "Son, can you hear me? Squeeze once for yes and twice for no."

— RICHARD CORBIN

We brought our newborn son, Adam, to the pediatrician for his first checkup. As he finished, the doctor told us, "You have a cute baby."

Smiling, I said, "I bet you say that to all new parents."

"No," he replied, "just to those whose babies really are good-looking."

"So what do you say to the others?" I asked.

"He looks just like you."

— MATT SLOT

During the year that my husband, Bob, was undergoing expensive dental reconstruction, he got to know everyone in the dentist's office. When a couple of staffers teased him about his garbled speech after he got a mouth-numbing anaesthetic, Bob replied, "Well, it's hard to talk with $3,000 in your mouth."

— MARY W. MATHIS

Although I knew I had put on a little weight, I didn't consider myself overweight until the day I decided to clean my refrigerator. I sat on a chair in front of the appliance and reached in to wipe the back wall.

While I was in this position, my teenage son came into the kitchen. "Hi, Mom," he said. "Whatcha doin', having lunch?"

I started my diet that day.

Betty Strohm

When I walked into a small café in rural P.E.I., I had no trouble distinguishing the non-smoking area from the smoking area. There before me were two neatly printed signs: "Coffee Corner" and "Coughy Corner."

— R. W. WILLE

My husband bought an exercise machine to help him lose weight. He set it up in the basement but didn't use it much, so he moved it to the bedroom. It gathered dust there, too, so he put it in the living room.

Weeks later I asked how it was going. "I was right," he said. "I do get more exercise now. Every time I close the drapes, I have to walk around the machine."

— PHYLLIS OLSON

My mother and my wife— both nurses—were shopping together when a woman in a nearby dressing room fell unconscious. Mom discovered that the woman wasn't breathing, so she and my wife started CPR and revived the shopper just as paramedics arrived.

They loaded the woman onto a gurney and were rolling her out of the store when she yelled, "Stop!" My mother and my wife thought maybe she wanted to thank them, but instead she said, "I still want to buy those dresses."

— JOSEPH O'CONNOR

"You get it all...the diet book, which you won't read; the diet motivation tape, which you won't listen to; the exercise video, which you won't watch; and the meal planner, which you won't follow, all for only $69.95."

© A. BACALL

During an attack of laryngitis I lost my voice completely for two days. To help me communicate with him, my husband devised a system of taps.

One tap meant "Give me a kiss." Two taps meant "No." Three taps meant "Yes"—and 95 taps meant "Take out the garbage."

— MILDRED BALDWIN

Enticed by a television promotion, my wife ordered a popular exercise machine on a 30-day trial offer. Two weeks later she decided not to buy it, and called UPS to arrange for a pickup.

The next day the UPS driver arrived at our house. "Oh, no, not another one of these," he said. "All I've been doing is delivering these machines, then picking them up. The only person getting exercise from these things is me!"

— JEROME M. RICKS

My wife, an exercise enthusiast with a gorgeous figure, had me on a diet. I had trouble staying motivated until one midnight when I sneaked out to the kitchen for another snack.

Taped to the refrigerator were a picture of her in a bikini and a sign that read "Reach for your mate instead of your plate."

Since then I've lost 10 kilos.

— EDWARD R. DESYLVIA

To confirm her suspicions, my sister needed to purchase a pregnancy test. Since I was going to the pharmacy, she asked me to pick one up. I didn't stop to think how I appeared to the clerk when I waddled up—nine months pregnant—to pay for the kit.

"Honey," she said, "I can save you $15 right now. You're definitely going to have a baby."

— ESTHER ERBLICH

I discussed peer pressure and cigarettes with my 12-year-old daughter. Having struggled for years to quit, I described how I had started smoking to "be cool."

As I outlined the arguments kids might make to tempt her to try it, she stopped me mid-lecture, saying, "Hey, I'll just tell them my mom smokes. How cool can it be?"

— JUDI MOORE

Nearing 40 and woefully out of shape, I resolved to buy a bicycle and begin an exercise regimen. As I browsed in the bike shop, a young, athletic-looking clerk approached. "What do you have for a fat old lady with a big, tender posterior who hasn't ridden in years?" I asked.

He didn't even blink. "Well, why don't you bring her in, and we'll see what we can do," he said, clinching the sale.

— KAREN BATEMAN

My diminutive aunt Flora, just four feet, nine inches tall, accepted an offer to visit a health club for a free session. After being greeted heartily, she was shown where she could change and told an instructor would soon be with her.

Having changed her clothes, Aunt Flora went back to the exercise area. Along one wall she noticed a silver bar that was not in use, and decided to try her hand at chin-ups while she waited. She jumped up, barely reaching the bar, and managed to strain through two chin-ups before the instructor came to her side.

Smiling politely, the instructor said, "If you want to let go of the coat rack and follow me, I'll be glad to help you get started."

— MYRTA McQUEEN

When a woman called 911 complaining of difficulty breathing, my husband, Glenn, and his partner—both EMTs—rushed to her home. Glenn placed a sensor on her finger to measure her pulse and blood oxygen. Then he began to gather her information. "What's your age?" he asked.

"Fifty-eight," answered the patient, eyeing the beeping device on her finger. "What does that do?"

"It's a lie detector," said Glenn with a straight face. "Now, what did you say your age was?"

"Sixty-seven," answered the woman sheepishly.

— SARAH SCHAFER

After noticing how trim my husband had become, a friend asked me how I had persuaded him to diet. It was then I shared my dark secret: "I put our teenage son's shorts in his underwear drawer."

— RUTH J. LUHRS

With five kids at home and one more on the way, I wasn't quite sure what to think when I was assigned the following password for my computer at work: "iud4u."

— CAROLYN THOMAS

"If we hurry, I can still catch the third period."

Television remote controls encourage couch potatoes to exercise their options while broadening their base.

— WILLIAM ARTHUR WARD

Happiness is good health and a bad memory.

— INGRID BERGMAN

I don't work out. If God wanted us to bend over, he'd put diamonds on the floor.

— JOAN RIVERS

Smoking means always having to say you're sorry.

— TOM FERGUSON

I'd rather wear black in August than do one sit-up.

— JOY BEHAR of ABC's talk show The View

I'm paranoid about everything. On my stationary bike I have a rearview mirror.

— RICHARD LEWIS

My metabolism stinks. I can gain weight just listening to dinner music.

— RON DENTINGER

It's time to diet and exercise when you accept the fact that you can fool some of the people all of the time and all of the people some of the time—but not while you're wearing a bathing suit.

— GENE PERRET

Pregnant with our second child, I was determined to ride my exercise bike at least two kilometres a day. Late one night, having put it off all day, I climbed aboard the noisy contraption in our bedroom, where my husband was reading a book.

After about 20 minutes of listening to the squeaky machine, he glanced up, somewhat annoyed. "Don't you think it's time you turned around and headed for home?" he asked.

— MARGARET KOCH

I was in a department store when I heard on the public-address system that the optical department was offering free ice cream. I headed down the escalator to take advantage of the offer, trying to decide on vanilla or chocolate. I was nearly drooling when I got to the optical section and said to the clerk, "I'm here for my ice cream."

"Ice cream?" came the reply. "Sorry. What we have is a free eye screening."

— ROSEANNE L. BARNETT

As a lawyer in a major New Brunswick law firm, I have many colleagues who work long hours. However, the reputation of one of my partners' workaholic ways even extended beyond the office. He not only had to leave work early one day because of a medical problem, but was also told by his doctor to stay home until the end of the week. He grudgingly agreed to comply.

In the middle of the week, our receptionist received a call for him. She announced that the partner was out of the office until Friday. "Good," the caller said. "That's all I wanted to know."

It was my partner's doctor.

— DON DECANDIA

Needing to shed some weight, my husband and I went on a diet that had specific recipes for each meal of the day. I followed the instructions closely, dividing the finished recipe in half for our individual plates. We felt terrific and thought the diet was wonderful—we never felt hungry!

But when we realized we were gaining weight, not losing it, I checked the recipes again. There, in fine print, was "Serves 6."

— BARBARA CURRIE

My daughter couldn't muster the willpower to lose unwanted kilos. One day, watching a svelte friend walking up our driveway, she lamented, "Linda's so skinny it makes me sick."

"If it bothers you," I suggested gently, "why don't you do something about it?"

"Good idea, Mom," she replied. Turning to her friend, she called out, "Hey, Linda, have a piece of chocolate cake."

— DORIS E. FLETCHER

ANXIETY CLINIC

ONE THING

THE OTHER

While a woman is keeping vigil beside her husband's deathbed, he says to her, "Before I die, I have something to confess to you."

"Shh, not now," she replies.

"But I need to tell you: I cheated on you," he admits.

"Yes, I know," she replies.

"I need to clear my conscience before I die…"

"Shh," she counters. "Just lie back and let the poison work."

— DIANNE GREENLAY

At the age of 64 Uncle Wally had to have a wisdom tooth removed. What was supposed to be a simple extraction proved to be a four-hour ordeal.

As my uncle, pale and a bit unsteady, prepared to leave the dentist's office, the attractive young receptionist expressed her concern. "Would you like me to walk home with you?" she asked.

He considered the offer carefully. "Not today," he said, "but maybe sometime when I'm feeling better."

— WILLIAM J. HARTMAN

As a dental hygienist, I had a family come in one day for cleanings. By the time I was ready for the father, he informed me I had a lot to live up to. His six-year-old daughter kept commenting that a "very smart lady" was cleaning their teeth today.

The father said she kept going on about my intelligence until he finally had to ask what she was basing her opinion on.

The little girl replied, "I heard people in here call her the Dental High Genius."

— BARBARA GIVENS

My sister decided to go on a diet, and that first evening she phoned me. I could tell her mouth was full, so I asked her what she was eating.

"A cupcake," she mumbled. "I just got on the scale, and it read 149½ pounds. I decided that was no place to start a diet, so I'm rounding it off to 150."

— SHARON E. ASKEGREEN

In an attempt to keep our rowdy coed health class focused, our teacher was giving us random facts about the body's ability to burn calories. "Kissing," she said, "can burn up to 45 calories."

"Hey," a boy called out, "any of you girls want to lose weight?"

— STEPHANIE FEIST

When my wife sent our bills to the insurance company, she accidentally enclosed a veterinary bill for our dog, Duster. The vet's statement was returned with this note: "Sorry, Duster. You're barking up the wrong tree."

— WILLIAM STARBODY

When my wife was about to have our first baby, we brought a tape recorder to the delivery ward to capture the sounds of the birth, the baby's first cry and our doctor's voice saying, "It's a boy!" or "It's a girl!" We intended to use the tape as a fun message on our answering machine to help announce the birth to friends and relatives.

My wife's labour went relatively smoothly and, when it seemed appropriate, I inserted the blank tape and began recording. Shortly thereafter, our baby was born and we all heard the first cry. The doctor held up the baby and, with tape rolling, loudly proclaimed, "Wow, will you look at the scrotum on him!"

— R. FISHMAN

sign language

A navy dentist's licence plate:

"TOP GUM."

Our local newspaper ran several stories about a study that tied male obesity to a virus. One evening my brother came in exhausted from a long day at work. "Did you read the paper?" he asked.

"I won't be going in to work tomorrow. I'm calling in fat."

— MARY C. LEANDERTS

Mother and I were discussing our mutual weight problem one evening, when I challenged her to a contest. If I lost the most weight in the next month, I wouldn't have to pay her the $6 that I owed her. If she lost the most weight, I would have to pay up. Anything for an incentive!

"All right," said Mother happily. "But let's wait two weeks before we start. There are some things I have to eat first."

— IRENE LANE

While I waited in our high school health office, I overheard another student explain to the nurse how badly his eyes hurt. "My head is spinning," he moaned, "and I can't see straight."

After listening to his ailments for ten minutes, even the often-skeptical nurse was convinced. "I am calling your mother to come pick you up," she said, dialing the telephone.

"Oh, that won't be necessary," the student instantly replied. "I can drive myself home."

— LEEANNE BATEMAN

"Chest pains? Have you tried loosening your belt?"

The new phone book arrived with a handy blank emergency-number form attached to the front page. I guess everyone's notion of an emergency is different. The categories for phone numbers were listed in this order: 1. Pizza, 2. Takeout Restaurants, 3. Taxi, 4. Poison Control, 5. Doctor.

— MEGHAN HUNSAKER

As an X-ray technician, I always ask female patients of childbearing age if they are pregnant before I proceed. I've received many responses, but my favourite was when a young woman looked at me with a straight face and replied, "If I am, it isn't mine!"

— KAYNE DARRELL

Customer-service reps repeat the same tired phrases so often that we can do the job in our sleep. We hear a beep telling us a customer's on the line, and we're on. I never knew how this humdrum routine affected us until a co-worker had heart surgery.

She was coming to, following her operation, when she heard the beep of the heart monitor. In her anaesthetized stupor, she groggily said, "This is Sue. Can I help you?"

— S.B.

The contest was simple: Which department in the hospital where I worked as a nurse could create the best Christmas decorations? While they didn't win first prize, the members of the proctology department did receive high honours with their distinctive sign, "Christmas is a good time to look up old friends."

— PAT INGELS

A customer walked into my pharmacy asking for a particular nasal spray. "You know, that brand is very addicting," I warned her. "If it's used for a prolonged period of time, your congestion can come back worse than before, prompting even further use."

"That's ridiculous," scoffed the woman. "I've been using it every day for years."

— CHARLES FREED

In hindsight I should have been more specific. I was visiting my doctor as part of a checkup after surgery.

"When can I resume regular activities?"

I asked.

He blushed slightly.

"You mean like sex?"

"Actually, I was thinking of vacuuming."

PATTY KEBERLE

One evening I was commenting on my bad exercise habits and tight clothes. Whenever I criticize myself, my four-year-old son always has something charming to say.

Using a new word this time, he smiled and said, "Oh, no, Mommy! You look flabulous!"

— JILLYNNE M. BAILEY

The orthodontist and his assistants were removing my ten-year-old son's dental appliance. Because it was cemented to his upper teeth, they had to use some pressure to release it. When it finally popped out, three of his baby teeth came out as well.

My boy was horrified when he saw the gaps. "Well," he said to the staff gathered around him, "who do I see about getting dentures?"

— KIM JAWORSKI

At the hospital where my wife is an X-ray technician, patients hit the "call light" to get a nurse's attention. To underscore the need to respond rapidly, a snappy catchphrase was created and printed on buttons.

But the campaign came to an abrupt halt. The staff feared that patients might misunderstand if nurses entered their rooms wearing a button that read "Go to the Light!"

— JAMES PARK

The voice-dictation program a physician friend of mine purchased for his computer often misinterpreted words. Once, my friend dictated, "Recommend CAT scan if symptoms persist."

The program typed out, "Recommend casket if symptoms persist."

— JASON SUROW

At the salon where I was a hairstylist, the conversation turned to smoking and its ill effects on our bodies. Even after hearing one woman reveal that she had survived cancer of the uterus, another customer lit up a cigarette. "Aren't you afraid of getting cancer of the uterus?" she was asked.

"Oh, no, dear," the smoker replied, without batting an eye. "I don't inhale that far down."

— MARY ARTERBURN

When I was on duty in the maternity ward, one of my patients was a woman who was having her first child. Because of her medical situation, she had to undergo a Caesarean section. After the operation, I handed her the newborn child and declared, "Congratulations! You have a healthy baby boy."

Still a little groggy from the anesthesia, she responded, "That's great. What's his name?"

— WENDY REYNOLDS

My friend read her son's horoscope and thought it quite appropriate. "You've spent the last few weeks looking for escape," it said. "But now it's time to get on with your life."

She had just given birth to him that morning.

— SUYEE KAOR

Traditional Chinese drugstores are always filled with bizarre remedies for everyday ailments. So while travelling in the Far East, I couldn't resist going into a drugstore to look around. There were rows and rows of jars filled with dried herbs, powders, and exotic oils. But one jar really caught my attention. The label said it was a guaranteed cure for stomach ache.

The jar was filled with chocolate chip cookies.

— FLORANTE F. FLORES

Timeless Humour from the '70s

Several months ago, my daughter and I had similar virus symptoms. She decided to consult a doctor so as not to lose any more time from her job.

"I'll see the doctor," she said, "and then tell you what's wrong with us."

The next day she called to say, "Guess what, Mom. We're pregnant!"

— HOPE SULLIVAN

"The good news is we're pretty sure we're going to name this disease after you."

As a dentist, I recently tried out a new chocolate-flavoured pumice paste on my patients. No one liked it except for a six-year-old boy. While I polished his teeth, he continued to smile and lick his lips. "You must really like this new flavour," I said.

"Yep," he replied, nodding with satisfaction. "It tastes just like the time I dropped my candy bar in the sandbox."

— JEFFERY K. LEIBFORTH

The commercial for Viagra with the middle-aged men running happily through the streets to the song "We Are the Champions" came on while my husband and ten-year-old son were watching TV. After seeing these jubilant men kicking up their heels, my son turned to his father and said, "Dad, would you be that happy if you got rid of your heartburn?"

— GRACE COTTON

The clinic where I work promoted a co-worker to head the payroll department, or Payment Management Systems. The title on his door now reads "PMS Director."

— MARILYN PEARSALL

My 60-year-old mother-in-law, completing two years of wearing orthodontic braces, was in the office having them adjusted. As she sat in one of the waiting-room chairs, the teenager next to her looked at my mother-in-law in astonishment. "Wow," he said. "How long have you been coming here?"

— DAVID REEVES

After my wife had a sonogram, I asked my mother-in-law to guess the sex of the twins her daughter was carrying.

"Two boys," she said.

I shook my head.

"It must be two girls," she offered.

Again I told her no.

"Well, then," she asked, "what are they?"

— FRANK WATESKA

"I'm prescribing a squiggly line, two slanted loops, and something that looks like a P or a J."

Timeless Humour from the '70s

Just before Easter I remarked to my husband that, with the children grown and away from home, this was the first year that we hadn't dyed eggs and had an Easter-egg hunt. "That's all right, honey," he said. "We can just hide each other's vitamin pills."

— MRS. ROBERT S. KING

One of our regular patients at the counselling centre had complained of hearing voices. So the doctor gave him medication. When the man came back for a follow-up, I asked if the prescription helped.

"I don't know," he said. "Now I'm having hallucinations."

"Well, make sure to tell the doctor so he can change the medication."

"I don't know if I want to change," he joked. "Finally, I get to see who's talking to me."

— BARBARA ALLEN

All
Creatures
Great and Small

Dogs, cats and countless common critters are all part of our everyday lives. Here's the funny stuff that happens when animals cross paths with us humans.

"I'd get so much more done if only I could get by
on seventeen hours of sleep."

A man is standing on the curb, getting ready to cross the street. As soon as he steps down onto the pavement, a car comes screaming straight at him. The man picks up speed, but so does the car. So the man turns around and heads back, but the car changes lanes and keeps coming. Now the vehicle is so close and the pedestrian is so scared that he freezes in the middle of the intersection. The car closes in on him—then swerves at the last possible moment and screeches to a halt.

The driver rolls down the window. Behind the wheel is a squirrel. "See," sneers the squirrel, "it's not as easy as it looks, is it?"

One beautiful morning, my husband and I decided to go for a drive in the country. Unfortunately, no matter which road we took, we kept seeing dead possums lying on the shoulder.

After several kilometres of this, my husband turned to me and said, "Now I think I know the answer to the age-old question 'Why did the chicken cross the road?'"

"What is it?" I asked.

"Well," he replied, "it was to prove to the possums that it could be done."

— JUANITA PAGE

My father's secretary was visibly distraught one morning when she arrived at the office and explained that her children's parrot had escaped from his cage and flown out an open window. Of all the dangers the tame bird would face outdoors alone, she seemed most concerned about what would happen if the bird started talking.

Confused, my father asked what the parrot could say.

"Well," she explained, "he mostly says, 'Here, kitty, kitty.'"

— TERRY WALKER

A man walks into a pub with a salamander on his shoulder and takes a seat at the bar.

"Nice pet," the bartender says. "What's his name?"

"I call him Tiny," the man replies.

"Why's that?"

"Because he's my newt."

— BARNEY WELLS

In good weather, my friend Mark always let his yellow-naped Amazon parrot, Nicky, sit on the balcony of his tenth-floor apartment. One morning, Nicky flew away, much to Mark's dismay. He searched and called for the bird, with no luck.

The next day when Mark returned from work, the phone rang. "Is this Mark?" The caller asked. "You're going to think this is crazy, but there's a bird outside on my balcony saying, 'Hello, this is Mark.' Then it recites this phone number and says, 'I can't come to the phone right now, but if you will leave a message at the tone, I will call you back.'"

Nicky's cage had been kept in the same room as Mark's answering machine.

— ANNE R. NEILSON

sign language

I was editing classified ads for a small-town newspaper when a man called to place an ad. "It should read," he said, "'Free to good home. Golden retriever. Will eat anything, loves children.'"

— ELLEN YOUNG

At a workshop on dog temperament, the instructor noted that a test for a canine's disposition was for an owner to fall down and act hurt. A dog with poor temperament would try to bite the person, whereas a good dog would lick his owner's face or show concern.

Once, while eating pizza in the living room, I decided to try out this theory on my two dogs. I stood up, clutched my heart, let out a scream and collapsed on the floor.

The dogs looked at me, glanced at each other and raced to the coffee table for my pizza.

— SUSAN MOTTICE

Once while riding the bus to work, I noticed a man at a stop enjoying a cup of coffee. As we approached the stop, he finished drinking and set the cup on the ground. This negligence surprised me, since it seemed to be a good ceramic cup.

Days later I saw the same man again drinking his coffee at the bus stop. Once again, he placed the cup on the grass before boarding. When the bus pulled away, I looked back in time to see a dog carefully carrying the cup in his mouth as he headed for home.

— VALERIE A. HUEBNER

My neighbour's son picked up a stray dog and named it Sam. Some time later, I was having coffee at their house and inquired about Sam.

"Oh, the dog is fine," my neighbour said. "She had puppies, and so we fixed the problem. Now we call her Sam Spayed."

— JUDY CHRISTENSEN

A snake slithers into a bar and the bartender says, "Sorry, buddy. I can't serve you."

"Why not?" the snake asks.

"Because you can't hold your liquor."

— LYNDELL LEATHERMAN

When my daughter and I caught only one perch on our fishing trip—not enough for even a modest lunch—we decided to feed it to her two cats. She put our catch in their dish and watched as the two pampered pets sniffed at the fish but refused to eat it.

Thinking quickly, my daughter then picked up the dish, walked over to the electric can opener, ran it for a few seconds, then put the fish back down. The cats dug right in.

— SUSAN WARD

"I wasn't chewing it, I was editing it."

You know why fish are so thin? They eat fish.

— JERRY SEINFELD

If dogs could talk, it would take a lot of fun out of owning one.

— ANDREW A. ROONEY, from "Not That You Asked" (Random House)

I feel strongly that the visual arts are of vast importance. Of course I could be prejudiced. I am a visual art.

— KERMIT THE FROG

Does it ever amaze and delight you that of all the places in the world—cold grassy nests under hedgerows, warm patches of sun on a carpet—the cat chooses to sit on your lap?

— NEVADA BARR, Seeking Enlightenment (Putnam)

A racehorse is an animal that can take several thousand people for a ride at the same time.

— MARJORIE JOHNSON

The cat could very well be man's best friend but would never stoop to admitting it.

— DOUG LARSON, United Feature Syndicate

The turkey is living proof that an animal can survive with no intelligence at all.

— HARVEY D. COMSTOCK

A truck ran a red light, almost sideswiping our car. As my husband veered away, he threw his arm across me, protecting me from a possible collision. I was ready to plant a big kiss on my hero's cheek when he apologized.

In his haste, he admitted, he had forgotten it was me in the front seat and not our black Labrador, Checkers.

— APRIL COLE

I worked at a boarding kennel where people leave their dogs and cats while on vacation. One morning I had taken a cat out of his cage, and after playing with him and replenishing his food and water, I put him back in.

A few minutes later, I was surprised to see the feline at my feet, since the cage doors lock automatically when they're shut. I couldn't figure out how the cat escaped, until I bent down to pick him up and spied his nametag: "Houdini."

— BARBARA ROHRSSEN

On a recent trip to the post office, I took a few minutes to read the notices posted on the public bulletin board in the lobby. One in particular caught my eye.

It read "Lost in post-office parking lot, small boa constrictor, family pet, will not attack. Reward."

Below the notice someone had written, in what appeared to be very shaky handwriting: "Please, would you mind posting another notice when you find your boa? Thank you."

— SUSAN ESBENSEN

In his younger days our golden retriever, Catcher, often ran away when he had the chance. His veterinarian's office was about a kilometre down the road, and Catcher would usually end up there. The office staff knew him well and would call me to come pick him up.

One day I called the vet to make an appointment for Catcher's yearly vaccine. "Will you be bringing him?" asked the receptionist. "Or will he be coming on his own?"

— LAURA STASZAK

"How can I ever live up to all this hype?"

"Have someone force one of these down your throat every six hours."

My son is an avid listener to our city's police frequency, and he leaves the scanner on all the time. One morning while making his bed, I heard the dispatcher say, "Car 34, there is a metre-long boa constrictor in a front yard. The resident wants a policeman to remove it."

There was a long pause, then some static. Slowly, a voice said, "We can't get the car started."

— JANET R. SMITH

Living in a household with eight indoor cats requires buying large amounts of kitty litter, which I usually get in 10-kilogram bags—50 kilograms at a time. When I was going to be out of town for a week, I decided to go to the supermarket to stock up. As my husband and I both pushed shopping carts, each loaded with five large bags of litter, a man looked at our purchases and queried, "Bengal or Siberian?"

— JUDY J. HAGG

Sitting with her cat, an old woman was polishing a dusty lamp she had found in the attic, when a genie popped out and offered her three wishes. Thinking quickly, she said, "I'd like to be rich. I'd like to be young and I'd like my cat to turn into a handsome prince." There was a puff of smoke and the woman found herself young and surrounded by riches. The cat had gone; a gorgeous prince stood beside her, holding out his arms. She melted into his embrace. "Now," he whispered, "aren't you sorry you had me neutered?"

When a rattlesnake got loose in the second-floor hall of the science building at my university, it created quite a furor. Fortunately, one of the professors was an expert on snakes. An agitated student ran to fetch him, urging him to come quickly, as a dangerous snake was loose, terrorizing everyone in the building.

The professor leisurely strolled out into the hall, examined the snake from head to tail, and calmly returned to his office. "It's not one of mine," he said, and closed the door.

— CARL ADKINS

sign language

From the classifieds:

"Ferret, likes kids, nice pet, but chewed the guinea pig's ear off. Also, partially deaf guinea pig."

— BILL PORTER

At the end of a visit to Amsterdam, a friend borrowed an old suitcase from his hosts to carry home his souvenirs. At the airport, however, a customs officer subjected our friend's luggage to a thorough search and even sent for a drug-sniffing dog. Sure enough, the dog entered the area, headed straight for the borrowed bag and went into a frenzy. The customs officer now intensified his search, but ultimately he found nothing.

After arriving home, the young man immediately phoned his hosts and told them how puzzled he'd been by the dog's behaviour.

"Perhaps," the owner of the suitcase said, "it was because that's the bag our cat usually sleeps in."

— J. RIETDIJK-SHEPHERD

I like hunting fossils, a hobby that isn't exactly my wife's favourite. On one excursion, I found the petrified bones of a squirrel-like mammal. When I brought them home and told my wife what they were, she squelched my excitement.

"I've heard of many a squirrel bringing a nut home," she remarked, "but this is the first time I've heard of a nut bringing a squirrel home."

— J. H. HILL

One night while I was cat-sitting my daughter's indoor feline, it escaped outside. When it failed to return the following morning, I found the beast clinging to a branch about 10 metres up in a tree. Unable to lure it down, I called the fire department.

"We don't do that anymore," the woman dispatcher said. When I persisted, she was polite but firm. "The cat will come down when it gets hungry enough."

"How do you know that?" I asked.

"Have you ever seen a cat skeleton in a tree?" she said.

Two hours later the cat was back, looking for breakfast.

— TERRY CHRISTIANSEN

The drive-up window at the bank where I'm a teller has an outside drawer to accept customer transactions. A woman once drove up with her dog in the front passenger seat, and the pet eagerly jumped over onto the driver's lap when the car reached my window. He looked excited to see me.

"Your dog is so friendly!" I said to the owner.

"He thinks he's at McDonald's," she replied.

— MARILYN BOURDEAU

I always scoffed when my sister insisted that our three dogs are computer literate. Then one day when I was signing on to AOL, I noticed that when the "welcome" voice came on, the dogs immediately settled down. Later, when they heard the "goodbye" sign-off, all three dogs rushed to the door expecting to be walked.

— MARGUERITE CANTINE

sign language

In the classifieds:

"Homing pigeons free to good home. Must live far, far away."

— CHRISTY SELTER

Finding Soda

▶ BY BILL RICHARDSON

Soda, whose mother was a careless Himalayan and whose father was a passing rogue, went out Monday evening, just after supper. I saw him round about ten, walking shoulder to shoulder down the alley with a couple of his homies, a fat black Manx of easy disposition and a bellicose tortoiseshell with well-aerated ears. They had a ready-to-rumble look. Where they were going and what they had in mind, I didn't care to know.

Tuesday morning, no sign of Soda. A spontaneous sleepover with his buddies? Maybe. It happens, but rarely. Usually I wake to the thud of him hitting my chest. He is the first thing I see when I open my eyes—his hot pink nose, his cool blue peepers—and I'm the last thing he sees when he drifts into diurnal dreaming. It's a bond. Absence is aberrant. Worry stirred in its dark corner. I told it to hush. "For heaven's sake," I said to myself, "he's a cat. This is what cats do. Vanish and reappear. He's fine, just fine."

The day evolved. I walked to the corner store, making a studied point of not fearing the worst. I looked up, rather than at the pavement over which so many cars speed. I surveyed his favourite rooftops, alert for his signatory silhouette. No sign. A disappointment. On the way home, I allowed my eyes to drift to the asphalt. No sign. A relief.

Noon gonged. I quizzed the other animals.

"Where's Soda?" I asked his sister, Trout. She glanced at me without even feigned interest, then returned to the business of supplementing her furball saving account.

The dogs were no more forthcoming. If they were receiving the psychic signals of distress that so often figure in Disney movies and that lead to much barking and carrying on—"This way, master, this way!"—they weren't letting on. As hunters, it must be said, they're a dead loss. They were apparently bred to herd canapés.

Worry stirred. I let it.

Time and again, as day waned, I went to the porch and unleashed my vast repertoire of "puss come home" noises. Dusk came. I took my act on the road, trawling the lanes and by-ways, shaking a tin of catnip treats, maraca-style, a low-rent Ricky Ricardo. I chirped and cooed and trilled soprano halloos.

"Puss-puss-puss-puss-puss-cat!"

Nothing.

I went home. I found a photo and a black felt marker. I got to work.

"Lost cat, huh?" said the guy at the all-night grocery where I stopped for tape. "Saw one get run down the other day."

The weather was no more accommodating than the clerks. The wind rose. The rain poured. Undaunted by storm and glade, and mindless of bylaws prohibiting the use of lamp standards for such purposes,

... been to London to visit the queen

I postered the neigh-bourhood. A girl on the stroll stopped to see what I was about.

"Awww," she said, "you've lost your pussy."

I gave her a look that said, "Just don't go there."

"You know what I do when my cat goes missing?"

"What?" I said.

"I pray, sort of. I get a picture of her in my mind. I think of her being safe and in one piece. I surround her with light. And I tell her to come home."

"That works?"

"Seems to. You want me to try it for you?"

"Sure," I said. What could it hurt? She looked hard at the picture. She closed her eyes, just for a few seconds.

"Okay," she said. "Take care, now."

"You too," I said, and we went about our respective business.

Soda was on the bed when I came home. He answered my many inquiries with a look of bland disregard. No explanation was forthcoming, not even a "been to London to visit the queen."

In the morning, I went around and removed the posters, picked up the ones the rain had washed down, which was most of them. REWARD! I'd written, in big black letters. I think I know who should get it. If ever our paths cross again, I'll do the right thing. In the meantime, I'll remember her face. I'll surround it with light. I'll imagine her safe. ▲

I saw two dogs walk over to a parking meter. One said to the other, **"How do you like that? Pay toilets."**

My father-in-law had prostate surgery. We brought him to the hospital at 7:30 a.m., and he was operated on at eight. We were amazed when the hospital called at noon to tell us he could go home. Two months later our beagle, Bo, also had prostate surgery. When I brought him in, I asked the veterinarian what time I should pick him up. The vet told me Bo would remain overnight. "Overnight?" I said. "My father-in-law came home the same day." The vet looked at me and said, "Bo's not on Medicare."

— CLYDE DYAR

An adorable little girl walked into my pet shop and asked, "Excuse me, do you have any rabbits here?"

"I do," I answered, and leaning down to her eye level I asked, "Did you want a white rabbit or would you rather have a soft, fuzzy black rabbit?"

She shrugged. "I don't think my python really cares."

— CINDY PATTERSON

Each morning at 5:30, I take my Lhasa Apso, Maxwell, for a walk. He has the bad habit of picking up bits of paper or other trash along the way. When he does, I command him to "drop it," and he usually complies. One morning, though, he absolutely refused to drop a piece of litter. So I told him to "sit" and then approached him to see what his treasure was. It was a $10 bill.

— ELSA BOGGS

Lost in the woods, a hiker spends two days wandering around with no food. Finally, he spots a bald eagle, hits the bird with a big rock and eats it. A park ranger stumbles on the scene and arrests the man for killing an endangered species. In court, the hiker explains that he was on the edge of starvation and had no choice.

"Considering the circumstances, I find you not guilty," says the judge. "But I have to ask—what did the eagle taste like?"

"Well, Your Honour," the hiker replies, "it tasted like a cross between a whooping crane and a spotted owl."

— ERIC FLEMING

A French poodle and a collie were walking down the street. The poodle turned to the collie and complained, "My life is such a mess. My owner is mean, my girlfriend is having an affair with a German shepherd and I'm as nervous as a cat."

"Why don't you go see a psychiatrist?" asked the collie.

"I can't," replied the poodle. "I'm not allowed on the couch."

— JOHN W. GAMBA

"I'll negotiate, Stan, but I won't beg."

We visited our newly married daughter, who was preparing her first Thanksgiving dinner. I noticed the turkey thawing in the kitchen sink with a dish drainer inverted over the bird. I asked why a drainer covered the turkey.

Our daughter turned to my wife and said, "Mom, you always did it that way." "Yes," my wife replied, "but you don't have a cat!"

— A. C. STOKERS, JR.

My friend's husband, Ray, is a police officer and enjoys sharing the excuses people use when stopped for speeding. One day, however, the tables were turned. Ray maintains an aquarium of exotic fish, and a prized specimen had threatened to turn belly up. The off-duty officer called a pet store, and they advised him to immediately purchase a special additive that would correct the water's pH.

Ray and his wife jumped into the car and rushed to the store. A police officer pulled them over. "Go ahead," Ray's wife said. "Tell him you've got a sick fish!"

— DEBRA McVEY

"I could swear that box of frozen fish sticks was here a minute ago."

A couple of dog owners are arguing about whose dog is smarter. "My dog is so smart," says the first owner, "that every morning he waits for the paper boy to come around. He tips the kid and then brings the newspaper to me, along with my morning coffee."

"I know," says the second owner.

"How do you know?"

"My dog told me."

"Nice dog. What's its name?" I asked my friend's 10-year-old son.

"Bob," he said.

"And your cat?"

"Bob."

"How do you keep them straight?"

"Well one is Bob Cat and the other is Bob Barker," the boy answered.

"Tell him your rabbit's name," his father suggested.

The kid smiled and said, "Dennis Hopper."

— MIKE HARRELSON

After our dog died, my parents had her cremated, and they placed the ashes in a special box on the fireplace mantel. One day the boy next door came over to play and noticed the fancy container. "What's in the box?" he asked.

"That's our dog," my mom replied.

"Oh," the boy simply said. A minute later he remarked, "He's awfully quiet, isn't he?"

I was at a yard sale one day and saw a box marked "Electronic cat and dog call—guaranteed to work." I looked inside and was amused to see an electric can opener.

— BRET SOHL

257

Enclosed with the heartworm pills my friend received from a veterinarian was a sheet of red heart stickers to place on a calendar as a reminder to give her pet the medication. She attached these stickers to her kitchen calendar, marking the first Saturday of every month. When her husband noticed the hearts, he grinned from ear to ear, turned to his wife and asked, "Do you have something special in mind for these days?"

— MARY LOUISE RUSSO

A friend of mine is an officer with the police department's canine division. One evening, the officer was dispatched to the scene of a possible burglary, where he discovered the back door of a building ajar. He let the dog out of his patrol car and commanded it to enter and seek.

Jumping from the back seat, the dog headed for the building. After lunging through the doorway, the dog froze and backed out. My friend was puzzled until he investigated further. Then he noticed the sign on the building: "Veterinarian's Office."

— ELIZABETH BENNETT

Snake 1:
Are we poisonous?

Snake 2:
I don't know. Why?

Snake 1:
I just bit my lip.

FAITH LACKEY

"Maybe aerobics wasn't such a good idea."

My niece bought her five-year-old daughter, Kayleigh, a hamster. One day he escaped from his cage. The family turned the house upside down and finally found him. Several weeks later, while Kayleigh was at school, he escaped from his cage again. My niece searched frantically but never found the critter. Hoping to make the loss less painful for Kayleigh, my niece took the cage out of her room.

When Kayleigh came home from school that afternoon, she climbed into her mother's lap. "We've got a serious problem," she announced. "Not only is my hamster gone again, but this time he took the cage."

— PATSY STRINGER

When my kid sister and my mother bought three exotic birds, they named them This, That and The Other. After a few months, This died, and they buried the bird in the backyard. A few more months later, The Other passed away and they buried it next to This. Then the last bird died.

Mom called my sister and tearfully announced, "Well, I guess that's That."

— GLORIA VITULANO

"You have just one more wish. Are you sure you want *another* belly rub?"

The Great Hamster Caper

▶ BY JIM GROVE

Friday. The weekend beckoned. But when I walked through the door, I heard a traumatized child. Amy, our eight-year-old, was sobbing. Hammie the hamster was inside our bathroom wall.

One major complicating factor: Hammie was not ours. He was the class hamster. He had come to our house as part of the great second-grade pet cultural exchange, having survived more than a dozen home visits with the kids in Mrs. Blackwell's class. A hamster with peer pressure attached.

Now, though he had been in our house only a few hours, Hammie was where no paw should tread—on and under pipes, stirring up drywall dust, munching on whatever looked tasty.

As great tragedies often do, this one started with a small act of kindness. Amy had uncaged Hammie in the bathroom for an early evening romp as she guarded the door. Unfortunately there was the teeniest hole where the sink cabinet meets the wall. We'd never known it was there, but to Hammie, it must have looked like a highway. A quick sprint and he was gone: down the linoleum, over the baseboard and into the wall. And now the little squirt's telltale scratching seemed to move in rhythm to the sobs outside.

Midnight. The family was fast asleep while I maintained the hamster watch. Poking my finger into the hole, I felt a hamster paw. I bent over and, startled, gazed right into Hammie's eyes. He seemed to be smiling.

At first I thought that by baiting Hammie with some hamster fast food—carrots, apple, a huge piece of lettuce—the little guy would pitter-patter back into the bathroom. He went for the lettuce. Unfortunately, he took it right back into the hole.

After a restless night we swore one another to a tell-and-you-die oath. We had 48 hours to capture Hammie. It would be bad enough without kick-starting the second-grade rumour mill.

Saturday afternoon. The plan of attack: Lure Hammie into the Mice Cube, a small plastic rectangle. Bait it, and the hungry rodent goes in the trapdoor, but he doesn't come out.

This night brought less sleep—more scratch, scratch, scratch—no Hammie. I guessed he still had plenty of lettuce.

Sunday morning. We prayed for Hammie. Amy said that under no circumstances would she ever attend school again if we didn't catch him. The pressure was on.

No pint-size rodent would ruin my daughter's reputation

A key to successful parenting, I'm told, is having a complete support network. A visit to Dad's secret weapon, The Pet Store Guy, now seemed crucial.

When I told him of our crisis, he barely batted an eye. Clearly he knew a lot about hamster psychology. In his opinion, Hammie was either a) on the lam and loving it, b) playing a game of catch-me-if-you-can or c) lost in the wall. But he would come out. Hunger would win.

The Pet Store Guy told me to take a bucket and place an apple inside. Douse a towel in apple juice. Put the bucket a few hamster steps from the hole and drape the towel over the side—a kind of hamster ramp, if you will. Just enough towel should stick into the bucket to allow the hamster to fall in but not crawl out.

Bedtime Sunday. The trap was in place, but the bathroom wall was eerily quiet. Was Hammie alive in there? I sat in a chair, feeling defeated. I had been beaten by a pint-size rodent.

Then, in what seemed like one of those slow-motion *Chariots of Fire* moments, my hamster-loving, sweet-hearted girl was motioning to us from the door. Amy had heard the hamster drop in the bucket.

She looked first. Her anxiety as she peered over the edge of the bucket, followed by the sheer euphoria of her realization that he was there, was indescribable. My wife and I savoured every second, as a living page of our family journal unfolded.

Hugs and kisses. Hero Dad. Hero Mom. Hamster high-fives.

There are moments in your children's lives when your heart bounces through your throat—the first step, the first bike ride, the first sentence read, the first hamster drop.

I never did win a stuffed animal at the carnival for my sweetheart. But now I know how it feels. ▲

My father and a friend were talking about the doors they had installed so their animals could let themselves in and out of the house. My dad asked his friend, who had two massive Great Danes, "Aren't you afraid that somebody might crawl through the dogs' door and steal something?"

"If you saw an opening that big," said his friend "would you crawl through it?"

— HORST JENKINS

Squirrels had overrun three churches in town. After much prayer, the elders of the first church determined that the animals were pre-destined to be there. Who were they to inter-fere with God's will? they reasoned. Soon, the squirrels multiplied.

The elders of the sec-ond church, deciding they could not harm any of God's creatures, humanely trapped the squirrels and set them free outside of town. Three days later, the squirrels were back.

It was only the third church that succeeded in keeping the pests away. The elders baptized the squirrels and registered them as members of the church. Now they only see them on Christmas and Easter.

— E. T. THOMPSON

"It's my way of showing support."

I bought my sons a pet rabbit after they promised they would take care of it. As expected, I ended up with the responsibility. Exasperated, one evening I said, "How many times do you think that rabbit would have died if I hadn't looked after it?"

"Once," my 12-year-old son replied.

— L. BARRY PARSONS

One day while we were doing yard work, my nine-year-old daughter found a baby snake, and I encouraged her to catch it and put it in a jar. Later she found a huge bullfrog and got another jar to put it in.

After dark I told her she would have to set them free. With the frog in one hand and the snake in the other, she started down the porch steps. Suddenly she screamed wildly, dropped both the snake and the frog, and ran into the house.

"What happened?" I asked, my heart thumping.

"Did you see that?" she replied. "That moth almost got me."

— CASSANDRA DALZELL

One afternoon I was walking on a trail with my newborn daughter, chatting to her about the scenery. When a man and his dog approached, I leaned into the baby carriage and said, "See the doggy?"

Suddenly I felt a little silly talking to my baby as if she understood me. But just as the man passed, I noticed he reached down, patted his dog and said, "See the baby?"

— CATHERINE REARDON

As I was walking through a variety store, I stopped at the pet department to look at some parakeets. In one cage a green bird lay on his back, one foot hooked oddly into the cage wire.

I was about to alert the saleswoman to the bird's plight when I noticed a sign taped to the cage: "No, I am not sick. No, I am not dead. No, my leg is not stuck in the cage. I just like to sleep this way."

— JOAN DEZEEUW

A hypnotist was visiting the aquarium during feeding time. "You know," the hypnotist said to the man feeding the fierce shark, "I could hypnotize that shark."

"You're crazy! He'll rip you limb from limb," the feeder said, laughing. "But, hey, if you're so brave, be my guest."

The hypnotist jumped in, swam to the shark and stared it in the eye for a full minute. The animal paused, blinked, and then tore into him. The bleeding man slowly made his way out of the tank.

"I thought you could hypnotize him," sneered the feeder.

"I did," the hypnotist said, holding his arm. "Now he thinks he's an alligator."

— JOHN CASON

My brother adopted a snake named Slinky, whose most disagreeable trait was eating live mice. Once I was pressed into going to the pet store to buy Slinky's dinner.

The worst part of this wasn't choosing the juiciest-looking creatures or turning down the clerk who wanted to sell me vitamins to ensure their longevity. The hardest part was carrying the poor things out in a box bearing the words "Thank you for giving me a home."

— JOANNE MITCHELL

sign language

In Motorola's employee ad publication, *Tradewinds*:

"Freshwater piranha fish— $4.50 each. Free to good home—one-legged duck named Betsy."

"How many times have I told you— No coffee after September!"

"Oh, yeah, like the stripes help."

One of the highlights of the freshman university biology class was the monthly feeding of a caged rattlesnake kept in the laboratory. One time, the entire class gathered around the cage and, in complete silence, watched as the feeding took place.

"I'm jealous of the snake," the instructor said. "I never get the class's undivided attention like this."

A student answered matter-of-factly, "You would if you could swallow a mouse."

— DIANE TALBOTT-MOSIER

Dave's parrot was always using bad language, so he asked the vet how he could stop it. "Every time the bird swears, put it in the freezer for 15 seconds," advised the vet.

The next time the parrot uttered an expletive, Dave did as the vet said. Then, feeling guilty, Dave opened the freezer.

Shivering, the parrot came out saying, "I'm sorry for all the bad language I've been using." Dave was astounded at the sudden change. Then the parrot said, "By the way, what did the chicken do?"

— PAUL IRWIN

My sister-in-law, a truck driver, had decided to get a dog for protection. As she inspected a likely candidate, the trainer told her, "He doesn't like men."

Perfect, my sister-in-law thought, and took the dog.

Then one day she was approached by two men in a parking lot, and she watched to see how her canine bodyguard would react. Soon it became clear that the trainer wasn't kidding. As the men got closer, the dog ran under the nearest car.

— DANNY ARIAIL

The vet prescribed daily tablets for our geriatric cat, Tigger, and after several battles my husband devised a way to give her the medication. It involved wrapping Tigger in a towel, trapping her between his knees, forcing her mouth open and depositing the pill on the back of her tongue.

David was proud of his resourcefulness until one hectic session when he lost control of both cat and medicine. Tigger leaped out of his grasp, paused to inspect the tablet—which had rolled across the floor—and then ate it.

— MADI LEGERE

The Truth About Cats

JERRY H. SIMPSON, JR., AND LOUIS M. BUZEK

Broadway's longest-running show, *Cats,* brought audiences a romanticized view of these well-loved pets. Despite the elaborate costumes, popular songs and lively dancing, the play didn't quite capture the essence of our feline companions. Here is what *Cats* should have done:

▲ Audience members should have entered the theatre only to find their seats had been clawed and covered with fur.

▲ Sometimes the actors would have performed, but sometimes not—depending on their mood.

▲ The show would have had to stop several times to allow cast members to bathe and groom themselves.

▲ When certain audience members opened their playbills, cast members should have attempted to lie down on them.

▲ For no apparent reason, the actors should have randomly run to the lobby and then back to the stage at top speed. They then should have continued as if nothing had happened.

▲ A special audience member might have found a headless bird in his or her seat after intermission.

▲ Most of the final act should have consisted of the cast just staring at the audience.

Sounds of crashing and banging in the middle of the night sent me and my husband out to our garage. There we spotted three raccoons eating out of the cat dish. We shooed them away and went back to bed.

Later that week we were driving home and I noticed three fat raccoons ambling down the road. "Do you think those are the same ones we chased off?" I asked.

"Hard to tell," said my husband. "They were wearing masks."

— CHERIE KONVICKA

Our cat, Figaro, comes home between 10 or 11 at night to eat. If he's late, I turn on the carport light and call him until he appears.

One day my daughter was explaining to a friend where we live, and her friend said, "Is that anywhere near the house where the woman stands on her steps late at night and sings opera?"

— MARGARET MATHES

"He likes you!"

Jim strolls into the paint section of a hardware store and walks up to the assistant. "I'd like a pint of canary-coloured paint," he says.

"Sure," the clerk replies. "Mind if I ask what it's for?"

"My parakeet," says Jim. "See, I want to enter him in a canary contest. He sings so sweet I know he's sure to win."

"Well, you can't do that, man!" the assistant says. "The chemicals in the paint will almost certainly kill the poor thing!"

"No, they won't," Jim replies.

"Listen, buddy, I'll bet you ten bucks your parakeet dies if you try to paint him."

"You're on," says Jim.

Two days later he comes back looking very sheepish and lays $10 on the counter.

"So the paint killed him?"

"Indirectly," says Jim. "He seemed to handle the paint okay, but he didn't survive the sanding between coats."

As spring migration approached, two elderly vultures doubted they could make the trip north, so they decided to go by airplane.

When they checked their baggage, the attendant noticed that they were carrying two dead armadillos.

"Do you wish to check the armadillos through as luggage?" she asked.

"No, thanks," replied the vultures. "They're carrion."

— FRED BRICE

sign language

I was waiting in line at a government office one afternoon and noticed a hand-lettered sign that read

"Any child left unattended will be given a free kitten."

— JEANNE MAULTSKY

"Botox"

Law and Disorder

The law is on your side—except when it isn't. Amusing misdemeanours, comical cops and the lawyers we love to hate.

"We can have a long, expensive trial or you can save the taxpayers some money
and spin the Wheel of Justice."

The lady drove through a red light and was motioned over to the curb by a police officer on the corner. Finding no place to pull up, she drove on to the next corner and made a U-turn to come back. A second policeman, seeing this illegal manoeuvre, flagged her down.

As she drove by him, she called out, "Please wait your turn! There's one ahead of you down the street."

— F. A. APPLEGATE

Any time the alarm goes off after-hours at the municipal office where I work, the security company calls me at home and I have to go back and reset it. Late at night I got one of those calls. As I was getting ready to head out the door, my husband groggily said, "You're not going down there by yourself at this hour."

Just as I was thinking, How thoughtful of him, he added, "Better take the dog with you."

— RUTH RODDICK

Our friend, a lawyer, was defending a man accused of sending obscene literature through the mail. Deciding to base his case on whether the material really was obscene, he asked court officials if he could see a copy. So they mailed it to him.

— ALAN BAINBRIDGE

Early in my career as a judge, I conducted hearings for those involuntarily committed to a psychiatric hospital. On my first day, I asked a man at the door of the hospital, "Can you tell me where the courtroom is?"

"Why?" he asked.

"I'm the judge."

Pointing to the building, he whispered, "Don't tell them that. They'll never let you out."

— CHRISTOPHER DIETZ

I was once a legal secretary to a young law clerk who passed the bar exam on his third try. This fledgling attorney worked hard on his initial pleading, which should have read "Attorney at Law" at the top of the first page.

After I submitted the finished document for his review and signature, I was embarrassed when he pointed out a critical typing error. "Must you rub it in?" he asked.

I had typed: "Attorney at Last."

— DONNA GRIEVE

Having successfully passed all the written exams and physical requirements to join the Royal Canadian Mounted Police, my daughter was now being interviewed. One of the questions was, "What would you do if you were out on patrol with a male officer and he drove to a secluded area and started making advances to you?"

My daughter didn't hesitate, "Is this before or after I'm issued a pistol?" she replied.

She's now a Mountie.

— FLOYD KELLY

It was just another day at the DMV. I had taken a woman out on her driving test when a police cruiser came up behind us— sirens wailing, lights flashing.

"Was I speeding?" she asked the officer after both cars pulled over.

"No," said the officer. "But you are driving a stolen vehicle."

Smiling awkwardly, the woman turned to me. "Does this mean I failed my test?"

— NADINE CARMOUCHE

sign language

On a billboard ad for a safe company:

"If your stuff is stolen, it's not our vault."

— HELEN McDANIEL

Dad's pager beeped, summoning him to the hospital, where he is an anaesthetist. As he raced toward the hospital, a patrol car sped up behind him—lights flashing, siren blaring. So Dad hung his stethoscope out the window to signal that he was on an emergency call.

Within seconds came the policeman's response: a pair of handcuffs flapping outside the police car window.

— NICHOLAS BANKS

Our community still has teenage curfew laws. One night I was listening to my scanner when the police dispatcher said, "We have a report of a 14-year-old male out after curfew. The subject, wearing jeans and a grey sweatshirt, is six-foot-four and weighs 265 pounds."

After a long pause, one of the patrols replied, "As far as I'm concerned, he can go anywhere he wants."

— JAMES VAN HORN

My son, a police officer, stopped a woman for going 20 km over the speed limit. After he handed her a ticket, she asked him, "Don't you give out warnings?"

"Yes, ma'am," he replied. "They're all up and down the road. They say, 'Speed Limit 100.'"

— PATRICIA GREENLEE

After practising law for several months, I was talking with my brother, John, a doctor. "My work is so exciting," I said. "People come into my office, tell me their problems and pay me for my advice."

As older brothers will, John took the upper hand. "You know," he said, "in my work, people come into my office, tell me their problems, take off all their clothes and then pay me for my advice."

— DAVID PAUL REUWER

"Use POLITICAL PULL to get OUT?... POLITICAL PULL is how I got IN!"

Timeless Humour from the '50s

I was hauled before the judge for driving with expired licence plates. The judge listened attentively while I gave him a long, plausible explanation.

Then he said with great courtesy, "My dear sir, we are not blaming you—we're just fining you."

— DON F. CROWHURST

QUOTABLE QUOTES

I wanted a man who wouldn't stray so I'm dating a guy on house arrest.
— KIM BOVE

Trust in God— but tie your camel tight.
— PERSIAN PROVERB

I'm convinced that every boy, in his heart, would rather steal second base than an automobile.
— TOM CLARK

People say New Yorkers can't get along. Not true. I saw two New Yorkers, complete strangers, sharing a cab. One guy took the tires and the radio; the other guy took the engine.
— DAVID LETTERMAN

If you obey all the rules, you miss all the fun.
— KATHARINE HEPBURN, The Making of the African Queen (Knopf)

Lawyers are like beavers: They get in the middle of the stream and dam it up.
— DONALD RUMSFELD
in The Wall Street Journal

Once when I was lost I asked a police-man to help me find my parents. I said to him, "Do you think we'll ever find them?" He answered, "I don't know, kid. There are so many places they can hide."
— RODNEY DANGERFIELD

My husband, Joe, is a police officer in a small town. He receives many phone calls at home about his work and decided to get an answering machine to screen them, especially the threatening or harassing ones.

This is the greeting he prepared: "You have reached the home of a police officer. You have the right to remain silent. If you wish to give up this right, leave your message after the beep. Anything you say can, and probably will, be held against you."

The phone calls became much friendlier.

— SUSAN ESCUJURI

Three lawyers—an American, a Russian and a Czech—went bear hunting in Canada. After three weeks they hadn't returned, so the authorities got up a search party and went looking for them.

At the attorneys' campsite they found signs of a violent struggle. And then, to their horror, they spotted two well-fed bears not far from the camp. Fearing the worst, the rangers shot them both. After cutting open the female and finding the American and Russian inside, they concluded that, in true lawyer fashion, the Czech was in the male.

— LUKE BREWER

Timeless Humour from the **'50s**

A man entered a shop in London, Ontario, picked up a suitcase and fled with it. The manager pursued, calling a cop. They soon ran down the culprit.

"I don't know what made me do it," the man cried. "If only you won't arrest me, I'll be glad to pay for it."

The manager agreed, so they returned to the shop to complete the transaction. Once there, the customer grew cautious.

"As a matter of fact," he said, "this bag is a little better than I had in mind. I wonder if you could show me something cheaper?"

— THOMAS B. LOGUE

272

Late one night, a mugger wearing a ski mask jumped into the path of a well-dressed man and stuck a gun in his ribs. "Give me your money," he demanded.

Indignant, the affluent man responded, "You can't do this. I'm a Member of Parliament!"

"In that case," replied the mugger, "give me my money."

One snowy evening my brother, a police officer, stopped a car at a roadside check for drunk drivers. "Good evening, ma'am," he greeted the lady. "How are you this evening?"

"Fine, thank you," she replied.

My brother continued, "Anything to drink this evening?"

Surprised, the lady answered, "No, thank you."

— DONNA FILSHIE

Driving across the country, my husband and I were admiring one beautiful old Quebec town while stopped at a red light. We sat there taking in the elegant storefronts, the beautiful trees and other sights, not noticing that the light had turned green and back to red again.

It was then that a police officer walked up to the car and tapped on my husband's window. "That's all the colours we got here," he said.

— MARY SHORES

My cousin was behind the bakery's cash register one morning when a gunman burst in and demanded all the cash. As she nervously handed over the money, she noticed the rolls of coins in the back of the register. "Do you want the rolls too?" she asked.

"No," said the robber, waving his gun. "Just the money."

— PHIL LEMAN

I'm a police officer, and was training a new recruit when we were assigned to transport a prisoner to headquarters. The guy was verbally abusive, and my recruit seemed to be getting upset as he drove the squad car into an intersection and then quickly changed lanes. Another car almost hit us, so after a screech of brakes I shouted, "Don't you know that it's illegal to change lanes in the middle of an intersection?"

"I was already through the intersection, sir," the recruit replied.

"Maybe," came a shaky voice from the backseat. "But I wasn't!"

— TIM FILKINS

Dear CRA: I'm sending you this money because I cheated on my income tax and my conscience has been bothering me. If it doesn't stop, I'll send you the rest.

— ROY PATE

I picked up the phone one day in the law office where I worked, and the caller asked to speak with an attorney. I didn't recognize the voice, so I asked his name.

He gave it to me, saying our office had just served him with divorce papers. I couldn't place his name right away because this was a new case.

Eager to talk, he blurted out, "I'm the despondent!"

— CAROLINE NIED

Driving my car one afternoon, I rolled through a stop sign. I was pulled over by a police officer, who recognized me as his former English teacher.

"Mrs. Brown," he said, "those stop signs are periods, not commas."

— GAIL BROWN

sign language

A sign on the highway, featuring an illustration of a police car with lights flashing, reads

"If you drink and drive, we'll provide the chasers."

— JOANN BERNTSEN

As a lawyer, I am perhaps more used to being criticized than praised. At the end of a difficult case I once received a letter of thanks from a client that concluded, "I shall always think of you as a friend and not as a good lawyer."

— PETER WILKINSON

In honour of my brother's retirement from the police force, my sister-in-law decided to throw a surprise party for him. Plans made in secrecy over a two-month period included catering and entertainment decisions as well as travel accommodations for over 100 friends and relatives from around the country.

At the party, my brother stood up to address his guests. As he looked around the room at everyone who had secretly gathered on his behalf, he shook his head and said, "After 25 years on the police force, I finally know why I never made detective."

— LAWRENCE WRIGHT

Our chief financial officer was giving a tour of corporate headquarters to a special group of senior executives from whose bank we had recently received a loan. As our CFO came to the jewel of the tour, the computer centre that had been financed with the bank's help, he proudly pointed to a small metal box on the wall next to the entrance.

"This box," he boasted, "is part of our new security system. The only way to gain admittance to the computer room is by inserting a properly encoded card in the slot."

He pressed a button next to the box, and a buzzer sounded. His face went pale when a voice from the other side of the door shouted, "Come on in. It's open!"

— BILL MIDWIG

As a policeman, I occasionally work off-duty as a security officer in stores. I was handling crowd control for a going-out-of-business sale, and people were massed around the two cash registers. Determined to establish order, I climbed onto the checkout counter and announced, "Please, I want to organize you into two lines, one for each register. Remember, you all can't be first—someone has to be second."

A woman in back raised her hand and called out, "I volunteer to be second!"

— NICK WALTMAN

"He's good, Nicky, really good. But how do we know he won't go dancing to the Feds?"

A friend of mine, a policeman, responded to an accident call one day. When he arrived, he noticed an emergency medical technician (EMT) trying to apply a spine board to a man standing near one of the cars involved in the accident. The patient appeared to be resisting.

"Really," he objected, "I ..."

The EMT interjected, explaining that because of regulations, he had to take necessary precautions.

"No, I'm okay, really, I am."

Again the EMT cut him off, explaining the rules he had to follow.

By then, my friend had reached them and, recognizing the patient, asked, "Are you sure you're okay? The accident looks pretty nasty."

"I reported the accident—I wasn't in it," he was finally able to explain.

— DAVID BLOOM, JR.

A police officer heard this plea on his radio: "Does anyone know where I'm at? I'm all screwed up." It was a policeman who had lost his way.

Another voice rang out, bold and authoritative: "Would the officer making that last transmission please identify himself?"

After a short silence, a third unidentified voice said, "He's not that screwed up."

— MICHAEL VIOLET

I was a brand-new attorney in practice alone, and I had a likewise inexperienced secretary fresh out of high school. The importance of proofreading the results of my dictation was highlighted one day when a reminder to a client's tenant to pay her rent or suffer eviction was transcribed as follows: "You are hereby notified that if payment is not received within five business days, I will have no choice but to commence execution proceedings."

— MARY E. RASAMNY

As a potential juror in an assault-and-battery case, I was sitting in a courtroom, answering questions from both sides. The Crown prosecutor asked such questions as: Had I ever been mugged? Did I know the victim or the defendant?

The defence attorney took a different approach, however. "I see you are a teacher," he said. "What do you teach?"

"English and theatre," I responded.

"Then I guess I better watch my grammar," the defence attorney quipped.

"No," I shot back. "You better watch your acting."

When the laughter in the courtroom died down, I was excused from the case.

— MACEY LEVIN

Timeless Humour from the '60s

A young man I know, who recently became law clerk in a large municipal courthouse, was asked to prepare a suggested opinion in an important case. After working on the assignment for some time, he proudly handed in a 23-page document.

When he got it back, he found a terse comment in the judge's handwriting on page 7: "Stop romancing—propose already."

— SELMA JANOFF

Most of us in the driver-safety class were stumped. We simply didn't have an answer for the instructor's question. So he called on a soft-spoken man and posed the situation to him. "What's the difference between an aggressive driver and a driver suffering from road rage?"

"A pistol," came the answer.

— JERRY HICKS

In the news the other day, a tractor-trailer loaded with brand-new file folders was hijacked. Later the same day, a truck carrying boxes of Post-its was stolen. Authorities are still investigating, but they believe the robberies were the work of organized crime.

— RON DENTINGER

On our way to the United States, we had to stop at the border for an agricultural inspection. We had been to the same border check before, but this time the inspector's line of questioning was a bit different. "Are you folks carrying any citrus fruit, citrus plants or citrus seeds, or any cotton, cotton plants or cotton seeds?"

"No, sir," I answered.

"Are you carrying any ham or tuna sandwiches?"

"No," I replied.

"Any fried chicken?"

"No, Officer," I said. "Is there a new restriction on these items in United States?"

"No, not really," he sighed. "It's just that I left my lunch at home this morning, and it's getting close to noon."

We happily gave him two bologna sandwiches, and went on our way.

— FRANK E. DENT

A woman was driving down the street and got stopped by a police officer.

"May I see your driver's licence?"

he said.

She looked at him with disgust.

"What's the matter with you guys? I wish you'd make up your minds. You took my licence from me yesterday."

LOA I. BENTON

A highway-patrolman friend of ours had stopped at our café for coffee and was getting ready to leave. "Go out and get 'em!" I said. "I suppose everyone gets a ticket today?"

"I don't really give out many tickets," he said seriously.

"Oh, come on," I teased, "you'd give your own mother a ticket."

"No, my mother never drove a car," said Bill, still serious. Then a grin spread over his face. "I did catch her jaywalking once," he said, "and I issued her a warning. But that's all."

— D. S. JONES.

A group of prospective jurors was asked by the judge whether any of them felt they had ever been treated unfairly by an officer of the law. "I once got a ticket for running a stop sign," offered one woman, "even though I definitely came to a complete stop."

"Did you pay the ticket?" the judge questioned.

"Yes."

"If you thought you were innocent," the judge went on, "why didn't you contest it?"

"Your Honour," she replied, "there have been so many times I didn't get a ticket for running a stop sign that I figured this evened things out a little."

— CHARLES KRAY

During his spare time my brother, a lawyer, volunteers on his town's fire and rescue squad. When I mentioned this to a friend, he smiled and said, "Let me get this straight. Your brother is a lawyer and an EMT? So he doesn't have to chase the ambulance—he's already in it?"

— DALE BIRCH

While I was serving as a juror, I chanced to share the elevator one morning with a visiting judge. He asked me where the jurors parked, and I informed him that we had our own lot several blocks away.

Then it occurred to me that he might be having a problem finding a place for his car, so I continued, "but, Your Honour, they have a special place reserved for judges down below."

"Yes," he said dryly, "I'm sure they do."

— HELEN BAYS

I once called upon an elderly lawyer, who greeted me warmly and invited me to be seated. As I was about to take the chair in front of his desk, he motioned me into a different one. Before I left, however, he invited me to try the first chair. I did so, and after a short time noticed an uncomfortable desire to rise.

"I have that chair for law-book sellers, bill collectors and pesky clients," he explained. "The front legs are sawed off five centimetres shorter than the back ones."

— ROBERT J. DEMER

While taking a routine vandalism report at an elementary school, I was interrupted by a little girl about six years old. Looking up and down at my uniform, she asked, "Are you a cop?"

"Yes," I answered, and continued writing the report.

"My mother said if I ever needed help I should ask the police. Is that right?"

"Yes, that's right," I told her.

"Well, then," she said as she extended her foot toward me, "would you please tie my shoe?"

— CAROL WIRGES

L. LIPSCHITZ
ATTORNEY AT LAW

"Don't worry about a thing. NOTHING is anyone's fault anymore."

The Dumbest Criminals

▶ BY WILLIAM BEAMAN

Who knew that shoplifting could be a perfect Kodak moment?

A thief and his sidekick seemed pretty savvy when they entered a Wal-Mart and swept the shelves of $2,000 worth of digital cameras. A store worker found only an abandoned shopping cart filled with empty camera boxes.

Meanwhile, the store's surveillance tape looked like it was going to be useless: The video showed the suspects, a man and a woman, but the images were far too grainy to identify them.

Then security officials noticed that, at one point, the tape showed the woman picked up a demonstration camera that was chained to a counter, and pointed it at her partner. No, she couldn't have . . . Yes, she did.

The store's manager called over to the Wal-Mart photo centre and asked about the camera. The guy operating the photo centre, Brian Mikucki, said they were in luck: The camera had batteries and a disc. What's more, it was hooked up to a printer. All they had to do was press the print button to see exactly what the picture on the disc looked like.

Out popped a clear colour image of a balding man with a mustache, looking straight at the camera. The police couldn't ask for a better mug shot.

It didn't take a master sleuth to catch these bumbling crooks.

Shortly after the robbery, Police Detective Sgt. Paul Dodorico said he thought the couple "will be kind of surprised. I'm sure they thought there was nothing in the camera."

No sooner did police go public with the photograph than calls poured in to a tip line, identifying the man as 36-year-old James Stissi. Less than three weeks later, detectives arrested Stissi at his home and charged him with grand larceny.

And your previous jobs?

It may be tough for Alejendro Martinez to clear himself of charges that he robbed a pizza parlour after allegedly leaving behind a crucial piece of evidence. According to prosecutors, the 23-year-old Martinez entered the parlour, ordered a pie and requested a job application. "The cashier immediately gave him an application and a pen, so he started filling it out," said prosecutor Frank Coumou. "Then, when he thought the moment was right, he lifted his shirt, exposed the butt of a firearm, and told her to give him all of the money."

> When police returned to the pizza parlour after the arrest, they found Martinez's job application still on the counter.

After stuffing over $200 in his pocket, Martinez hustled out to a waiting car, authorities say. But a witness followed the gunman and jotted down the licence plate. An easy trace of that number led police to Martinez, whom they found sitting at home.

None of that has made it easy for the public defender who has taken on the case. But the evidence left behind could make his job nearly impossible. When police returned to the pizza parlour after the arrest, they found Martinez's job application still on the counter. He had dutifully written down on it his real name and address. "I'd chalk it up to either inexperience or plain stupidity," said prosecutor Coumou. Martinez has pleaded not guilty and his case is now pending in district court. ▲

Ha, Ha! Hee Hee Hee! Ho! Ha, Ha, Ha, Ha! Hee-Hee! Ha, Ha!

A guy I know was towing his boat home from a fishing trip to Lake Huron when his car broke down. He didn't have his cellphone with him, but he thought maybe he might be able to raise someone on his marine radio to call for roadside assistance.

He climbed into his boat, clicked on the radio and said, "Mayday, Mayday."

A Coast Guard officer came on and said, "State your location."

"Highway 21, two kilometres south of Bayfield."

After a very long pause, the officer asked, "How fast were you going when you reached shore?"

— MARY MARINEAU

On a long drive from Nova Scotia, I thought I was driving at a reasonable speed. But the flashing blue lights in my rearview mirror made me realize that I'd been over the limit.

I handed the officer my licence and made small talk while my wife dug through the glove compartment for the registration. "I am usually very careful about my speed," I told him as my wife handed me the paperwork.

The officer studied it and then gave it back. "Sir," he said gruffly, "this is not your registration." It was a warning ticket I had gotten for speeding in New Brunswick.

— A. ABERCROMBIE

Some years ago, my dad, an attorney, took me to a fancy restaurant. When the bill arrived, there was a $1.50 charge for bread and butter. Dad paid the bill, including the charge for bread and butter. However, the next day, he sent a letter to the restaurant stating that the charge was uncalled for. Enclosed in the same envelope was a bill for $500 in legal services.

Someone from the restaurant called immediately and asked, "What is this $500 bill for? We never ordered any legal services."

Dad replied, "I never ordered any bread and butter."

The $1.50 was returned without delay.

— CARL FIELD

"I've got a funny feeling about this, Dave. Are you sure you ran it by legal?"

Phil was driving down a country road late one night when he felt a big thud. He got out of the car and looked around, but the road was empty. Since there was nothing else to be done, Phil drove on home. In the morning a police officer was standing at his doorstep. "You're under arrest for hitting a pig and leaving the scene," the lawman told him with a frown. "Please come with me."

Phil couldn't believe his ears. "But how could you possibly know that's what happened?" he asked.

"It wasn't hard," the police officer replied. "The pig squealed."

— SANDRA BINGHAM

A female attorney in a law office found a typewriter on her desk with this note: "We are short of secretarial help and need your assistance."

Recognizing that this was yet another prank by her male colleagues, she quickly typed a response that forever squelched the jokes: "I wold lov to hep out eny wey I kan."

— BRENDA L. OLIVER

When a friend received a traffic ticket, he promptly sent the policeman an orchid. Asked why, he explained: "I figure that when he gets the orchid, he will give it to his wife or his girl, who will make him take her out for the evening to show it off—and that will probably cost him more than I have to pay for the ticket he gave me."

— JANET CHRISTIE

My husband, an attorney, is frequently consulted by clients who, after learning what the cost of legal services will be, decide to do without his aid. Recently the elderly minister of a small, struggling church came in with a legal problem.

After patiently listening to an explanation of my husband's fees, he left the office with a prudent: "Thank you, sir, but I believe I'll just pray this one through."

— JAN LYONS

While discussing the plight of driver's-licence examiners, a former motor-vehicle-bureau director told about a woman who was parallel parking. "Could you get a little closer?" the examiner asked.

And she slid over.

— NEIL MORGAN

Fellow employees at the international company where I work know I'm a notary public and have me certify personal documents. One day, two Swedish men asked me to witness signatures on an automobile title.

"I'm selling my car to this guy," one of them explained. "We came here because we heard you were notorious."

— BARBARA FRIEDEWALD

A man is pulled over by a police officer for a broken headlight. The cop looks in the car and sees a collection of knives on the backseat. "Sir," he says. "Why do you have all those knives?"

"They're for my juggling act," the man replies.

"Prove it," says the cop.

The man gets out of the car and begins juggling the knives just as two men drive by.

"Man," says one guy. "I'm glad I quit drinking. These new sobriety tests are hard."

— BASIL W. HENDRICKSON

Timeless Humour from the '60s

As we approached a small town in Ontario, my wife and I were amazed at the crudely painted signs along the road, warning "Speed Trap Ahead!" I cautiously slowed down, and we entered the city limits at a sedate crawl.

When we stopped for gas, I mentioned the signs to the station attendant. "Yep, our police department put those signs up themselves," he said, chuckling. "And they do a darn sight better job than the regular speed-warning signs."

— RICHARD H. SCHNEIDER

One weekend, a doctor, a priest and a lawyer were out in a fishing boat. Their motor had conked out and one of the oars had drifted off. Just as the doctor was about to dive in to retrieve the oar, the boat was surrounded by sharks.

"I can't go now," the doctor said. "If someone gets bitten, you'll need my services."

"I can't go either," said the priest. "If the doctor fails, I'll need to give last rites."

"Fine," said the lawyer. "I'll get it."

He dove in, the sharks moved, he retrieved the oar and climbed back into the boat. The doctor and priest looked flabbergasted. The lawyer just smiled and said, "Professional courtesy."

— MELODY LEE

Our son and his friends had recently earned their driving privileges. They were hanging out at our house comparing family cars when one of the fellows bragged that his parents' car could really move.

"How fast does it go?" my husband chimed in.

Without missing a beat, our quick-thinking young friend replied, "One hundred."

— SANDI WALLESTAD

As a freelance secretary, I type story manuscripts. When an author pays me, I print the name of the story across the top of his cheque. Once when I took a cheque to the bank, the teller suddenly froze. Only after I had explained my procedure to a bank officer did the reason for the teller's reaction become clear.

The story was called "Your Money or Your Life," and that, of course, was what I had written in bold letters across the top of the cheque.

— ELIO DESIDERIO

sign language

Sign in a police station:
"In God we trust—others we polygraph."
— RON HUDSPETH, *Atlanta Journal*

My son, a lawyer, was approached by his friend, a priest, who wanted a will drawn up. When the work was completed and ready to be mailed, my son could not resist inserting this note: "Thy will be done."

— MARJORIE SUMMERS

My law partner was presenting a no-fault divorce case in court. The couple involved had no children, but they did have a dog, of whom both were very fond.

My partner stated that both parties agreed to share whatever medical expenses might be necessary for the care of the animal. They also agreed that the wife would have custody, but that the husband would be allowed visitation rights.

The judge, looking somewhat startled, peered down at the husband and asked, "Is this true?"

The husband replied, "Yes, Your Honour."

"Well," intoned the judge, with a trace of a smile on his face, "you should know that there is nothing this court can do for you if the dog refuses to see you."

— STEPHEN G. MECKLER

On a curvy mountain highway late one night, my dad was complaining about the car behind us. "That guy must be drunk!" he said. "Every time I move over to let him pass, he slows down. When I get back on the road, he gets closer and stays on my tail."

Thirty minutes later, the car turned on a set of flashing blue lights. Coming up to our window, the officer said, "Sir, I'd like you to take an alcohol test. You've been swerving on and off the road for half an hour."

— PRISCILLA YEN

As a police officer, I hear many excuses by those caught speeding. Once, the driver ran back to my patrol unit to tell me someone in the car was sick and he was taking her to the hospital. I let the man go, but was suspicious when he declined my offer of a police escort. I decided to follow him.

By the time we reached the emergency entrance of the local hospital, I was feeling a little foolish about not trusting the man. When I noticed he was having difficulty getting an elderly woman out of his car, I walked over to offer my assistance. It was then that I overheard the struggling woman say, "Leave me alone. You told him someone was sick, so you be the sick one."

I wrote the ticket.

— DARRELL GUILLORY

"Why are you asking for a divorce?" the judge enquired. "Because all my husband wants to do is make love," the woman said. "Most women would be pleased about that!" "They are!" the woman shot back. "That's why I want a divorce."

My father was the presiding judge in a case involving a man charged with tax evasion. As the defendant stood before him alone, Dad asked if he had counsel.

Looking toward the ceiling, the man replied, "Jesus Christ is my counsellor and defender."

My father nodded slowly while framing his next question, which was, "Do you have local counsel?"

— TOM CECIL

The civil trial dragged on and on and everyone in the courtroom, including my former boss, the judge, found themselves waging a losing battle against boredom. The first one to fall asleep was the bailiff.

After his snoring began to interrupt testimony, one of the attorneys addressed the bench. "Um, Your Honour," he asked, "should I wake him up?"

"Leave him alone," answered the judge. "He's the only one in the courtroom enjoying himself."

— JACKIE REEVES

Sidewalks were treacherous after a heavy snowstorm blanketed McGill University. Watching people slip and slide, I gingerly made my way to class.

Suddenly I found myself on a clean, snow-free section of walkway. This is weird, I thought— until I noticed that it was directly in front of the Faculty of Law building.

— REBECCA HARRIS

Timeless Humour from the '70s

The judge had not yet put in an appearance in the Sarnia traffic court. When the bailiff entered the courtroom, he sensed the nervousness of the traffic offenders awaiting their ordeal.

"Good morning, ladies and gentlemen," he said. "Welcome to 'What's My Fine?'"

— W. W. McFARLAND

"Red means stop—not attack."

A police officer stopped me for speeding and told me I was travelling 110 k.p.h. in a 100-k.p.h. zone. "I don't see how I could have been," I told him. "I had my cruise control set."

We talked for a few minutes, and he asked if I had had my tires rotated. "My wife just had them done last week," I replied, "but I guess I have to get the speedometer checked."

The officer grinned and said, "Sir, you just did have your speedometer checked."

— LARRY GRIMES

Two convicts are working on a chain gang. "I heard the warden's daughter up and married a guy down on cellblock D," the first con says to the other. "The warden's mighty upset about it too."

"Why?" asks the second prisoner. "Because she married a con?"

"No. Because they eloped."

— ADAM JOSHUA SMARGON

When a thief snatched a chain necklace a friend of mine was wearing, she grabbed at his collar, trying unsuccessfully to stop his getaway. Asked for the thief's description later, she said, "Don't bother looking for him. He only got a costume-jewellery chain of mine. But when I grabbed him by the collar, I got his chain, and it's real gold!"

— ROCHELLE ADELMAN

A police officer pulled us over for speeding on a deserted road in southern Alberta. The road was empty, and he was almost apologetic about writing the ticket. He even complimented us for wearing our seat belts.

At that point, my wife leaned over and said, "Well, Officer, when you drive the speeds we do, you've got to wear them."

— CHANCE HUNT

Timeless Humour from the '70s

For the second consecutive year, a Drummondville, Quebec, man listed his occupation as "hired killer" when he filed his federal income tax. The listing elicited no response from the Canada Revenue Agency last year, the man says, so he decided to pull the same gag again. He is a pest exterminator.

— ROBERT McMORRIS

A five-year-old boy got lost in a shopping mall. Remembering what his mother had told him to do in these circumstances, he went up to a policeman and said, "Officer, did you happen to see a lady without a boy like me?"

"One minute I'm fanning my plumage and the next thing I know I'm a registered sex offender!"

284

Amen
to That

A minister, a priest and a rabbi walk into a bar…
and what comes next is always hilarious.
From the pulpit to the Pearly Gates, higher humour at its best.

"I wrote assembly instructions for children's toys. What did you do?"

During his children's sermon, our assistant pastor asked the kids, "What is grey, has a bushy tail, and gathers nuts in the fall?"

One five-year-old raised his hand. "I know the answer should be Jesus," he began, "but it sounds like a squirrel to me."

— REV. RICHARD E. O'HARA

My wife and I arrived late to a crowded religious convention where there was standing room only. We noticed some people get up to leave, and after they hadn't returned for several minutes, we took their seats. The woman next to us insisted that the chairs were taken. I assured her that we'd be glad to move if the people came back.

Moments later we sang a hymn, and at its conclusion the music director asked all of us to turn to our neighbours and say that we loved them. The woman at my side faced me and said, "I love you, but those seats are still taken."

— CRAIG L. SAMPLES

While waiting in line to check out at a Christian bookstore, a man in front of me asked the clerk about a display of hats with the letters WWJD on them. The clerk explained that WWJD stands for "What would Jesus do?" and that the idea is to get people to consider this question when making decisions.

The man pondered a moment, then replied, "I don't think he'd pay $17.95 for that hat."

— TODD ASH

As part of his talk at a banquet, our minister told some jokes and a few funny stories. Since he planned to use the same anecdotes at a meeting the next day, he asked reporters covering the event not to include them in their articles.

Reading the paper the following morning, he noticed that one well-meaning cub reporter had ended his story on the banquet with the observation "The minister told a number of stories that cannot be published."

— DAN BETTS

Our synagogue was throwing a coming-out party of sorts for our new officiant, which was to be billed as "Coffee With the Cantor." The guest of honour, an Argentine, suggested that rather than coffee we serve mate, a variation of a South American tea.

That idea was quickly nixed, however, when we realized that we would be inviting congregants to "Mate With the Cantor."

— PHILLIP HAIN

We were celebrating the 100th anniversary of our church, and several former pastors and the bishop were in attendance. At one point, our minister had the children gather at the altar for a talk about the importance of the day. He began by asking them, "Does anyone know what the bishop does?"

There was silence. But finally, one little boy answered gravely, "He's the one you can move diagonally."

— LILLIE LAMPE

At an ecumenical round-table discussion, various religious leaders tried to answer the question "When does life start?"

"At conception," said the Catholic priest.

"No, no," said the Presbyterian minister. "It begins at birth."

"It's in between," said the Baptist. "Life begins at 12 weeks when the fetus develops a functional heartbeat."

"I disagree with all of you," said the rabbi. "Life begins when your last child leaves home and takes the dog with him."

— LYNDELL LEATHERMAN

Prior to our wedding, David and I met with the minister to discuss our marriage ceremony and various traditions, such as lighting the unity candle from two individual candles. Couples usually blow out the two candles as a sign of becoming one. Our minister said that many people were now leaving their individual candles lit to signify independence and personal freedom.

He asked if we wanted to extinguish our candles or leave them burning.

After thinking about it, David replied, "How about if we leave mine lit and blow out hers?"

— CARA SUE TAUCHER

Shortly after my husband passed away, one of my daughter's Jewish friends approached her with a question. "Kate," he said, "I've never attended a Catholic wake before. What is the significance of the widow not wearing shoes?"

Kate replied, "My mom's feet hurt."

— MARIE MAY

A distinguished minister and two elders from his congregation attended an out-of-town meeting that did not finish until rather late. They decided to have something to eat before going home, but unfortunately, the only spot open was a seedy bar-and-grill with a questionable reputation.

After being served, one of the elders asked the minister to say grace. "I'd rather not," the clergyman said. "I don't want him to know I'm here."

— PHYLLIS R. MARTIN

When the minister agrees to marry the young couple in his church, he stipulates that they remain abstinent during their engagement. A week before the wedding he asks, "Have you remained chaste?"

"I'm afraid not, Reverend," the groom-to-be answers.

"What happened?"

"My fiancée dropped a box of light bulbs, and when she bent over to pick it up, I was overcome with lust and we lost all control."

"I'm sorry," the minister says, "but I can't marry you in this church."

"That's what I figured," the young man sighs. "We're not welcome at Home Depot anymore, either."

One Sunday our priest announced he was passing out miniature crosses made of palm leaves. "Put this cross in the room where your family argues most," he advised. "When you look at it, the cross will remind you that God is watching."

As I was leaving church, the woman in front of me walked up to the priest, shook his hand, and said, "I'll take five."

— AARON RUPP

My six-year-old son was excited about his Halloween costume. "I'm going to be the Pope," he said.

"Ian, you can't be the Pope," I said. "You're not Catholic. You're Lutheran."

Ian hadn't thought about that. So he considered his alternatives. After a few minutes, he asked, "Is Dracula a Lutheran?"

— JENNY CRANE

Our minister's sermon was about how the institution of marriage is under assault in popular culture. He cited the show *Desperate Housewives*. "How many are going to watch the season finale this week?" he challenged.

When no one raised a hand, he smiled. "Nobody's willing to admit to being a fan?"

My mom whispered to me, "Actually, the finale was last week."

— DIANA JUE

During a Sunday service, the pastor asked the congregation for their intentions. We heard the usual requests to pray for sick people and the acknowledgments for those who helped when a parishioner died. The somber mood was broken when the last intention was heard.

A woman stood up and said, "My granddaughter turned 16 this week and received her driver's licence. Let us pray for us all."

— KEN MALLORY

A young parish minister about to deliver his first sermon asked a retired cleric for advice on how to capture the congregation's attention. "Start with an opening line that's certain to grab them," the older man said. "For example: 'Some of the best years of my life were spent in the arms of a woman who was not my wife.'" He smiled at the younger man's shocked expression before adding, "She was my mother."

The next Sunday the young clergyman nervously clutched the pulpit rail in front of the congregation. Finally he said, "Some of the best years of my life were spent in the arms of a woman."

He was pleased at the instant reaction—then became panic-stricken. "But for the life of me, I can't remember who she was!"

— GIL HARRIS

"Good to see you in church, Frank—but it doesn't change anything, I'm afraid . . . you're still going to hell."

One Sunday I asked our pastor to announce that the church softball team had won its league championship. As he did, he asked team members to stand up.

Although there were usually ten to twelve of us at Sunday service, I was embarrassed to see only four of us standing.

Not missing a beat, the pastor continued, "And what is most amazing is that they won with such a small team."

— JEFF LAKE

Sharma, my cousin, was telling me about an evening service at the church we've both attended for years. She and her husband usually sat in the back, but this time they moved up front to be sure to hear the Scripture reading. They sat beside a long-time church member who cheerfully said, "Good to have ya with us! Where y'all from?"

Taken by surprise, Sharma mumbled, "The back."

— LAUREN GRISHAM

"Honey, I'm afraid the children aren't forming the **right** values."

Not long after I resigned as pastor of a small community church, the phone rang. "Is the reverend there?" a man asked.

I explained that I was a minister, though not the current pastor.

"You'll do," he said. The man wanted to know which Scripture verses applied to funeral services.

I gave him several references, and he jotted them down.

"What about the 'ashes to ashes, dust to dust' part?" he asked.

I read it to him slowly. Then, intending to offer him some sympathy, I inquired, "And who is the deceased?"

"My daughter's rabbit," he replied.

— FRED FIRSTBROOK

The ordination of women as Anglican priests occasionally presents awkward situations as to what to call us. "Father" sounds inappropriate to some; "Mother" is traditionally used for unordained women overseeing religious communities.

Last year, one of my colleagues, dressed in her clerical garb, was in an airport. A man summoned the courage to ask her, "Pardon me, but what do you call a female father?"

My colleague smiled mischievously and replied, "Ambisextrous."

— MARY ELLEN APPLETON

The phone rings at the synagogue office.

"Hello, is this Rabbi Schwartz?" The caller asked.

"It is."

"This is the Canada Revenue Agency. We wonder if you can help us."

"I'll try."

"Do you know Herman Cohen?"

"I do."

"Is this man a member of your congregation."

"He is."

"Did he donate $10,000?"

"He will."

JONATHAN POWELL

In the newsroom of a metropolitan Ontario newspaper, my colleagues and I were busily working during an afternoon thunderstorm. Suddenly an unusually loud clap of thunder rattled the windows, and every light in the place went out—save one.

Bathed in the glow of the remaining light sat our religion writer, a minister, at his desk. Apparently not surprised, he stood and bowed, receiving our applause with aplomb.

— JEAN D. GIGANTE

I was working as a phone-order representative for a textbook publisher. One very busy day, many customers had been put on hold. When I took my next call, I heard a soft yet annoyed voice on the line muttering, "Darn, darn, damn, darn, darn it!"

I chuckled and said, "What may I help you with today?"

There was a brief silence, followed by, "I'm so sorry. I wish to place an order."

"Don't be sorry," I replied. "That's hardly the worst thing I've heard today. Now, first I need your name."

"Oh, dear," she said, "how embarrassing. My name is Sister Patience."

— RAYELYNNE WINGROVE

Do you know how to make holy water? You take some regular water and you boil the hell out of it.

— JACKIE MARTLING

Sitting by the convent window one evening, Sister Barbara opened a letter from home and found a $100 bill her parents had sent. Sister Barbara smiled at the gesture. But, as she read the letter, she noticed a shabbily dressed man leaning against the lamppost below.

Quickly she wrote, "Don't despair. Sister Barbara," on a piece of paper, wrapped the $100 bill in it, got the man's attention, and tossed it out the window to him. He picked it up with a puzzled expression and went off down the street.

The next day, Sister Barbara was told there was a man at the door to see her. She went down, and found the stranger waiting. Without a word, he handed her a huge wad of $100 bills.

"What's this?" she asked.

"That's the $8,000 you have coming, Sister," he replied. "Don't Despair paid 80 to 1."

— SEAN CONROY

Two priests died at the same time and met St. Peter at the Pearly Gates. "Our computer's down," said St. Peter. "You'll have to go back for a week, but you can't go back as priests. What'll it be?"

The first priest said, "I've always wanted to be an eagle, soaring above the Rocky Mountains."

"So be it," said St. Peter, and off flew the first priest.

The second priest thought for a moment and asked, "Will any of this week count?"

"No," said St. Peter.

"Well," the priest said, "I've always wanted to be a stud."

"So be it," said St. Peter. A week later, the computer was fixed, and the Lord told St. Peter to recall the two priests. "Will you have any trouble locating them?" he asked.

"The first one should be easy," said St. Peter. "He's somewhere over the Rockies, flying with the eagles. But the second one could prove more difficult."

"Why?" asked the Lord.

"He's on a snow tire somewhere in northern Ontario," said St. Peter.

— RUMESA KHALID

"Somehow, I thought it would be different up here."

My first pastoral ministry was as an assistant pastor to youth at a large church in northern British Columbia. In the fall of that first year, an evangelist was having a Saturday breakfast meeting with our group.

I was anxious for every detail of this event to be flawless and elegant, so the lay youth workers and I agreed to bring the last of the fall flowers from our gardens for floral arrangements.

The next morning, I decided to walk to church. There I was, dressed in a dark suit, a tie, hat and overcoat, walking down the street at 6:30 a.m. with a bouquet of chrysanthemums tucked under my arm.

As I strolled along, a car passed me from behind. Then, as though an afterthought, the driver stopped, backed up, rolled down the window, gestured to the flowers, and quipped, "If you're just getting home, buddy, you'd better take her more than those."

— WILLIAM C. SCHMIDT

As the golfer approached the first tee, a hazardous hole with a green surrounded by water, he debated if he should use his new golf ball. Deciding that the hole was too treacherous, he pulled an old ball out and placed it on the tee. Just then he heard a voice from above say loudly, "Use the new ball!"

Frightened, he replaced the old ball with the new and approached the tee. Now the voice from above shouted, "Take a practice swing!"

With this, the golfer stepped backward and took a swing.

Feeling more confident, he approached the tee when the voice again rang out, "Use the old ball!"

— KEVIN KUBALA

My husband is a preacher. At a revival meeting, the visiting choir sang at the beginning and then turned the service over to him. Wanting to compliment them, my husband said, "The singing was so good, we could all leave right now without any preaching."

A parishioner called out, "Amen, brother!"

— PAM LOCKE

sign language

A church bulletin listed hymns for the service. The last one was

"Jesus, Remember Me (if time permits)."

— RUTH HEINECKE

Our pastor was teaching Proverbs 16:24: "Pleasant words are as an honeycomb, sweet to the soul, and health to the bones."

The minister then added, "You can catch more flies with honey than with vinegar."

My wife leaned over, put her head on my shoulder, and whispered in my ear, "I just love to watch your muscles ripple when you take out the garbage."

— TOM KOLOSICK

A motorist was driving in the country when he came upon a priest and a rabbi standing on the shoulder of the road, fishing. Next to them was a sign that read "Turn Around. The End Is Near."

The motorist didn't like to be preached to, so he rolled down the window and yelled, "Mind your own business, you religious nuts!"

A few seconds later the two fishermen heard tires screech, then a splash.

The rabbi turned to the priest and said, "I told you we should've just written, 'Bridge Out.'"

— CHRISTI RIGGS

The newly appointed priest was being briefed by the housekeeper on problems in the rectory that required immediate attention. "Your roof needs repair, Father," she said. "Your water pressure is bad and your furnace is not working."

"Now, Mrs. Kelly," the priest allowed, "you've been the housekeeper here five years, and I've only been here a few days. Why not say our roof and our furnace?"

Several weeks later, when the pastor was meeting with the bishop and several other priests, Mrs. Kelly burst into the office, terribly upset. "Father, Father," she blurted, "there's a mouse in our room and it's under our bed!"

— DORIS CYPHER

" 'Coulda, woulda, shoulda.' Yeah, we get a lot of that."

A preacher was asking for contributions to the church's program to buy food for the needy. The town gambler, who also owned the saloon and several other shady operations, offered the preacher $500.

"You can't take that," a scandalized deacon told the preacher. "That's the devil's money."

"Well, brother," said the preacher, cheerfully accepting the gift, "in that case, the devil has had his hands on it long enough. Now let's see what the Lord will do with it."

— JAMES DENT

Henry goes to confession and says, "Bless me, Father, for I have sinned. Last night I was with seven different women."

The priest says, "Take seven lemons, squeeze them into a glass, and drink the juice."

"Will that cleanse me of my sins?"

"No," replies the priest. "But it'll wipe that silly grin off your face."

— JAY TRACHMAN IN ONE TO ONE

QUOTABLE QUOTES

The bulletin board on the lawn of a New Jersey church reads "We reserve the right to accept everybody."

— JOHN KAZMARK

An eye for an eye only leads to more blindness.

— MARGARET ATWOOD

Did you hear that the atheists have produced a Christmas play? It's called *Coincidence on 34th Street*.

— JAY LENO

For two people in a marriage to live together day after day is unquestionably the one miracle the Vatican has overlooked.

— BILL COSBY, Love and Marriage (Doubleday)

And did you hear about the bishop who hired a secretary who had worked for the Pentagon? She immediately changed his filing system to "Sacred" and "Top Sacred."

— IRA N. BRIGGS

The true measure of a man is how he treats someone who can do him absolutely no good.

— ANN LANDERS

If Adam and Eve were alive today, they would probably sue the snake.

— BERN WILLIAMS

A man goes to church one Sunday and hears a sermon about the Ten Commandments. He has an epiphany and goes to confession. "Forgive me, Father, for I have sinned," he begins.

"Go ahead, son," the priest says.

"Well, I lost my hat and I came to church to steal one. But then I heard your sermon and I changed my mind."

"That's great," the priest replies. " 'Thou shalt not steal' is a powerful commandment."

"True," the man says. "But it was when you said, 'Thou shalt not commit adultery' that I remembered where my hat was."

The teenager asked his father for a car. "Not until you start studying your Talmud and get your hair cut," his father said.

A month later the boy approached his father again. "Well," the father said, "I know you've been reading the Talmud quite diligently, but your hair's still long."

"You know, Dad," the boy replied, "I've been thinking about that. All the prophets had long hair."

"That's true," the boy's father said. "And everywhere they went, they walked."

Kevin was not an ideal child. He managed to get into mischief frequently, and was always trailed by his younger brother, Ken. Finally, at her wits' end, his long-suffering mother took him to see their parish priest. The father decided to focus Kevin's mind on higher levels.

"Kevin," he asked with great seriousness, "where is God?"

Kevin gave no reply.

"Kevin, where is God?"

Again there was silence.

For a third time the priest asked the question, and this time Kevin bolted out of the office and ran all the way home. He burst into his brother's room.

"Ken," he panted breathlessly, "Father can't find God and he thinks we had something to do with it!"

— JAN SCHREDL

Desperate for a child, a couple asked their priest to pray for them. "I'm going on sabbatical to Rome," he replied. "I'll light a candle in St. Peter's for you."

When the priest returned three years later, he found the wife pregnant, tending two sets of twins. Elated, the priest asked to speak to her husband and congratulate him.

"He's gone to Rome," came the harried reply, "to blow out that candle."

— KATLYN YODER

"The meaning of life is location, location, location."

After my five-year-old, Ryan, had told me what I assumed to be his first little fib, I decided it was time to tell him about the boy who cried wolf. He liked the story and had me tell it to him several times. Hoping the moral would sink in, I asked if he had learned anything.

"Yes," Ryan answered. "You can only tell a lie twice."

— KELLY SARE

In December at our church, we collect frozen turkeys from generous parishioners, and I drive the turkeys to the Calgary Food Bank in time for Christmas. Contributions are left in the church kitchen's freezer. On checking the freezer the day of delivery, I was pleased to find not only several turkeys, but an extremely large goose with a note attached saying it was from Mary B., one of our most active parishioners.

Arriving back home after the delivery, I had a call from our church secretary. "Do you know what happened to Mary's goose? It disappeared!"

The goose had been for Mary's Christmas dinner and was being stored at the church because it was too big for her own freezer.

— DERYK BODINGTON

A computer salesman dies and meets St. Peter at the Pearly Gates. St. Peter tells the salesman that he can choose between heaven and hell. First he shows the man heaven, where people in white robes play harps and float around.

"Dull," says the salesman.

Next, St. Peter shows him hell: toga parties, excellent food and wine, and everyone looking as though he's having a wonderful time.

"I'll take hell," he says.

He enters the gates of hell and is immediately set upon by a dozen demons who poke him with pitchforks. "Hey," the salesman demands as Satan walks past, "what happened to the party I saw going on?"

"Ah," Satan replies. "You must have seen our demo."

— DIGITAL REVIEW

Moses was walking down the street when he bumped into George W. Bush. "Hello," Bush said. "Nice weather we're having, huh?" Moses took one look at the president, turned, and ran in the other direction.

The next day Moses was walking down the same street and there was Bush. Again he tried to initiate a conversation. Again Moses turned and ran away.

Bush was tired of this bizarre treatment, so the next time Moses ran away from him, Bush followed. When he caught up, he asked Moses what was wrong.

Moses said, "The last time I talked to a bush I spent 40 years in the desert."

— DON NGUYEN

sign language

The sentence in the Thanksgiving edition of my church bulletin intended to say "Thank you, Lord, for the many miracles we are too blind to see." But in what might have been a classic Freudian slip, the sentence read

"Thank you, Lord, for the many miracles we are too blond to see."

— ANITA DAUGHERTY

A big, burly man paid a visit to a pastor's home. "Sir," he said, "I wish to draw your attention to the terrible plight of a poor family. The father is unemployed, and the mother can't work because of the nine children she must raise. They are hungry and soon will be forced onto the street unless someone pays their $500 rent."

"How terrible!" exclaimed the preacher. Touched by the concern of a man with such a gruff appearance, he asked, "May I ask who you are?"

The visitor sobbed, "I'm their landlord."

The ten-year-old boy was failing math. His parents tried everything to get him to do well in school, but nothing worked. Finally they enrolled him in a Catholic school. From his first day, the boy spent every night poring over books. When his first report card came, he had received an A in math.

"Son," his father asked, "what made the difference in math class? The nuns? The textbooks?"

"Dad, I had never taken math seriously before," the boy admitted. "But when I walked in and saw that guy nailed to the plus sign, I knew this place meant business!"

— SCOTT BIHL

The young couple met with their pastor to set a date for their wedding. When he asked whether they preferred a contemporary or a traditional service, they opted for the former.

On the big day, a major storm forced the groom to take an alternate route to the church. The streets were flooded, so he rolled up his pants legs to keep his trousers dry. When he finally reached the church, his best man rushed him into the sanctuary and up to the altar, just as the ceremony was starting. "Pull down your pants," whispered the pastor.

"Uh, Reverend, I've changed my mind," the groom responded. "I think I want the traditional service."

— FAITH AT WORK

Jesus, Moses, and an old bearded guy were playing golf. On the first tee, Moses shanked his ball into a lake. He parted the water and hit his ball onto the green.

Jesus teed off, hitting his ball into another water hazard. But he walked on water and stroked his ball just short of the cup.

Then the old man with the beard stepped up for his tee shot. He hit the ball with tremendous force, but hooked it badly. The ball bounced off the clubhouse roof, hit the cart path, and rolled down a hill into a pond, coming to rest on a lily pad. A frog hopped over and picked up the ball, then an eagle swooped down, snatched the frog, and flew over the green. The frog dropped the ball, and it rolled into the cup for a hole in one.

Moses turned to Jesus and said, "I hate playing golf with your dad."

— RICHARD WRIGHT

We accompanied our son and his fiancée when they met with her priest to sign some pre-wedding ceremony papers. While filling out the form, our son read aloud a few questions. When he got to the last one, which read "Are you entering this marriage at your own will?" he looked over at his fiancée.

"Put down 'yes,' " she said.

— LILYAN VAN ALMELO

My co-worker and I were making a sales call to a rural Baptist church. We gave our presentation to the church committee, and then the group's chairman walked to the altar and knelt down. After about a minute of silent prayer, he returned and announced in a solemn tone, "The Lord tells me we should wait."

My colleague responded by walking to the altar and kneeling down himself. Then he returned to the group, looked at the chairman, and declared, "He wants to talk with you again."

— HAROLD LAMB

Walking through the forest, an atheist hears a rustling in the bushes. Turning, he sees a massive grizzly charging toward him! He runs as fast as he can but trips over a stump and falls. As the bear raises a huge paw to strike, the atheist screams: "God! Help me!"

Time freezes. The bear becomes immobile, the forest is silent, and the river stops running. Then the atheist hears a powerful voice: "You have denied my existence for years, taught others I don't exist and credited my creation to a cosmic accident. Why should I help you?"

"It would be hypocritical to ask you to show mercy on me," the atheist agrees. "But perhaps you could make the bear a Christian?"

At that, the noise of the forest resumes, the river runs, and the bear drops to its knees, brings its paws together, and says, "Lord, for this food which I am about to receive, I am truly thankful."

— EARL BOWES

IF YOU DON'T WISH YOUR SINS TO BECOME COMMON KNOWLEDGE - TICK BOX

A Biblical Traffic Jam

▶ BY BRUCE CARLSON

Hearken unto my voice, all of you, and I learn from my misfortune. For I have dallied too long over Good Morning America and now I pay the price. Yea, verily, it is rush hour. And though I falleth upon my steering wheel and weep most piteously, I goeth not forward upon the highway. And lo! There is wailing and gnashing of teeth, for clients do await me at the office, and my boss does curse my name most horribly.

And woe unto us all who do travel in the valley of the shadow of road construction. For verily, I am stopped near the Machine That Makes Pounding Noises for No Reason, and soon the pain in my head is as a spike through my temple.

I look around myself, and I seeth also the doom of others. For there are many children who frolic in back seats, and who do cry out with much noise as an angry multitude: "I am hungry," "He's sitting on my side!" "She is touching me!" and "Are we there yet? For pee we must, and mightily!"

Soon it comes to pass that I do howl and the hair of my flesh stands up. For my coffee has fallen into my lap, and there are many foul curses, and lo! I am most grievous sore. For unto my loins there is a great desolation.

And after having suffered these trials and tribulations, I arrive at my company's parking lot; but there are those who parketh crookedly, and do taketh up two spaces with one car, for fear others will smite their doors. And there are those vehicles of an unnaturally large aspect that are puffed up and bear a multitude of bumper stickers. These cars are an abomination and a pestilence in my eyes, for they causeth me to park far from all mankind, out in the blasted wilderness. I must walk many leagues, with my briefcase heavy upon me, and the lessons of this day burned into my soul and other parts with letters of fire.

When at last I reach my office, I fall upon my brother's neck and weep with joy. For I know that at the end of the day, I shall not wander about as a sheep who has not a shepherd. My car will not be lost in the wilderness and hidden unto me, because by the time I am freed from my great travails, evening rush hour will be long over, and mine will be the only car left in the parking lot. ▲

One of my friends is in charge of the part-time help hired by an old-age home run by an order of nuns. She confided to the Mother Superior, a feisty little nun of 70, that she always felt uncomfortable giving the young girls the obligatory lecture about the need to be careful around certain of the older male patients.

The Mother Superior volunteered to give it for her, and eventually reduced my friend's 30 minutes of embarrassed rambling to a one-liner that has now become famous around the place. "Girls," she announced. "Just remember—old ain't dead."

— EUGENE M. GRACZYK

My friend and I delivered a large refrigerator to the local priest's home. With difficulty we had managed to get the fridge into the porch, but struggled for over 20 minutes to make the 90-degree turn through the narrow door. The priest, seeing our difficulty, asked what we usually did when confronted with such a situation.

Rubbing some badly skinned knuckles, I replied, "Well, Father, at this point we usually start cursing."

"Well, gentlemen," Father replied, "allow me time to move out of earshot so you can continue your work."

— JOHN GILLIS

When Travis Wolfe was the editor of religious news for a municipal newspaper, he would receive photographs from clergymen, church musicians, and speakers on religion. Wolfe made it a point to return all such photographs to their owners.

With a flourish of his pen, he would inscribe this commandment to the post office on the envelopes in which the pictures were returned: "Thou shalt not bend."

— GEORGE SHORT

The funeral directors of the mortuary where I am a receptionist were asked by a grieving family if they could place a golf club in the casket alongside their uncle, who had been an avid golfer.

"Of course," was the answer.

On the day of the funeral, as the pallbearers descended the steps toward the hearse, a loud rattling and rolling came from the coffin. "Sounds like a pinball machine," murmured one startled director.

Later a family member of the deceased came to the chapel office to apologize. At the last minute, they had decided to place in the casket, along with the club, a half-dozen golf balls.

— SHIRLEY THOMPSON

Vacationing in Hawaii, two priests decide to wear casual clothes so they won't be identified as clergy. They buy Hawaiian shirts and sandals, and soon hit the beach. They notice a gorgeous blonde in a tiny bikini. "Good afternoon, Fathers," she says as she strolls by.

The men are stunned. How does she know they're clergy? Later they buy even wilder attire: surfer shorts, tie-dyed T-shirts, and dark glasses. The next day, they return to the beach. The same fabulous blonde, now wearing a string bikini, passes by, nods politely at them, and says, "Good morning, Fathers."

"Just a minute, young lady," says one of the priests. "We are priests and proud of it, but how in the world did you know?"

"Don't you recognize me? I'm Sister Kathryn from the convent."

— MICHAEL RANA

Jake, Johnny, and Billy died and went to heaven. "Welcome," St. Peter said. "You'll be very happy here if you just obey our rule: Never step on a duck. If you step on a duck, the duck quacks, they all start quacking and it makes a terrible racket."

That sounded simple enough until they passed through the Pearly Gates and found thousands of ducks everywhere. Jake

"The fool's paradise is the next gate down."

stepped on one right away. The ducks quacked, making an unholy racket, and St. Peter came up to Jake bringing with him a ferocious-looking Amazon woman. "I warned you if you broke the rule you'd be punished," St. Peter said. Then he chained the Amazon woman to Jake for eternity.

Several hours later, Johnny stepped on a duck. The duck quacked, they all quacked, and St. Peter stepped up to Johnny with an angry-looking, shrewish woman. "As your punishment,"

St. Peter told Johnny, "you'll be chained to this woman for eternity."

Billy was extremely careful not to step on a duck. Several months went by. Then St. Peter came up to him with a gorgeous blond and chained her to Billy, uniting them for all time. "Wow!" exclaimed Billy. "I wonder what I did to deserve this?"

"I don't know about you," said the beautiful woman, "but I stepped on a duck."

— PENNY WILLIAMS

The 104-year-old building that had served as the priory and primary student residence of the small Catholic university where I work was about to be demolished. As the wrecker's ball began to strike, I sensed the anxiety and sadness experienced by one of the older monks whose order had founded the college.

"This must be difficult to watch, Father," I said. "The tradition associated with that building, the memories of all the students and monks who lived and worked there. I can't imagine how hard this must be for you."

"It's worse than that," the monk replied. "I think I left my PalmPilot in there."

— P. J. BROZYNSKI

Sol strictly observed Jewish dietary laws. But one day he went to a restaurant by himself and noticed roast pig on the menu. *Just once, I'd like to try it,* he thought, and placed his order.

The pig was brought to his table with an apple in its mouth. Just then, Sol looked up, and there was a member of his synagogue staring at him. "I ordered a baked apple," said Sol. "Who knew how they'd serve it?"

— RUTH SCHWARTZ

I can't believe I locked my keys inside, again!

St. Peter

Reynolds

It was my friend's first night working at the nursing home run by an order of Catholic nuns. She was assigned Mr. Jones, a patient known for being difficult. No amount of persuasion could convince him that it was time to go to bed.

In desperation, my friend sought the night sister's help. "Now, now, Mr. Jones," the sister began as she bustled into the room. "It's time for us to go to bed."

Without hesitating, Mr. Jones answered, "Sure as we do, we'll get caught."

— RUTH WILLEMS

A lawyer I know once drafted wills for an elderly husband and wife who had been somewhat apprehensive about discussing death. When they arrived to sign the documents, he ushered the couple into his office.

"Now," he said to them, "which one of you wants to go first?"

— ROBERT W. CUNNINGHAM

You are driving along on a wild stormy night. You pass by a bus stop, and see three people waiting for the bus: 1. An elderly woman who is about to die. 2. An old friend who once saved your life. 3. The perfect mate you've been dreaming about.

Which would you choose, knowing there could be only one passenger in your car? Should you save the elderly woman or take the old friend because he once saved your life? You may never find your perfect dream lover again!

This quiz was given to 200 applicants for a single job. The one who was hired responded, "I would give the car keys to my friend and let him take the elderly woman to the hospital. Then I would stay behind and wait for the bus with the woman of my dreams."

— DICK BREIT

"Please serve me the fibrous chicken, give me a headset that cuts in and out, and ask the passenger in front of me to recline fully, that I may achieve the purified state of total suffering."

My husband, who believes in avoiding doctors and hospitals at all costs, had to have emergency surgery for an inflamed appendix. In pain, but still protesting the whole idea of an operation, he muttered, "When God gave man an appendix, there must have been a reason for putting it there."

"Oh, there was," said the surgeon. "God gave you that appendix so I could put my children through college."

— JUDITH STOLTZ

One night when my son was five years old, I told him the Bible story about Noah and the Ark. I gave him the full treatment, complete with animal sounds and howling winds and detailed descriptions of the beasts arriving two by two. I could tell he was captivated as he stared at me in wonder, and as I finished the story, I asked him if he had any questions.

His stare never wavered as he replied, "Where were you hiding?"

— BOBBIE WILLIAMS

"Frankly, I'm quite disappointed with the technology."

A man walks into a church one day and kneels down to pray. "Lord," he says, "I've made mistakes, but I'm determined to change. If you let me win the lottery, I promise to be a good servant and never bother you again."

Nothing happens. So the next week the man tries again. "Please, God, let me win the lottery, and I'll come to church every week."

Again nothing happens. So the man decides to try one last time. "Lord," he implores, "why haven't I won the lottery? Have you abandoned me?"

Suddenly a deep voice booms down from above. "My son, I have not abandoned you, but at least meet me halfway—buy a ticket!"

— SIMON McDERMOTT

As secretary of a church whose phone number differs by only one digit from that of a local bank, I receive many wrong numbers. One day, in response to my "Good afternoon, Christ Lutheran Church," a quick-witted caller responded exuberantly, "How about that! I called the money changers and got the temple."

— JOAN SOEBBING

"If I sold my house and my car, had a big garage sale, and gave all my money to the church, would I get into heaven?" a teacher asked the children in her Sunday school class.

"No!" the children all answered.

"If I cleaned the church every day, mowed the yard, and kept everything neat and tidy, would I get into heaven?"

Again the answer was, "No!"

"Well," she continued, "then how can I get to heaven?"

A five-year-old boy shouted out, "You gotta be dead!"

— R. WARNER

A human-resources director found herself at the Pearly Gates. "We've never had a human-resources director here before," said St. Peter. "So we're going to let you spend one day in heaven and one in hell, and you can choose where to spend eternity."

"I'll go to hell first and get it over with," said the HR director.

To her surprise she spent a wonderful day with her former fellow executives, playing golf on a beautiful course. The game was followed by a sumptuous meal at the clubhouse. When she returned to heaven, she spent her day there sitting in a cloud, playing a harp.

"Have you decided where you'd like to spend eternity?" St. Peter asked.

"Yes," she said, "heaven was great, but too boring. I choose hell."

"Okay," said St. Peter, "off you go."

This time when she arrived in hell, she found everything barren and desolate. Confused, she confronted Satan. "Where's the golf course?" she asked. "And where are my friends?"

Satan smiled. "Yesterday we were recruiting you; today you're staff!"

— STEVEN SCHWARTZ

An elderly couple, admitted by St. Peter through the Pearly Gates, found conditions there just heavenly. Said the man to his wife, "I could have been here two years ago if you hadn't fed me all that oat bran."

Paul Izdepski

Our priest suddenly became ill and asked his twin brother, also a priest, to fill in for him and conduct a funeral Mass scheduled for that day. His brother, of course, agreed. It was not until the brother was accompanying the casket down the aisle, however, that he realized that he had neglected to ask the sex of the deceased. This was information that he would need for his remarks during the service.

As he approached the first pew where the deceased's relatives were seated, he nodded toward the casket and whispered to one woman, "Brother or sister?"

"Cousin," she replied.

— GEORGE E. MILHAM

The custodian of our parish is a college student who struggles to fit his duties into a busy social and academic schedule. While on an errand for the rector, Father Peter, I spied a note on his desk from the young sexton: "Peter asked for a clean men's room and God harkened unto Peter's plea and the men's room was clean. Peter asked that the hallway be swept and God harkened unto Peter's plea and the hallway was swept. Peter asked for a clean office, but God was tired. He will clean Peter's office tomorrow."

— JAMES N. NAYLOR

My sister's dog had been deaf and blind for years. When she started to suffer painful tumours, it was time to put her down. As I explained this to my seven-year-old son, he asked if Jazzy would go to heaven.

I said I thought she would, and that in dog heaven, she would be healthy again and able to do her favourite thing: chase squirrels.

Jacob thought about that for a minute, then said, "So dog heaven must be the same as squirrel hell."

— JUDY SUTTERFIELD

My boyfriend was working in the souvenir shop at Canterbury Cathedral in Kent, England. One afternoon he was talking with an attendant who worked in the cathedral when they were approached by two tourists. "Are you a monk?" one of the women asked.

"No," the attendant explained, "I wear this robe as part of my job, but I'm not a member of any religious order."

"Then where are the monks?" asked the woman.

The man replied, "Oh, there haven't been any monks here since 1415."

Hearing this, the woman looked at her watch and announced to her friend, "Betty, we missed the monks."

— SHAWNDA URIE

Pope John Paul II gets to heaven.

"Frankly," St. Peter says, "you're lucky to be here."

"Why?" the Pope asks. "What did I do wrong on earth?"

"God's really angry with the stance you took on women being ordained into the priesthood," St. Peter tells him.

"He's mad about that?" the Pope asks.

"She's furious!" St. Peter says.

SHARON HENDRICKSON

On a visit to Canada, the Pope is riding in a limo when he gets an idea. "Driver? Can I take the wheel for a while?" he asks.

"Sure," says the driver. How can I say no to the Pope? he thinks. So the Pope starts driving—like a maniac. He ignores the speed limit, dodges in and out of traffic, cuts people off.

Before long, a police officer pulls him over. But when the Pope rolls down the window, the cop stops dead in his tracks and goes back to his squad car. "We've got somebody really important here," he radios in.

"Who?" the dispatcher asks. "An MP?"

"No. More important."

"The prime minister? Who?"

"I can't tell, but the Pope is his driver."

A Sunday school teacher was discussing the Ten Commandments with her five- and six-year-old charges. After explaining the commandment to "Honour thy father and thy mother," she asked, "Is there a commandment that teaches us how to treat our brothers and sisters?"

Without missing a beat, one little boy answered, "Thou shall not kill."

— JESSICA LASALLE

Bob is taking a walk when his foot gets caught in some railroad tracks. He tries to pull it out, but it gets wedged in tighter. Then Bob spots a train bearing down on him. Panicking, he starts to pray, "Please, Lord. Get my foot out and I'll stop drinking."

But it's still stuck. As Bob struggles to free himself, he prays again, "Please! Help me and I'll stop drinking and cussing." Still nothing.

"I'm begging you, Lord," Bob pleads. "Let me live and I'll stop drinking, cussing, and I'll give all my money to the poor."

Suddenly his foot slips free and Bob lunges to safety as the train thunders past. "Whew," says Bob. "Thanks anyway, God. I took care of it myself."

— CHRIS PARKE

At church recently, I stopped to study an announcement promoting the youth choir's sandwich sale. Being an English teacher, I couldn't resist the temptation to correct the last line, which read "Donations Excepted." I crossed out the misused word and penciled in "Donations Accepted."

After the service, I glanced at the announcement again, this time noting yet another pencilled-in correction. It now read "Donations Expected."

— LORI DIGBY

"If I hadn't yelled 'FIRE!' he'd still be talking."

One Sunday my teenage son was in church. When the collection plate was passed around, he pulled a loonie from his pocket and dropped it in. Just at that moment the person behind him tapped him on the shoulder and handed him a $20 bill.

Secretly admiring the man's generosity, my son placed the $20 in the plate and passed it on. Then he felt another tap from behind and heard a whisper: "Son, that was your $20. It fell out of your pocket."

— MARY C. LOWE

Finally! After 25 years on a desert island, Joe was being rescued. As he climbed onto the boat, the curious crew noticed three small grass huts. "What are those?" they asked.

"The first one is my home," Joe said. "The second is my church."

"What about the third hut?" the rescuers wanted to know.

"Oh," says Joe, "that's the church I used to belong to."

— THOMAS R. ALLEN

A pastor was preaching an impassioned sermon on the evils of television. "It steals away precious time that could be better spent on other things," he said, advising the congregation to do what he and his family had done. "We put our TV in the closet."

"That's right," his wife mumbled, "and it gets awfully crowded in there."

— SHERRI DORMER

It was a typical backseat scene between my two boys: Keaton was flicking Kade in the ear. "Stop!" said Kade, punching his brother lightly on the arm.

Immediately Keaton began to scream and cry as if his arm had been severed. I looked at him in the rearview mirror and said, "Did he really hurt you that badly?"

"Yes! He hit me very hard!"

"Keaton," I said, "Jesus knows when you're lying."

My son paused. "Well, yeah," he said. "But does he tell you?"

— MAJESTY COATES

The preacher, arriving in a small town to be guest speaker at a local church, wanted to mail a letter to his family back home. He stopped a young boy on a bike and asked him where the post office was. The boy gave him directions, and the preacher thanked him.

"If you come to church this evening," the preacher said, "I'll tell you how to get to heaven."

"I don't think I'll be there," the boy said. "You don't even know your way to the post office."

— ARTHUR GAMMON

Our Dixieland band was hired to perform at a funeral, but our stubborn bandleader flat-out refused to play any songs remotely religious.

"I don't believe in it, and I won't play it," he insisted.

"So what tune can you play?" he was asked.

After giving the question some thought, he said, "How about, 'Don't Get Around Much Anymore'?"

— CATHY REILLY

The pastor of my church hates to plead for money. But when the coffers were running low, he had no choice. "There's good news and there's bad news," he told the congregation. "The good news is that we have more than enough money for all the current and future needs of the parish. The bad news is, it's still in your pockets."

— GILES V. SCHMITT

At the gates of heaven, a woman asked St. Peter, "How do I get into heaven?"

"You have to spell a word," said St. Peter.

"Which word?" she asked.

"Love," he replied. She spelled it correctly and was welcomed into heaven.

A year later, she was watching the gates for St. Peter when her husband arrived. "How've you been?" she asked.

"Oh, I've been doing pretty well since you died," he answered. "I married the young nurse who took care of you while you were ill. I won the lottery, so I sold the house we'd lived in and bought a mansion. We travelled the world and were in Cancún when I fell and hit my head, and here I am. How do I get in?"

"You have to spell a word," she told him.

"Which word?" he asked.

"Czechoslovakia."

— KERRY BARNUM

"'You can't take it with you' means your cellphone too."

Word Play

Is English the easiest language to mangle? It sure seems so. Here are silly word plays, ridiculous euphemisms, hysterically flawed utterances, and other fun language twists and plays.

When our air conditioner broke down, we called for a serviceman to come and take a look at it. It turned out to be a high school classmate of my husband's named Love. He said next time we needed any repairs to ask for him. The next year when we needed service again, we requested Mr. Love. I took the day off from work and waited for him to arrive.

After he had worked on our air conditioner, he left his work order behind. It had my name and said: "Wants Love in afternoon."

— DONNA MELLER

A pregnant woman lapses into a deep coma. She awakens and frantically calls for the doctor. "You had twins. A boy and a girl. They're fine," he says. "Your brother named them."

sign language

Today was the day. I was going to get a tattoo. I walked into a local shop to check out their designs. But I had second thoughts when I noticed the two "artists" working there had the last names of **Pane and Burns.**

— LINDSAY HALVERSON

Oh no, the new mother thinks. He's an idiot. Expecting the worst, she asks, "What's the girl's name?"

"Denise," the doctor says. Not bad, she thinks. Guess I was wrong about him.

"And the boy?"

"DeNephew."

Pity the poor insomniac dyslexic agnostic. He stays up all night wondering if there really is a dog.

While I was driving through a seedy area of Toronto, I noticed that sandwiched between a strip bar and a beer store sat a storefront with all of its windows suspiciously blacked out. Over the door was a sign that proudly declared, "Welcome to Kink-o's. We have nothing to do with office supplies."

— DARLENE BENAVIDEZ

Our regimental sergeant major was well known for his abuse of the English language, and we all joked about it. At parade one morning, he announced in a stentorian voice, "Certain people have been making allegations about me. If I catch these alligators, they will be in for a hard time."

— C. G. MALEY

Can you be a closet claustrophobic?

GINA FADELY | **COSMIC QUESTION**

The patient walked into the doctor's office. "You've got to help me, Doc. It's my ear. There's something in there." "Let's have a look," said the doctor. "My goodness, you're right. There's money inside." The doctor proceeded to pull out a loonie. "I don't believe it," the practitioner exclaimed, "there's more in there." Out came a fifty, a twenty and some tens. Finally, all the money had been removed. The doctor counted it; "One thousand, nine hundred and ninety dollars." "Ah, yes, that sounds about right," nodded the patient. "I knew I wasn't feeling two grand."

New definitions to add to your vocabulary:

Arbitrator: A cook that leaves Arby's to work at McDonald's.

Bernadette: The act of torching your mortgage.

Parasites: What you see from the top of the Eiffel Tower.

Primate: Removing your spouse from in front of the TV.

Subdued: A guy that works on submarines.

— EDWARD THOMPSON

A Harley rider eating in a restaurant is checking out a gorgeous redhead. Suddenly she sneezes and her glass eye comes flying out of its socket. The biker reaches up, snatches it out of the air, and hands it back to her. "I am so embarrassed," the woman says. "Please join me for dinner."

They enjoy a wonderful meal together and afterwards she invites him to the theatre, followed by drinks. She pays for everything. Then she asks him to her place for a nightcap, and to stay for breakfast.

The next morning the guy is amazed. "Are you this nice to every biker you meet?" he asks.

"Not usually," she replies. "But you just happened to catch my eye."

— FROM THE INTERNET

HEALTH FOOD SUPPLEMENTS

"Do you have the root of all evil?"

There were only two people in line ahead of me at the electronics store, yet the wait was dragging on forever. Finally the customer behind me muttered, "Mr. Hare must be on vacation."

Only then did I notice the name tag on the man at the register. It read: "Mr. Turtle, sales associate."

— BRON WRIGHT

Hear about the guy who went to the library and checked out a book called *How to Hug*? He got home and found out it was volume seven of the encyclopedia.

Freshmen in a high school general-science class were studying astronomy. "What do we call a group of stars that makes an imaginary picture in the sky?" the teacher asked. "A consternation," one student replied.

— RALPH E. HEDGES

At the end of a long, hard day, I found myself standing in line at a fast-food restaurant with my husband, Stan, and our three-year-old daughter. The service was painfully slow, and my husband's temper began to mount.

"Look, honey, it's been a long day," I said, trying to console him. "You're tired, I'm tired, she's tired."

Before I could say another word, Stan interrupted me, smiling. "You conjugate well," he said.

— SHERRY DEPASSE

sign language

The New York-New Jersey Trail Conference was preparing to move from its longtime home in New York City to Mahwah, N.J. The day before the big move, the following sign appeared on the door:

"Here today, gone to Mahwah."

— JANICE CECHONY

For anyone who gets confused about proper grammar and style in writing, we offer, from the Internet, the following tip sheet, "How to Write Good":

- It is wrong to ever split an infinitive.
- Contractions aren't necessary.
- The passive voice is to be avoided.
- Prepositions are not the words to end sentences with.
- Be more or less specific.
- Who needs rhetorical questions?
- Exaggeration is a billion times worse than understatement.

What do fish say when they hit a concrete wall?…Dam!

What do you get from a pampered cow?…Spoiled milk.

What do you call cheese that isn't yours?…Nacho cheese.

What do you call four bullfighters in quicksand?…Quattro sinko.

What do you get when you cross a snowman with a vampire?…Frostbite.

— DUSTIN GODSEY

I went to the butcher's the other day and I bet him fifty bucks that he couldn't reach the meat on the top shelf.

He said, "No, the steaks are too high."

— ED THOMPSON

The police officer pulled up alongside a speeding car and was shocked to see that the little old lady behind the wheel was knitting. The officer switched on his lights and sounded his siren, but the driver was oblivious. So the officer cranked up the bullhorn and yelled to the woman, "Pull over."

"No," the old lady shouted back. "Cardigan."

Sitting at a stoplight, I was puzzling over the meaning of the vanity plate on the car in front of me. It read "Innie."

Then I got it. The make of the car was Audi.

— KATHY JOHNSON

If someone is addicted to eating Thanksgiving leftovers, can he quit cold turkey?

MICHAEL MORSE   COSMIC QUESTION

Most of my English literature classmates thought reading Melville's *Billy Budd* would be an easy task because the novel is only 90 pages long. One boy, however, complained that the text was heavy and hard to comprehend.

"Hey," another student suggested, "maybe you should try reading Budd Light."

— CARRIE L. BENSON

"The labs are back."

315

In our high school software-applications class we were running through a list of common computer lingo." There were many terms, including "Pentium," "motherboard" and "gigabyte." Skimming the list, one girl noticed the term "RAM."

"Isn't that a kind of truck?" she asked without thinking.

"Sure," replied another student. "You can rent them at a megahertz."

— HEATHER LESSIG

One morning a man is woken by a knock at the door. He gets up and goes downstairs to open the door. To his horror, he is met by a six-foot-six-inch spider which immediately head-butts him, runs inside, tramples all over the man, kicks him in the back, kicks his ribs and stamps all over him. Next thing the homeowner remembers is waking up in hospital. Turning to the doctor he says, "I feel terrible. I am sore all over. What's wrong with me?" The doctor tells him, "I'm afraid there's a vicious bug going around."

When someone offers you a penny for your thoughts, and you put in your two cents' worth, what happens to the other penny?

?

COSMIC QUESTION

According to the Internet: Students in a university English 101 class were asked to write a concise essay containing four elements: religion, royalty, sex and mystery. The only A+ in the class read: "'My God,' said the Queen, 'I'm pregnant! I wonder who did it.'"

— E. T. THOMPSON

News that her third child was going to be a girl thrilled my cousin, who already had two boys. "My husband wants to call her Sunny," she told me, "and I want to give her Anna as her middle name in memory of my mom."

I thought they might want to reconsider their decision, since their birth announcement would herald the arrival of Sunny Anna Rainey.

— CAROLYN WALLIS

Police are investigating the murder of Juan Gonzalez. "It looks like he was killed with a golf gun," one detective observes.

"A golf gun?" asks his partner. "What in the world is a golf gun?"

"I don't know. But it sure made a hole in Juan."

Two boll weevils grew up in rural Alberta. One moved to Calgary and became a famous actor. The other stayed in the wheat field and never amounted to anything.

He became known as the lesser of two weevils.

— DUSTIN GODSEY

"You have to admire the way she juggles family and career."

"We request low bail as my client is not a flight risk."

My friend John came into French class one Monday with a pillow that he placed on his seat. Over the weekend he had been skiing and mildly fractured his tailbone. Our teacher promptly asked him to explain, *en français,* why he was sitting on a pillow.

To our amusement, John answered, "Sorbonne."

— GEORGE B. SHUPING

Today in the markets, helium was up; feathers were down. Paper was stationary. Elevators rose, while escalators continued their slow decline. Mining equipment hit rock bottom. The market for raisins dried up. Coca-Cola fizzled. Balloon prices were inflated. And Scott Tissue reached a new bottom.

— ERIC CAMPBELL

A man walks into a bar, orders a drink and sits down. A few minutes later, he hears someone shouting abuse at him. "You look terrible in those jeans," says the voice. "Go to the gym and lose some weight!" The man turns around to find that the abuse is coming from the cigarette machine. The insults continue and the man finally goes up to the bar to complain. "I'm really sorry," says the bartender. "That machine has been out of order for ages."

Did you hear that NASA is planning to send a group of Holsteins into orbit? Apparently they're calling it the herd shot round the world.

While waiting in line for my new licence plate, I heard the clerk shout out, "E I E I O." "Here," the woman standing next to me answered.

Curious, I asked if she was married to a farmer, or maybe taught preschool.

"Neither," she replied. "My name is McDonald."

— JIM PIERCE

I took my high-school government class on a field trip to the local jail. Near the end of what was an eye-opening tour, we passed through the prison's recreation room. There I spotted two board games sitting on a table, selections that I thought were particularly appropriate to a correctional facility: Life and Sorry.

— CHRISTINA GUERLAND

As a fundraiser, the chemistry club designed and sold T-shirts. Written across the front were our top "Stupid Chemistry Sayings":

- Have yourself a Merry Little Bismuth
- What do you do with dead people? Barium
- You stupid boron!
- We hope your year is very phosphorous.

— SHANE HART

Stuck in rush-hour traffic, I couldn't help but stare when a burly biker wearing black leather jacket and chaps pulled up next to me on a shocking pink Harley Davidson. My first thoughts were, "Is that really a pink Harley? I wonder if he's…"

Just then the traffic cleared and he pulled in front of me. On the back of his helmet were stencilled the words "Yes it is. No I'm not."

— AMY CARPENTER

Driving through rural Ontario, I stopped at a roadside stand that sold fruit, vegetables and crafts. As I went to pay, I noticed the young woman behind the counter was painting a sign. "Why the new sign?" I asked.

"My boyfriend didn't approve of the old one," she said. When I glanced at what hung above the counter, I understood. It declared: "Local Honey Dates Nuts."

— THEODORE BOLOGNA

A man walked into a bar and ordered six whiskies. Lining them up on the bar, he downed the first glass, then the third and finally the fifth. "Excuse me," said the bartender as the man turned to leave. "But you've left three of the whiskies you ordered untouched." "Yes," said the man. "My doctor said it was OK to take the odd drink."

A favourite beach restaurant of ours has a simple way of advertising its hours. During the day, the window panes sport large letters spelling "Open."

After hours, the "N" is moved forward to spell "Nope."

— PHIL TRIPP

My high-school basketball team was scheduled to play in the district tournament, and when we got there we were all excited to find our pictures and our stats published in the glossy program. My friend Brian Bird, a senior who was having a great season, eagerly searched for his name. But then he threw the program down in disgust, and I figured that there must be some error in his entry.

Sure enough, his name appeared as "Bird, Brain."

— DARREN JOHNSON

Three vampires walk into a bar. "What can I get ya?" asks the bartender.

"Blood," orders the first vampire.

"Make it two," says the second.

The bartender looks at the third. "What about you, buddy?"

"Plasma," says the vampire.

"Okay," replies the barman. "Let me make sure I've got this straight. Two bloods and a blood light."

— WESTON DAVIS

If you arrest a mime, do you still have to tell him he has the right to remain silent?

MICHAEL MORSE   COSMIC QUESTION

I believe in an open mind, but not so open that your brains fall out.

— ARTHUR HAYS SULZBERGER

Polite conversation is rarely either.

— FRAN LEBOWITZ, Social Studies (Random House)

As far as I'm concerned, "whom" is a word that was invented to make everyone sound like a butler.

— CALVIN TRILLIN in The Nation

Baseball, it is said, is only a game. True. And the Grand Canyon is only a hole in Arizona.

— GEORGE F. WILL in Fast Company

If truth is beauty, how come no one has their hair done in the library?

— LILY TOMLIN

The problem with people who have no vices is that they're pretty sure to have some annoying virtues.

— ELIZABETH TAYLOR

My early choice in life was either to be a piano player in a whorehouse or a politician. And to tell the truth, there's hardly any difference.

— HARRY S. TRUMAN

I looked up the word *politics* in the dictionary. It's actually a combination of two words: *poli,* which means many, and *tics,* which means bloodsuckers.

— JAY LENO on "The Tonight Show"

Local government officials had just bought a new fire engine for their town and were discussing what to do with the old one. "I've got an idea," said one official "Why not keep it for false alarms?"

A policewoman stopped a car and found that the driver had been drinking. She told him to get out of the vehicle. "You're staggering," she said, when he did. "You're not so bad yourself," replied the driver.

Hoss drove over to the next county to buy a new bull for the farm. It cost more than expected, and he was left with only one dollar. This was a problem, since he needed to let his wife, Sue, know that he'd bought the bull so she could come get it with the truck—and telegrams cost a dollar per word. Hoss thought hard for a minute. Finally he said, "All right. Here's my dollar. Go ahead and just make it this one word: Comfortable."

"How's that going to get your point across?" the clerk asked.

"Don't worry," Hoss said. "Sue's not the greatest reader. She'll say it real slow."

— RICHARD H. SCHEUB

Did you hear about the satellite dishes who married?

The ceremony was awful, but the reception was great.

— SANDRA CORONA

The gladiator was having a rough day in the arena—his opponent had sliced off both of his arms. Nevertheless, he kept on fighting, kicking and biting as furiously as he could. But when his opponent lopped off both feet, our gladiator had no choice but to give up, for now he was both unarmed and defeated.

— TEDDEM YEE

"I think I'll just stay in tonight, maybe open a can of worms."

Our son recently married a Russian woman. During the reception, Russian and Canadian guests proposed toasts. As someone translated, my sister-in-law said, "Good health, good fortune. Go and multiply."

I couldn't help noticing that some of the guests looked confused. We found out later that this had been translated as, "Good health, good fortune. Go and do math."

— DAVID A. MACLEOD

Nancy was Catholic, but her fiancé, Chris, was not. Since my friends were planning to be married in the Catholic Church, Chris made sure to listen carefully throughout their prenuptial sessions. At one meeting the priest turned to Chris and told him, "Since you are not Catholic, we shall have the ceremony without Eucharist."

Later that day, Chris was noticeably upset, so Nancy asked what was wrong. "I don't understand," he said. "How can we have the ceremony without me?"

— KURT SHELLENBACK

People Who Become Words

▶ BY JAY HEINRICHS

There once was an original Maverick—Samuel A. Maverick, mayor of San Antonio in the mid-1800s—who, despite the name, was no maverick. He was just a small-town politician whose name lives on not because he was a great gunfighter—apologies to you, James Garner, and you, Mel Gibson—but because he was lazy. When Maverick bought a herd of cattle in 1847, he allowed the steers to roam on his ranch, unbranded. From then on, unbranded cattle—and, eventually, independent-minded humans—became known as mavericks.

As a household word, Mayor Maverick has some distinguished, if not always appreciative, company, including the likes of Mr. Boycott, Ms. Bloomer and Monsieur Leotard. There was a real guy named Silhouette and, for that matter, a real Guy. All of these people achieved a sort of immortality when their names were turned into everyday words called eponyms (from the Greek "upon a name").

Some 35,000 have made their way into English.

Murphy's Law is one of the most famous eponyms—the legacy of one very picky Air Force officer. In the late 1940s, Capt. Ed Murphy, an aircraft engineer by training, complained about an incompetent technician on his team. "If there is any way to do it wrong, he will," Murphy said. His co-workers began calling the captain's pessimism Murphy's Law, and mentioned it in a press conference. As long as people keep on making mistakes, Murphy will live.

More distant, but still enduring, is the memory of the original Guy, an Englishman named Guy Fawkes. On November 5, 1605, Fawkes attempted to blow up Parliament and King James I. The English still remember the date by burning stuffed dummies in effigy, and for years any bizarrely dressed person was known as a guy. Over time, and after crossing the Atlantic, the term picked up a less humbling connotation.

The British have a knack for punishing memorable characters with eponyms.

Charles Cunningham Boycott was an English estate manager who refused to lower rents for poor Irish tenant farmers, inspiring a rent strike and the first boycott. Thomas Derrick, another unpopular Brit, worked as executioner at London's Tyburn gallows, hanging hundreds of convicts before being convicted of rape and condemned to die. The Earl of Essex pardoned him, only to be executed in 1601 for treason—by Derrick. A derrick was once a gallows; now the word refers to any equipment used to hang something. (Mr. Derrick did not live long enough to hang any Hooligans, members of a rowdy Irish clan who, legend has it, terrorized a London neighbourhood in the 1890s.)

Also achieving dubious fame was Étienne de Silhouette. A deficit-fighting finance minister of France in 1759, he had the nerve to suggest raising taxes.

Meet the cobb in salad, the bloomer in underwear and the derrick in crane.

His name became a synonym for cheapness. There's debate among linguists about just how we got the contemporary usage of silhouette: Some say the black-on-white cut paper portraits then popular were named after the skinflint finance minister, while others insist he was known for making the cut-out portraits.

Shirley Temple has never liked Shirley Temples. ("Too sweet," she says).

Nonetheless, during the more than 60 years since a bartender at the Brown Derby restaurant in Hollywood mixed 7-Up and grenadine in her honour, people have pressed Shirley Temples on her. The retired diplomat Shirley Temple Black might well wish her name were Cobb. At least then she'd get a stick-to-your-ribs salad. That concoction began with Bob Cobb, owner of the Brown Derby restaurant in Los Angeles, who invented his salad in 1926.

If you're ambitious to become an eponym yourself, the fashion world might be a good start. Amelia Bloomer, an American feminist of the 1800s, championed the undergarment known as bloomers. And the French aerialist Jules Leotard, creator of the flying trapeze, popularized the even more daring tights.

The newest eponyms come from mass media and politics. People already talk about gumping through life—getting by on dumb luck, the way Forrest Gump did in the movie. "Doing a Homer" means smacking your head and saying, "D'oh!" Homer Simpson-style, either in frustration, or because you've done something dumb—or both.

Among the wonks in Washington, "to bork" is to viciously attack a candidate or appointee. That's in honour of Robert Bork, the Reagan nominee to the Supreme Court whose career was torpedoed in the Senate. One day we may find that people use marthastewart as a single word to mean to arrange with excruciatingly good taste. (As in "I'm marthastewarting his party.")

Over time, eponyms may change meaning dramatically. That was the happy outcome for Bertha Krupp, a German military manufacturer during World War I. Her firm made a giant howitzer that British soldiers dubbed Big Bertha. But the hefty arms merchant has been redeemed through sport: Contemporary golfers refer to her fondly as they swing the innovative driver named—what else?—Big Bertha. ▲

After a long career of being blasted into a net, the human cannonball was tired. He told the circus owner he was going to retire. "But you can't!" protested the boss. "Where am I going to find another man of your calibre?"

Searching in my library for two books by communications expert Deborah Tannen turned into an Abbott and Costello routine. "What's the first book?" the librarian asked.

"*That's Not What I Meant,*"
I said.

"Well, what did you mean?"

"That's the title of the book," I explained.

"Okay." She looked at me a little skeptically. "And the other book?"

"*You Just Don't Understand.*"

"Excuse me?"

I got both books. Eventually.

— NORM WILLIAMS

Tiffany adopts two dogs, and she names them Rolex and Timex. "Where'd you come up with those names?" asks her friend Mandy. "HellOOOOOO," Tiffany replies. "They're watchdogs!"

— GUSTAVO YEPES

Aoccdrnig to rscheearch at an Elingsh uinervtisy, it deosn't mttaer in waht oredr the ltteers in a wrod are, the olny iprmoetnt tihng is taht teh frist and lsat ltteer is at the rghit pclae. The rset can be a toatl mses and you can sitll raed it wouthit a porbelm.

Tihs is bcuseae we do not raed ervey lteter by istlef but the wrod as a wlohe.

Johnathan Powell

"I'm sorry."

A man was sent to court for drunk and disorderly conduct. The judge inquired where the defendant worked. "Here and there," he replied. "And what do you do for a living?" "This and that," came the answer. The judge turned to a policeman and instructed him to take the man straight to jail. "Wait," implored the accused. "When will I come out?" "Sooner or later."

When my wife and I were vacationing in the eastern part of our state, our car's licence plate was stolen. We planned to go to a local office for a replacement, but then we discovered that our registration had expired. The new one was at home in a pile of mail.

After much thought, we came up with a solution. Taping a sign over the empty licence-plate space on the rear of the vehicle, we made the eight-hour trip home safely. Not a single state trooper stopped us, but many passing motorists took great pains to honk and wave at us.

Our sign read "Just Married!"

— GARY FROEHLICH

"Try double **clucking** on it."

My wife walked into a coffee shop on Halloween to find the woman behind the counter with a bunch of sponges pinned to her uniform.

"I'm assuming this is a costume," said my wife. "But what are you supposed to be?"

The waitress responded proudly, "I'm self-absorbed."

— SCOTT PIPER

Rick, a banker, is showing off his fancy new boat to his friend Jim. But the boat sinks, and Rick can't swim. So Jim starts pulling him to shore.

Finally, with only 10 metres to land, Jim says, "So do you think you could float alone?"

Rick gasps back, "This is a heck of a time to be asking for money!"

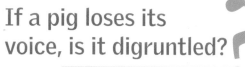

If a pig loses its voice, is it digruntled?

COSMIC QUESTION

One day, the president of the company came upon a young man who was expertly counting out a large wad of the firm's cash. The boss asked, "Where did you get your financial training, young man?"

"Yale," the young man answered proudly.

"Ah, a fellow Ivy Leaguer! What's your name?"

"Yack Yackson."

— ADAM JOSHUA SMARGON

The zookeeper needed to purchase some new animals, so he started composing a letter: "To whom it may concern, I need two mongeese." That doesn't look right—too bad I don't have a dictionary, thought the zookeeper.

So he started over: "To whom it may concern, I need two mongooses." That doesn't look right either, he thought.

Finally he got an idea: "To whom it may concern, I need a mongoose. And while you're at it, make it two."

"Honey, I'm taking the dog out to do his business."

The new composers' dictionary:

Adagio Frommagio—
To play in a slow and cheesy manner.

Angus Dei—
To play with a divine, beefy tone.

A Patella—
Unaccompanied knee-slapping.

Frugalhorn—
A sensible, inexpensive brass instrument.

Dill Piccolino—
A wind instrument that plays only sour notes.

Approximento—
A musical entrance that is somewhere in the vicinity of the correct pitch.

— E. T. THOMPSON

Did you hear about the self-help group for compulsive talkers? It's called On & On Anon.

— SALLY DAVIS

A policeman looked up to see a woman racing down the centre of the road at 200 k.p.h. He pulled her over and said, "Hey, lady, would you mind telling me why you're going so fast down the middle of the road?"

"Oh, it's okay, Officer," she replied. "I have a special licence that allows me to drive like that."

"Oh, yeah?" Let's see it." The cop looked at the licence and then concluded, "Ma'am, there's nothing special about this. It's just a temporary licence."

"Look at the very bottom, though," the woman insisted. "See? It says 'Tear along the dotted line.'"

— ROCKY MEYERSON

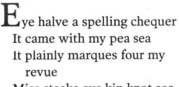

E ye halve a spelling chequer
It came with my pea sea
It plainly marques four my revue
Miss steaks eye kin knot sea
Eye strike a key and type a word
And weight four it two say
Weather eye am wrong oar write
It shows me strait a weigh
As soon as a mist ache is maid
It nose bee fore two long
And eye can put the error rite
Its rarely ever wrong
Eye have run this poem threw it
I am shore your pleased two no
Its letter perfect in it's weigh
My chequer tolled me sew.

— SAUCE UNKNOWN

When the waitress in a Halifax restaurant brought him the soup du jour, the Englishman was a bit dismayed. "Good heavens," he said, "What is this?"

"Why, it's bean soup," she replied.

"I don't care what it has been," he sputtered. What is it now?"

— MARGARET OLDERROG

"I fear that one day I'll meet God, he'll sneeze, and I won't know what to say."

— RONNIE SHAKES,
SUBMITTED BY SHARON KANSAS

Speak the truth, but leave immediately after.

— SLOVENIAN PROVERB

327

Why did the French train derail?

Toulouse-Lautrec.
JOHN KELL

What do you call a Far Eastern monk who
sells reincarnations?

A used karma dealer.
RICHARD SELTZER

How many ears did Davy Crockett have?

Three—his left ear, his right ear, and his wild front ear.
MUZAMMIL PATEL

Why did the cowboy buy a dachshund?

Someone told him to get a long little doggy.
SAVANNA SMITH

What do you call someone who has just
printed 1,000 puns off the Internet?

Well e-quipped.
J. C. PICKETT

What did the scientist say to his stubborn,
argumentative clone?

"Why can't you be a reasonable facsimile?"
MARK SOLOMON

What do you call a rap star who has
studied classical music?

Yo Yo Ma Ma.
FRANK J. PLAZA

I was waiting to board a plane in Houston when a flight attendant stopped a woman in front of me to question her about the number of carry-on bags she had. The woman vehemently defended herself, claiming the extra bag was really her purse. It was the size of a large briefcase, but she insisted that it shouldn't count as a carry-on item. The flight attendant finally let the woman pass.

As the next man stepped up, the flight attendant's gaze settled on his bags. Immediately, he held up his briefcase and exclaimed, "This is my wallet."

— KIMBERLEY LEVACY

Everything is expensive in the upscale resort town where we live, and part of what you pay for is attitude. I realized this after I bought a couple kilograms of hamburger at the fancy market on Main Street.

When I was taking the meat out of the bag at home, I noticed the label, "Ground Charles."

— FRAN COPELAND

While redecorating my bathroom, I phoned a store to see if it stocked a particular model of toilet. "We haven't got one here," said the clerk.

"Oh, no!" I said, crestfallen. His number had been the fourth one I'd called.

"Don't worry," he added helpfully. "I'll contact our other outlets to see if there's anybody out there sitting on one."

— DOUG BINGHAM

Things you need to know if your son wants to quit school and become a rock star:
- What do you call a guitar player who breaks up with his girlfriend? Homeless.
- What's the difference between a rock musician and a large pizza? The pizza can feed a family of four.
- What's the definition of an optimist? A rock musician with a mortgage.
- How do you define perfect pitch? It's when you throw your son's guitar into the Dumpster and it lands right on top of his amplifier.

If athletes get athlete's foot, do astronauts get mistletoe?

E. T. THOMPSON   COSMIC QUESTION

A man walked into a bar carrying a checkered flag. "I hope you're not going to start anything in here," warned the bartender.

— JIM LEACH

Sitting in the first row of coach class during a lengthy flight, my wife and I were able to hear a flight attendant as he pushed a wine cart down the aisle in the first-class section. "Would you care for Chardonnay or Burgundy?" he asked the high-paying passengers.

A few minutes later the attendant opened the curtain between the two sections, offered wine to one final first-class patron, then wheeled the same cart forward to our aisle. "Excuse me," he said, looking down at us, "would you care for a glass of wine? We have white and red."

— WILLIAM V. COPELAND

Following months of marijuana drug busts, the police took the contraband into a remote region to burn. The fire was blazing brightly when an agent noticed that a flock of terns was flying around the area. Concerned about the effects of the smoke on the birds, they called the Audubon Society.

Their worst fears were confirmed. There was not one tern left unstoned.

— JOHN ARENDS

Fear factor. Are you scared of heights? Cramped spaces? If so, you've got plenty of company. Some people, though, have to wrestle with phobias that may surprise you.

- Automatonophobia = fear of ventriloquist dummies
- Ecclesiophobia = fear of church
- Aulophobia = fear of flutes
- Selenophobia = fear of the moon
- Venustraphobia = fear of beautiful women
- Logizomechanophobia = fear of computers.

Reporter: "Brzinlatow-skiczinina is the name of the guy on the west side who was struck by lightning."

City editor: "What was his name before he was struck?"

Did you hear about the Buddhist who refused his dentist's novocaine? He wanted to transcend dental medication.

Did you hear about the college professor who was involved in a terrible car wreck? He was grading papers on a curve.

— JACK R. KISER

Vancouver has a reputation for rainy weather, so it wasn't surprising when Wong's Chinese Buffet restaurant started advertising "Dim Sun on Weekends."

— MARGUERITE POUGH

Does Santa call his elves "subordinate clauses"?

DOUG HECOX **COSMIC QUESTION**

A man called the phone company to complain about his listing in the directory. "I told you that my last name is Sweady," he said, "but you have it listed as Cyirwu."

"I'm sorry, sir," the phone-company rep said. "I'll fix it so it'll be correct the next time we publish the directory. Now how do you spell your name?"

"Just like I told you before," the customer said. "It's S as in sea, W as in why, E as in eye, A as in are, D as in double-u and Y as in you."

— BILL GAULEY

A man walks into a bar with a snake and orders two beers. The man drinks his, but the snake struggles with his glass and eventually smashes it on the floor. The man orders another two beers and the same thing happens. "I'm afraid I'm going to have to ask you to leave," says the bartender to the snake. "I'm so sorry," apologizes the man. "But he just can't hold his liquor."

Words that aren't in the dictionary but should be:

Bozone—n.
The substance surrounding stupid people that stops bright ideas from penetrating.

Decafalon—n.
The gruelling event of getting through the day consuming only those things that are good for you.

Maypop—n.
A bald tire.

Pajangle—n.
Condition of waking up with one's pajamas turned 180 degrees.

Snackmosphere—n.
The empty but explosive layer of air at the top of a potato chip bag.

— BERT CHRISTENSON

"Doc, you've got to help me. Every time I drive down a country lane, I find myself singing 'Green Green Grass of Home.' Every time I see a cat I sing 'What's New Pussycat?' And last night I sang 'Delilah' in my sleep. I tell you, Doc, my wife was not at all amused."

"I wouldn't worry. It seems you have the early symptoms of Tom Jones syndrome."

"I have never heard of that. Is it common?"

"It's not unusual."

The fur began to fly when my fellow airplane passengers learned there was a chance they might miss their connecting flights out of Montreal. When we finally landed, I found out just how nasty things got.

Over the intercom, a harried flight attendant announced, "Those of you continuing on to Charlottetown, please wait outside next to the boarding ramp and we will have a shuttle run you over."

— ALAINA WAGNER

"His personals ad said he was solid."

332

Last Laughs

Jest the facts: Laugh-out-loud humour we couldn't resist.

Did you hear about the doctor who went on a ski trip and got lost on the slopes? He stamped out "help" in the snow, but nobody could read his writing.

— HAROLD ZUBER

When the patrolman saw the man speed past, he pulled him over and asked for his licence and registration. "I lost my licence after my last DUI," the guy replied calmly. "I'll give you the registration, but don't freak out when I open the glove box because I've got a couple of guns in there. And if you should search the car, don't be surprised if you find a some drugs and illegal aliens in the trunk."

Alarmed, the patrolman went back to his car and called for backup. Moments later a SWAT team swept down on the car. The driver was handcuffed as the team searched the vehicle.

"There's no drugs or guns in this car, buddy'" the SWAT leader said to the driver.

"Of course there aren't," the driver replied. "And I suppose that cop told you I was speeding, too."

— DARRELL ELMORE

It's Tuesday. Three in the afternoon. Moncton police pick up a con artist on a section 836, the old Fountain of Youth scam. The con artist is selling bottles filled with a liquid that he claims slows the aging process.

The detective tells his partner, "Frank, check his record. My gut tells me that our boy has played this game before."

Frank reports back. "You're right, he's got priors. He was busted for the same thing in 1815, 1887, 1921…"

— RON DENTINGER

Joe and Dave are hunting when Dave keels over. Frantic, Joe dials 911 on his cellphone and blurts, "My friend just dropped dead! What should I do?"

A soothing voice at the other end says, "Don't worry, I can help. First, let's make sure he's really dead."

After a brief silence the operator hears a shot ring out. Then Joe comes back to the phone. "Okay," he says nervously to the operator. "What do I do next?"

An older father noticed his son's Viagra tablets in the medicine cabinet. "Could I try one?" he asked. "Sure," his son said, "but make the most of it. Each of those pills costs ten bucks."

His dad was shocked by the price. "Don't worry," he promised, "I'll pay you back."

The next morning the son found an envelope under his breakfast plate. Inside was $110.

"Dad," he said, "that pill only cost $10."

"I know," his father said, smiling. "The ten is from me. The hundred is from your mother."

— DON KELLY

Vacationing in the Prairies, a group of British tourists spots a cowboy lying by the side of the road with his ear to the ground. "What's going on?" they ask. "Two horses—one grey, one chestnut—are pulling a wagon carrying two men," the cowboy says. "One man is wearing a red shirt, the other a black shirt. They're heading east."

"Wow!" says one of the tourists. "You can tell all that just by listening to the ground?"

"No!" replies the cowboy. "They just ran over me."

— JOHN GAMBA

Timeless Humour from the **'50s**

"For 20 years," mused the man at the bar, "my wife and I were ecstatically happy."

"Then what happened?" asked the bartender.

"We met."

On business in Mexico, three men get drunk and wake up in jail to learn they will be executed, though none of them can recall what they did to deserve it. The first man put in the electric chair is asked for his last words. "I'm from the Toronto School of Theology, and believe in the power of God to intervene on behalf of the innocent." The switch is thrown, but nothing happens. The jailers figure God wants the man alive and let him go.

The second man is strapped in. "I'm from UBC's Faculty of Law, and believe in the power of justice to intervene on behalf of the innocent." The switch is thrown; again, nothing. The jailers think the law is on this man's side, so they let him go.

The last man says, "Well, I'm an electrical engineer from McGill, and you're not electrocuting anybody if you don't connect those two loose wires down there."

I got thrown out of a mime show the other day for having a spasm. They thought I was heckling.

— JEFF SHAW

"If I've only got two weeks to live, I'll take the last week in July and first week in August."

"When I press my forehead with my finger, it really hurts," a patient complained to his doctor. "And when I do the same to my cheek, it's also painful. Even if I press on my stomach, I suffer. What can it be?"

Stumped, the physician sent the patient to a specialist. The man returned to his doctor the following week.

"What did the specialist say?" the doctor asked.

"I have a broken finger."

— GEORGE RUSSELL

A woman goes to the drugstore and asks for arsenic. "What do you want that for?" the pharmacist asks.

"I want to kill my husband," she replies. "He's having an affair with another woman."

"I can't sell you arsenic to kill your husband," says the pharmacist, "even if he is cheating."

The woman pulls out a picture of her husband with the pharmacist's wife. The druggist turns pale and replies, "Oh, I didn't realize you had a prescription."

— MARSHA SCHÄUER

The 16th tee featured a fairway that ran along a road fenced off on the left. The first golfer in a foursome teed off and hooked the ball. It soared over the fence and bounced onto the street, where it hit the tire of a moving bus and ricocheted back onto the fairway.

As they all stood in amazement, one of his partners asked, "How did you do that?"

The golfer shrugged. "You have to know the bus schedule."

The police officer pulled over a guy driving a convertible because he had a penguin riding in the passenger seat. "Hey, buddy, is that an actual penguin?"

"Yeah. I just picked him up."

"Well, why don't you take him to the zoo?"

The guy agreed, but the very next day the cop saw him drive by again with the penguin sitting beside him. "I thought I told you to take that thing to the zoo," said the officer.

"I did," the guy replied. "And we had such a good time, tonight we're going to a hockey game."

An old man living alone on a farm wrote to his only son, Bubba, in prison. "Dear Bubba: I'm feeling pretty bad because it looks like I won't be able to plant my potato garden this year. I'm just getting too old to be digging up a garden plot. Wish you were here—I know you would take care of it for me. Love, Dad."

About a week later, the farmer received this letter. "Dear Dad: Don't dig up the garden! That's where I buried the bodies. Love, Bubba." The next day, the RCMP stormed the property and dug up the entire garden. They didn't find any bodies, though, so they apologized to the old man and left.

Soon the farmer received another letter. "Dear Dad: Go ahead and plant the potatoes now. It's the best I could do under the circumstances. Love, Bubba."

"Where did you get that great motorcycle?" the engineering student asked his friend.

"I was minding my own business," his fellow engineer replied, "when a gorgeous woman rode up on it, jumped off, threw the bike to the ground, tore off her clothes and said, 'Take what you want.'"

The first engineer nodded his approval. "Good choice," he said. "The clothes probably wouldn't have fit."

— ED PERRATORE

Six things you never want to hear at the tattoo parlour:
- "'Eagle'? I thought you said 'beagle.'"
- "Boy, I hate it when I get hiccups."
- "Hey, buddy, we ran out of red, so I used pink."

Timeless Humour from the '50s

The young bride noticed that her husband was depressed. "George, dearest," she whispered, "please tell me what is bothering you. Your worries are not your worries now—they are our worries."

"Oh, very well," said George. "We have just had a letter from a girl in Detroit, and she is suing us for breach of promise."

- "Two O's in 'Bob,' right?"
- "I bet you can't tell I've never done this before."
- "Anything else you want to say? You've got all kinds of room back here."

Nancy offers her friend Veronica a ride home from work. During the drive, Veronica notices a brown paper bag on the front seat between them. "It's a bottle of wine," says Nancy. "I got it for my husband."

Veronica nods. "Good trade."

— ALAN E. OWENS

One day a genie appeared to a British Columbia man and offered to grant him one wish. The man said, "I wish you'd build a bridge from here to Hawaii so I could drive over there anytime."

The genie frowned. "I don't know. It sounds like quite an undertaking," he said. "Just think of the logistics. The supports required to reach the bottom of the ocean, the concrete, the steel! Why don't you pick something else?"

The man thought for a while and then said, "Okay, I wish for a complete understanding of women—what they're thinking, why they cry. I wish I knew how to make a woman truly happy."

The genie was silent for a minute, then said, "So how many lanes did you want on that bridge?"

— LISA FREDERICK

A priest, a nun, a rabbi, a lawyer and a doctor walk into a bar. The bartender takes one look at them and says, "What is this? A joke?"

— SEAN MORRISON

A pair of cows were talking in the field. One says, "Have you heard about the mad cow disease that's going around?"

"Yeah," the other cow says. "Makes me glad I'm a penguin."

His wife was going into labour, and a man dialed 911 in a panic. When the dispatcher came on the line, he cried, "My wife is having a baby. Her contractions are only two minutes apart. What am I supposed to do?"

The dispatcher said, "Calm down, sir. Is this her first child?"

"No," the frantic man replied. "This is her husband!"

Up in heaven, the pastor was shown his eternal reward. To his disappointment, he was given only a small shack. But down the street he saw a taxi driver being shown a lovely estate with gardens and pools.

"I don't understand it," the pastor said. "My whole life, I served God with everything I had and this is all I get, while a mere cabby is given a mansion?"

"It's quite simple," St. Peter said. "When you preached, people slept; when he drove, people prayed."

— JOEL BERGMAN

Timeless Humour from the '60s

Breathless scientist, to returning spaceman: "Is there any life on Mars?"

Spaceman: "Well, there's a little on Saturday night, but it's awfully dead the rest of the week."

"This Heimlich instructional video just won't stay in the VCR."

A local charity had never received a donation from the town's most successful lawyer. The director called to get a contribution. "Our records show you make $500,000 year, yet you haven't given a penny to charity," the director began. "Wouldn't you like to help the community?"

The lawyer replied, "Did your research show that my mother is ill, with medical bills several times her annual income?"

"Um, no," mumbled the director.

"Or that my brother is blind and unemployed?"

The stricken director began to stammer out an apology.

"Or that my sister's husband died in an accident," said the lawyer, his voice rising in indignation, "leaving her penniless with three kids?"

The humiliated director said simply, "I had no idea."

"So," said the lawyer, "if I don't give any money to them, why would I give any to you?"

The dying penny pincher told his doctor, lawyer and pastor, "I have $90,000 under my mattress. At my funeral I want each of you to toss an envelope with $30,000 into the grave." And after telling them this, he died.

At the funeral, each threw his envelope in the grave. Later, the pastor said, "I must confess. I needed $10,000 for my new church, so I only threw in $20,000."

The doctor admitted, "I needed $20,000 for new equipment at the hospital, so I only had $10,000 in the envelope."

"Gentlemen, I'm shocked that you would blatantly ignore this man's final wish," said the lawyer. "I threw in my personal check for the full amount."

In the hospitality suite at a bar association convention, a young lawyer meets the Devil. The Devil says, "Listen, if you give me your soul and the souls of everyone in your family, I'll make you a full partner in your firm."

After mulling this over, the lawyer says, "What's the catch?"

Jim's doctor tells him he has only one day to live. When Jim goes home to share the bad news with his wife, she asks what he wants to do with the little bit of time he has left. "All I want," Jim tells his beloved wife, "is to spend my last few hours reliving our honeymoon." Which is exactly what they did.

But after four hours of blissful romance, she announces that she's tired and wants to go to sleep.

"Oh, come on," Jim whispers in her ear.

"Look," his wife snaps, "I've got to get up in the morning. You don't!"

A 75-year-old millionaire had just married a 20-year-old woman. "You crafty old thing," said his friend. "I am most jealous. How did you manage to get such a lovely young wife?" "Easy," replied the millionaire. "I told her I was 95."

The Japanese eat little fat and suffer fewer heart attacks than Canadians or Americans. The French eat a lot of fat and also suffer fewer heart attacks than Canadians or Americans. The Italians drink a lot of red wine and also suffer fewer heart attacks than Canadians or Americans.

Conclusion: Eat and drink what you like. Speaking English is apparently what kills you.

— IRWIN KNOPF

Jake: "Why are cowboys' hats turned up on the sides?"

Bill: "I don't know, Jake. Why?"

Jake: "So that three people can fit in the pickup."

— DONNA L. ANDERSON

Proudly showing off his new apartment to a friend late one night, the drunk led the way to his bedroom, where there was a big brass gong. "What's that big brass gong for?" asked the friend.

"It's not a gong. It's a talking clock," the drunk replied.

"A talking clock? How's it work?"

"Watch," said the drunk. He picked up a hammer, gave the gong an ear-shattering pound and stepped back.

Someone on the other side of the wall screamed: "Hey, you jerk. It's three in the morning!"

— E. T. THOMPSON

These two green beans are crossing the freeway when one of them is hit by an 18-wheeler. His friend scrapes him up and rushes him to the hospital. After hours of surgery, the doctor says, "I have good news and bad news."

The healthy green bean says, "Okay, give me the good news first."

"Well, he's going to live."

"So, what's the bad news?"

"The bad news is he'll be a vegetable for the rest of his life."

A junior manager, a senior manager and their boss were on their way to a lunch meeting. In the cab, they found a lamp. The boss rubbed it and a genie appeared. "I'll grant you one wish each," the genie said.

Grabbing the lamp from his boss, the eager senior manager shouted, "I want to be on a fast boat in the Bahamas with no worries." And, poof, he was gone.

The junior manager couldn't keep quiet. He shouted, "I want to be in Miami, with beautiful girls, food and cocktails." And, poof, he was gone.

Finally, it was the boss's turn. "I want those idiots back in the office after lunch."

— ASHFAQ AHMED

341

A woman bought a whole range of anti-aging cosmetics and spent a whole afternoon in the bedroom applying creams and potions to various parts of her body. Then she went downstairs and said to her husband, "Tell me honestly, darling—how old do I look?"

He replied, "From your skin—17; from your hair—20; from your figure—22."

"Ooh, you flatterer," she gushed.

"Wait a minute," he said. "I haven't added them up yet."

While a motorist was driving through the country, his car broke down by a gate to a field. He got out and lifted the hood. "Your distributor's loose," announced a voice. The man looked around in alarm, but could see nobody. He continued to inspect the engine. Again a voice said, "Your distributor's loose." Looking up, he saw a black horse standing by the gate. "It's definitely your distributor," said the horse. Stunned, he checked the distributor and sure enough it was loose. He quickly did the necessary repairs and drove to the next village. There he rushed to the nearest bar and ordered a double whisky. "You won't believe what

/ SMELTZER

I've just witnessed," he confided to the barman and told him about the incident. "It's a good job it wasn't the white horse you saw," said the barman. "Why's that?" asked the motorist. "Because he knows nothing about cars."

A thug and his girlfriend were strolling down the street late at night, holding hands and gazing into shop windows. Passing a jewellery store, the girlfriend spotted a shiny ring. "Oh!" she exclaimed. "I'd just love to have that."

The thug looked around, and without a word threw a brick through the window, reached in and grabbed the ring. "There you go, baby," he said. The girl was impressed.

They walked on until she spotted a leather jacket in another window. "Wow," she said. "It sure is beautiful."

"Hold on," said the thug. He threw another brick through the window and handed her the coat.

A few blocks later she spotted an attractive pair of boots. "Oh—" she began, but the thug interrupted. "C'mon, baby," he said. "You think I'm made of bricks?"

— STEPHEN McCULLOUGH

The blind man walks into a bar and says, "Wanna hear a blond joke?"

The bartender tells him, "Well, I'm blond and I won't appreciate it. The man sitting next to you is 265 pounds, and is also blond. The man behind you is 285 pounds, and he's a blond too. Do you still want to tell that joke?"

"No way," says the blind man. "Not if I have to explain it three times."

— PAT PATEL

Timeless Humour from the '60s

Did you hear they are putting a clock in the Leaning Tower of Pisa? Because what's the good if you have the inclination and don't have the time?

Reporter interviewing a 104-year-old woman: "What is the best thing about being 104?" She replies, **"No peer pressure."**

— SYLVIA R. SHINER

Abiologist assigned to work in deepest Africa hired a guide to take him upriver to the remote site where he would do his study. As they were making their way into the jungle, the scientist heard the sound of drums. "What is that drumming?" he asked his guide nervously.

The guide, who spoke little English, replied, "Drums okay, but very bad when they stop." The drumming continued for two weeks while the biologist conducted his fieldwork. Finally, on the last day, the drums suddenly stopped, and the forest fell eerily silent.

Alarmed, the scientist called out to his guide, "The drums have stopped! What happens now?"

The guide crouched down, covered his head with his hands and, with despair in his voice, answered, "Bass solo."

Phoning a patient, the doctor says, "I have some bad news and some worse news. The bad news is that you have only 24 hours left to live."

"That is bad news," the patient replies. "What could be worse?"

The doctor answers, "I've been trying to reach you since yesterday."

Lou sees a sign in front of a house: "Talking Dog for Sale." Intrigued, he rings the bell and the owner shows him the dog. "What's your story?" Lou asks.

The dog says, "I discovered I had this gift when I was just a pup. CSIS signed me up, and soon I was jetting around the world, sitting at the feet of spies and world leaders, gathering important information and sending it back home. When I tired of that lifestyle, I joined the RCMP, where I helped catch drug lords and gunrunners. I was wounded in the line of duty, received some medals, and now a movie is being made of my life."

"How much do you want for the dog?" Lou asks the owner.

"Ten dollars," says the owner.

Lou is incredulous. "Why on earth would you sell that remarkable dog for so little?"

"Because he's a liar. He didn't do any of that stuff."

— STEVE DERIVAN

So... which one is yours?

343

Everything is changing. People are taking their comedians seriously and the politicians as a joke.

— WILL ROGERS

Humour is a rubber sword— it allows you to make a point without drawing blood.

— MARY HIRSCH

Inviting people to laugh with you while you are laughing at yourself is a good thing to do. You may be the fool, but you're the fool in charge.

— CARL REINER, My Anecdotal Life (St. Martin's)

You know there is a problem with the education system when you realize that out of the three R's, only one begins with an R.

— DENNIS MILLER, "Dennis Miller Live," HBO

No matter what happens, somebody will find a way to take it too seriously.

— DAVE BARRY, Dave Barry Turns 50 (Crown)

Humour is always based on a modicum of truth. Ever heard a joke about a father-in-law?

— DICK CLARK

How come if you mix flour and water together you get glue? And when you add eggs and sugar you get cake? Where does the glue go?

— RITA RUDNER

A scoutmaster asks his troop to list three important things to bring in case they get lost in the desert. Food, matches, a bandana are all mentioned. Then Timmy suggests a compass, a canteen of water, and a deck of cards.

"I get the first two items," says the leader. "But what good are the cards?"

"Well, as soon as you start playing solitaire, it's guaranteed someone will come up to you and say, 'Put the red nine on top of the black ten.'"

John told the mortician to spare no expense for his father's funeral. So when a bill for $3,200 arrived after the funeral, John paid it. The next month, he received a bill for $85. He paid it, figuring it had been left off the original tally. But a month later, after receiving another bill for $85, John called the funeral director.

"You said you wanted the best funeral we could arrange," the director told him. "So I rented him a tuxedo."

— RICHARD REYNOSA

Last night I played a blank tape at full blast. The mime next door went nuts.

— STEVEN WRIGHT

"Knock, knock."

"Who's there?"

"Control freak. Now you say, 'Control freak who?'"

On the way home from work, Tom is stopped on the street by an attractive woman in a suggestive outfit.

"For $100, I'll do anything you ask in three words or less," she whispers.

"Okay," agrees Tom, handing over the cash. "Paint my house."

— BILL UPDIKE

At a convention of blonds, a speaker insisted that the "dumb blond" myth is all wrong. To prove it he asked one cute young volunteer, "How much is 101 plus 20?"

The blond answered, "120."

"No," he said, "that's not right."

The audience called out, "Give her another chance."

So the speaker asked the blond, "How much is 10 plus 13?"

Slowly the blond replied, "16."

"Sorry," he said, shaking his head.

Once again the crowd roared, "Give her another chance."

"This is your last try," warned the speaker. "How much is 2 plus 2?"

Carefully she ventured, "Four?"

And the crowd yelled, "Give her another chance!"

— JAMES T. DORSEY

A farmer on a tractor approached a driver whose car was stuck in a mud hole. "For ten bucks, I'll pull you out of there," the farmer said.

"All right," the driver agreed. After the farmer had pocketed the money, he said, "You know, yours is the tenth car I've rescued today."

"Wow," the driver said incredulously. "When do you have time to work on your land? At night?"

"No," the farmer replied. "Night is when I fill the hole with water."

— RODRIGO CAMARGO

This duck walks into a store one day and asks the clerk, "Do you have any grapes?"

The clerk replies, "Sorry, no."

The next day the duck walks into the same store and again asks, "Do you have any grapes?"

The clerk says, "No."

The next day the duck walks into the store and asks, "Do you have any grapes?"

This time the clerk says: "No. And if you ask me one more time, I'll staple your feet to the floor."

The next day the duck walks into the store and asks, "Do you have any staples?"

The clerk says, "No."

So the duck says, "Do you have any grapes?"

— GREG WILKEY

Overheard: "I hate talking cars. A voice out of nowhere says things like, 'Your door is ajar.' Why don't they say something really useful, like 'There's a cop hiding behind that bush.'?"

A businesswoman is sitting at a bar. A man approaches her. "Hi, honey," he says. "Want a little company?"

"Why?" asks the woman. "Do you have one to sell?"

— CAROLYN A. STRADLEY

So this neutron walks into a bar and orders a beer. "How much will that be?" the neutron asks.

"For you," replies the bartender, "no charge."

— LYNDELL LEATHERMAN

The man auditioning for the circus was confident, even though he'd been told the impresario had seen it all. "I have the most unusual act," the man said before he began. "Just watch. I'm sure you'll be amazed."

He proceeded to climb a tall tower, and then jumped off, his arms flapping wildly. Nearing the ground, the man's fall suddenly slowed and he soared upward. He swooped past the impresario twice and then fluttered gently to the ground, where he beamed triumphantly at his audience.

The impresario stood there for a moment staring at the man. Finally he said, "So is that all you've got? Bird impressions?"

Two lawyers walk into a diner, order drinks and pull their lunches from their briefcases. "Sorry," the bartender says, "but you can't eat your own food in here."

The guys look at each other, shrug their shoulders and swap sandwiches.

— LYDIA PRINCE

A man approaches the Gate of Heaven and asks to be let in. "Tell me one good thing you did in your life," St. Peter says to him.

"Well," replies the fellow, "I saw a group of punks harassing an elderly woman, so I kicked their leader in the shins."

"When did this happen?"

"About 40 seconds ago."

— MICHAEL S. COFFEY

In Niagara Falls two men were shutting down the casino at about 2 a.m. when a beautiful woman came in and said she wanted to gamble $2,000 on one roll of the dice. They said they were closed, but she insisted that one roll would only take a minute. The men figured why not, the odds were in their favour.

So the woman put her money down, and they put theirs down. Then she said, "Wait just a moment," and went to the restroom.

She came out a minute later, stark naked, and rolled the dice. "Seven," she said, and picked up the money, returned to the restroom, dressed and left.

"Did you see that seven?" one man asked the other.

"No," he replied. "I thought you did."

— BOYCE D. KESTERSON

Phil visits his doctor after weeks of not feeling well. "I have bad news," says the doctor. "You don't have long to live."

"How long have I got?" asks a distraught Phil.

"Ten," the doctor says sadly.

"Ten? Ten what? Months? Days?"

Suddenly the doctor interrupts, "Nine…"

Timeless Humour from the '70s

A mother was writing an excuse to the kindergarten teacher for her five-year-old daughter, who had been out of school with a cold.

"Okay," said the little girl. "But don't write that I threw up. I want to save that for show and tell."

"The first thing you have to understand is that when they throw your ball, they're not trying to get rid of you."

It was the annual grudge match football game between the large animals and the small animals. In the first half, the big animals crushed the little critters. But by the second half, things had turned around. The big animals' stars—the elephant, rhino and hippo—were all tackled for huge losses. "Who's making all those tackles?" asked the small critters' coach.

"I am," said the centipede.

"Why weren't you here earlier when we needed you?" the coach yelled. The centipede replied,

"I was having my ankles taped."

A scrawny little fellow showed up at the lumber camp looking for work. "Just give me a chance to show you what I can do," he said to the head lumberjack.

"All right," said the boss. "Take your ax and cut down that red-wood tree."

Five minutes later the skinny guy was back. "I cut it down," he said, "and split it up into lumber."

The boss couldn't believe his eyes. "Where did you learn to cut trees like that?"

"The Sahara," the man answered.

"The Sahara Desert?"

"Desert? Oh, sure, that's what they call it now!"

— KUMIKO YOSHIDA

Mother Teresa arrives in Heaven. "Be thou hungry?" God asks. Mother Teresa nods. He serves them each a humble sandwich of tuna on rye bread. Meanwhile, the sainted woman looks down to see gluttons in Hell devouring steaks, lobsters and wine.

The next day God invites her to join him for another meal. Again, it's tuna on rye. Again, she sees the denizens of Hell feasting.

The next day, as another can of tuna is opened, Mother Teresa meekly says, "I am grateful to be here with you as a reward for the pious life I led. But I don't get it: All we eat is tuna and bread while in the other place they eat like kings."

"Let's be honest," God says with a sigh, "for just two people, does it pay to cook?"

Two dogs were out for a walk. One dog says to the other, "Wait here a minute. I'll be right back." He walks across the street and sniffs a fire hydrant for about a minute, then rejoins his friend.

"What was that all about?" the other dog asks.

"Just checking my messages."

Alice and Ted went snow-boarding, and Ted brought along a litre-size thermos. Alice had never seen one, and asked what it was. "It's a thermos," replied Ted. "The guy at the store told me it's used for keeping hot things hot and cold things cold."

"Sounds great," said Alice. "What do you have in it?"

"Three coffees and a Popsicle."

— JEANNE STANTON

Do you know what you get when you play a country-and-western song backward? You get your job back, you get your house back, your wife back, your truck back...

The husband came home unexpectedly and found his wife in the arms of another man.

"What do you think you're doing?" he shouted.

"See?" the woman said to her companion. "I told you he was stupid."

349

I went on a 45-day diet. It's going great.
I've already lost 30 days.

A guy goes on vacation to the Holy Land with his wife and mother-in-law. Halfway through their trip, the mother-in-law dies. So the guy goes to an undertaker, who explains that they can ship the body home, but it'll cost $5,000. Or they can bury her in the Holy Land for $150.

"We'll ship her home," says the son-in-law.

"Are you sure?" asks the undertaker. "That's an awfully big expense. And I can assure you we do a very nice burial here."

"Look," says the son-in-law, "two thousand years ago they buried a guy here, and three days later he rose from the dead. I just can't take that chance."

— JASON TUTHILL

Two guys were discussing modern trends on sex and marriage. "I didn't sleep with my wife before we got married," Roy said. "Did you?"

"I'm not sure," Bobby replied. "What was her maiden name?"

— JONATHAN DURIA

"It's chilly in here," the wealthy customer sniffed. "Will you please turn down the air conditioner?"

"No problem, sir," said the waiter.

After a few minutes, the man flagged the server again. "Now I'm too warm."

"All right," said the waiter. But soon the customer was chilly again.

Finally a patron at a nearby table whispered to the waiter, "I commend you for your patience. That guy is certainly keeping you busy."

"No, he's not," the waiter said with a shrug. "We don't even have an air conditioner."

"Billy's opinions do not reflect the views of the Andersons, their affiliates or subsidiaries."

Lou, Sam and Joe walk into a bar and each orders a pint. Just as they're about to take their first sip, flies land in each of their drinks.

Lou, the most squeamish of the trio, pushes his beer away in disgust.

Sam, the thrifty one, fishes the fly out and drinks his beer.

And Joe, the lush, drags the fly out, holds it over the beer and yells, "C'mon, spit it out! Spit it out!"

Overheard: "If Batman is supposed to be so smart, how come he wears his underwear outside his clothes?"

— ASHLEY COOPER

"May I try on that dress in the window?" the gorgeous young woman asks the manager of the designer boutique.

"Go ahead," the manager replies. "Maybe it'll attract some business."

— HARRY BUCK

The nurse said to the doctor, "There's an invisible man in the waiting room."

The doctor replied, "Tell him I can't see him now."

— PAUL W. REGENESS

The devout cowboy lost his favourite Bible while he was mending fences out on the range. Three weeks later a cow walked up to him carrying the Bible in its mouth. The cowboy couldn't believe his eyes. He took the book out of the cow's mouth, raised his eyes heavenward and exclaimed, "It's a miracle!"

"Not really," said the cow. "Your name is written inside the cover."

— ROMAN WILBERT

At a gallery, a couple went to look at some paintings. One of the pictures was of a beautiful naked woman with only a little foliage covering the appropriate areas. The wife thought the picture was in bad taste and moved on quickly, but the husband lingered, completely transfixed. "What are you waiting for?" called his wife. "Autumn?"

They are making a new film about Moses. It's not finished yet, but apparently the baby looks just great in the rushes.

"Every time I drink a cup of coffee, doctor, I have a stabbing pain in my right eye. What should I do?"

"Take the spoon out of your cup."

— STEVE JARRELL

Shelley, a talent scout for a large recording studio, was walking by a convent when he heard someone singing in a voice so beautiful he couldn't believe his ears. He rang the bell and asked to speak to the woman with the amazing voice. Soon a young nun appeared.

"Sister," Shelley said, "I represent Euphonics, Inc., and I'd like you to make a tape of hymns. Your fee could be donated to charity."

"I'd be delighted," she replied, "but first I must get written permission from our Mother Superior."

"Okay, Sister, just give me a call." Shelley rushed back to the office and described his find to his boss. Then he asked for a raise.

Replied the boss, "Wait till the nun signs, Shelley."

— STEVE KEUEBEL

A doctor answered the phone and heard the familiar voice of a colleague on the other end of the line say, "We need a fourth for poker."

"I'll be right over," the doctor answered.

As he was putting on his coat, his wife asked, "Is it serious?"

"Oh, yes," the doctor answered gravely. "In fact, there are three doctors there already."

— DOROTHEA KENT

"I think Mary is getting suspicious about all the long walks."

Timeless Humour from the **'70s**

Then there's the story about the gossip columnist who asked comedian George Burns, 74, if he planned to marry the 19-year-old UCLA student he was dating. George took a long puff on his cigar and quipped, "I told her I might think it over if she gets all A's on her report card."

How many country and western singers does
it take to change a light bulb?

Five. One to put in the new bulb, and four to sing
about how much they long for the old one.

LESLIE R. TANNER

Who invented copper wire?

Two tax lawyers fighting over a penny.

EARLE HITCHNER

Why did the Pope cross the road?

He crosses everything.

TOM FLITTER

Why do some testing labs prefer to use lawyers
instead of mice?

Because there are more lawyers than mice,
the scientists don't get as attached to the lawyers,
and there are some things mice won't do.

How many lawyer jokes are there?

Only three. The rest are true stories . . .

What do you get when you cross a librarian
and a lawyer?

All the information you want, except
you can't understand it.

PRADHAN NAGESH

Ralph was on his way home from work one night when, to his horror, he suddenly realized that he'd completely forgotten his daughter's birthday. He rushed to the toy store and asked the manager, "How much is the Barbie in the window?"

"Which one?" the manager replied. "We have Workout Barbie for $19.95, Malibu Barbie for $19.95, Soccer Barbie is $19.95, Cinderella Barbie $19.95, Retro '70s Barbie $19.95, and Divorced Barbie is $375."

"Hold on," Ralph said. "Why is Divorced Barbie $375 when all the other Barbies are only $19.95?"

"Well," said the store manager, "Divorced Barbie comes with Ken's car, Ken's house, Ken's boat, Ken's dog, Ken's cat, Ken's furniture…"

Jack walked into his house breathless and exhausted. "What happened?" his wife asked. "It's a great idea I had," he gasped, smiling proudly. "I ran all the way home behind the bus and saved myself fifty cents."

His wife frowned. "That's just like you, Jack, always thinking small," she said, shaking her head disapprovingly. "Why couldn't you have run behind a taxi and saved yourself six dollars?"

One day, the general noticed one of his soldiers behaving oddly. He would pick up every piece of paper he saw, read it, frown and say, "That's not it," and drop it.

After a month of this, the general finally arranged to have the soldier tested. The psychologist found that the soldier was deranged, and wrote out his discharge from the army.

The soldier picked it up, smiled and said, "That's it."

Ten men and one woman are hanging on to a rope that extends down from a helicopter. The weight of 11 people is too much for the rope, so the group decides one person has to jump off. No one can decide who should go, until finally the woman volunteers.

She gives a touching speech, saying she will sacrifice her life to save the others, because women are used to giving up things for their husbands and children.

When she finishes speaking… all the men start clapping.

— MARGARET PITMAN

Babs couldn't understand why she was losing so badly at Trivial Pursuit. Nevertheless, she persevered, rolling the dice and landing on green—Science & Nature. Her question was, "If you are in a vacuum and someone calls your name, can you hear it?"

Babs mulled over the question for a minute, and then asked, "Is it on or off?"

A guy walks into a bank, points a gun at the teller and says, "Give me all your money, lady, or you're geography."

"Don't you mean 'history'?" the teller asks.

"Hey, lady," the thug replies. "Don't change the subject."

— MIRIAM HARTILL

The teacher asks, "If you had one dollar and you asked your father for another, how many dollars would you have?"

Vincent raised his hand and answered, "One dollar."

The teacher shook her head. "You don't know your math."

Vincent said, "You don't know my father."

Walking into the local chambre of commerce, the stranger obviously looked desperate. He approached the guy at the counter and asked, "Is there a criminal lawyer in town?" The guy behind the counter replied, "Yes, but we can't prove it yet!"

— JOHN G. STEEN

Louise came home and found Henry stalking around with a fly swatter. "Killed any yet?" she asked. "Yep," Henry answered. "Two males and a female."

"How could you tell?"

"Well," said Henry, "two were on a beer can and one was on the telephone."

Two friends were beginning a game of golf. The first man stepped up to the tee, hit the ball and got a hole in one. The other man said, "Now I'll take my practice swing, and then we'll start the game."

— EDWARD W. STRICKLER

Shakey said to the psychiatrist, "Doc, every time I get into bed, I think there's somebody under it. You gotta help me!"

"Come to me three times a week for two years and I'll cure your fears," said the shrink. "And I'll only charge you $200 a visit."

"I'll think about it," said Shakey.

Six months later the doctor met Shakey on the street and asked why he never came to see him.

"For two hundred bucks a visit? A bartender cured me for ten dollars."

"Is that so! How?"

"He told me to cut the legs off the bed."

"I got this great new hearing aid the other day. It really works fantastically."

"Are you wearing it now?"

"Yep. Cost me a small fortune, but it's really top of the line."

"What kind is it?"

"Twelve thirty."

A pastor, known for his lengthy sermons, noticed a man get up and leave for part of the service. After church, the pastor asked the man where he had gone. "To get a haircut," the guy said.

"But," asked the pastor, "why didn't you do that before the service?"

"Because," the gentleman replied, "I didn't need one then."

— RUBEN QUEZADA

"It's number two! That's the man who stole my identity."

Albert comes home, plops down in front of the TV and says to his wife, "Quick! Get me a beer before it starts." She rolls her eyes and brings him a beer.

Fifteen minutes later he says, "Get me another beer. It's going to start any minute now."

His wife is furious. "Is that all you're going to do tonight? Sit in front of that television drinking beer? You have to be the world's laziest, most—"

He interrupts her with a heavy sigh. "Well," he says. "It's started."

Two atoms are walking down the sidewalk when they accidentally bump into each other. "I'm really sorry!" the first atom exclaims.

"Are you all right?"

"Actually, no," the second atom replies. "I lost an electron."

"Oh, no! Are you sure?"

"I'm positive!"

— VYAS SARWESHWAR PRASAD

Bill walked into a bar with a lump of tarmac under his arm. "What can I do for you?" asked the bartender, looking him up and down. "A beer for me," Bill replied, "and one for the road."

— NIGEL PENN

A homeless beggar walked up to a well-dressed woman shopping in Beverly Hills and moaned, "I haven't eaten anything in four days."

The woman looked at him, sighed and said, "I wish I had your willpower."

— PAUL SILVEIRA

Clementine is driving home one night when her car is hit by a bad hailstorm, leaving hundreds of dents. The next day she goes to a body shop for a repair estimate. The repairman winks at his buddy and tells Clementine that if she blows into the tailpipe really hard, the dents will just pop out.

After she arrives home, she blows with all her might into the exhaust pipe. Her roommate asks what she's doing. Clementine explains the repairman's tip. "But it doesn't work," she says, pausing to catch her breath.

"Duh!" replies her friend. "You have to roll up the windows first!"

— MINDY VAUGHAN

The curvy redhead limped into the doctor's office complaining about a trick knee. The doctor stooped down, peering at the knee, and asked, "Now what's a joint like you doing in a nice girl like this?"

— JOHN DRATWA

Late one night the political candidate came home and gave his wife the glorious news: "Darling, I've been elected!"

"Honestly?" she replied.

"Hey," the politician said, frowning, "why bring that up?"

"At this point the Western influence starts to show."

Did you hear about the guy who froze to death at the drive-in? He went to see **Closed for the Winter.**

On their first date, a man asked his companion if she'd like a drink with dinner. "Oh, no, what would I tell my Sunday school class?" she said.

Later, he offered her a cigarette. "Oh, no, what would I tell my Sunday school class?" she said again.

On the drive home, he saw a motel. Figuring he had nothing to lose, he asked if she wanted to stop in there.

"Okay," his date replied.

"What will you tell your Sunday school class?" he asked, shocked.

"The same thing I always tell them. 'You don't have to drink or smoke to have a good time.' "

— GEORGE NORDHAM

A businessman taking an efficiency seminar presented a case study on his wife's routine for cooking breakfast: "After a few days of observation, I determined what was slowing her down and suggested ways to speed up the process."

"Did it work?" the teacher asked.

"It sure did. Instead of taking her 20 minutes to cook my breakfast, it takes me only seven."

Then there was the 85-year-old woman who found her husband in bed with another woman. She was so enraged that she dragged him to the balcony of their Regina high-rise and pushed him to his death. When she appeared in court, the judge asked if she had anything to say in her own defence.

"Well, Your Honour," she replied, "I figured if at 92 he could make love, he could fly too."

— ROB MARSHALL

Bob and Bill fly to B.C. for a fishing trip. They hire a bush pilot and rent a boat, rods and tackle. After two weeks, they've caught only one small salmon.

"Man, Bill," Bob says. "Do you realize this lousy fish cost us about $2,000 apiece?"

"Wow," Bill replies. "At that rate, it's a good thing we only caught one."

Howard dies and waits in line for judgment. He notices that some souls go right into heaven, while Satan throws others into a burning pit. But every so often, instead of hurling a poor soul into the fire, the devil tosses it aside.

Curious, Howard asks Satan, "Excuse me, but why are you tossing them aside instead of flinging them into hell with the others?"

"They're from Vancouver," Satan replies. "They're too wet to burn."

— ANNETTE JOHNSON

Jason showed his buddy the beautiful diamond ring he had bought his girlfriend for her birthday. "I thought she wanted a four-wheel-drive vehicle," ventured his friend.

"She did," Jason said. "But where am I going to find a fake Jeep?"

— ZHANG WENPENG

sign language

Church bulletin bloopers, courtesy of the Internet:

"Morning sermon: Jesus Walks on the Water. Evening sermon: Searching for Jesus."

"Ladies, don't forget the rummage sale. It's a chance to get rid of those things not worth keeping around the house. Don't forget your husbands."

A young woman was describing her date to a friend. "After dinner," she said, "he wanted to come back to my apartment, but I refused. I told him my mother would worry if I did anything like that."

"Then what happened?" asked her friend.

"He kept insisting, and I kept refusing," the young woman responded.

"He didn't weaken your resolve, did he?" the friend asked.

"Not a bit. In the end, we went back to his apartment. I figured, let his mother worry."

Sunday a minister played hooky from church so he could enjoy a round of golf, leaving his assistant to conduct the service. He drove to a faraway golf course to avoid bumping into any parishioners.

Looking down, St. Peter said to God, "You're not going to let him get away with this, are you?" The Lord shook his head.

The minister took his first shot, and scored a 420-yard hole-in-one. St. Peter was outraged. "I thought you were going to punish him!" he said to the Lord.

The Lord looked at St. Peter and replied, "So who's he going to tell?"

— CLAIRE PARKER

Visiting a restaurant, a couple decided to order steak. As the waitress put their plates on the table they noticed the strange way she was holding them. "You've got your thumbs on our steaks!" complained the wife. "Well, you don't want me to drop them again, do you?" the waitress replied.

Timeless Humour from the '70s

Comedian Woody Allen has never had good relationships with mechanical objects. "I have a tape recorder," he says. "I paid $150 for it, and as I talk into it, it goes, 'I know, I know.'"

So a guy walks into a bar with a pair of jumper cables hanging around his neck. The bartender gives him a look and says gruffly, "All right, pal, I'll let you stay, but don't start anything."

— SCOTT HOFFMAN

text credits

PAGE 16 "What I Really, Really Need Now Is the Padded-Cell Phone" © 2005 by Josh Freed, first published in *The (Montreal) Gazette* (September 3, '05). **PAGE 20** "Designer of Audio CD Packaging Enters Hell": Reprinted by permission of International Creative Management, Inc. © 1999 by Steve Martin. Originally appeared in *The New Yorker*. **PAGE 26** "In the Battle of Wits with Kitchen Appliances, I'm Toast": *Boogers Are My Beat,* © 2003 by Dave Barry. Used by permission of Crown Publishers, a division of Random House, Inc. Originally appeared in *Miami Herald*. **PAGE 50** "Don't Let Email Become Ejail" © 2005 by Josh Freed, first published in *The (Montreal) Gazette* (November 12, '05). **PAGE 62** "Caddy Hack": *Who's Your Caddy?* © 2003 by Rick Reilly. Used by permission of Random House. **PAGE 70** "Me and My Big Mouth": *It's Only a Game,* © 2001 by Terry Bradshaw, published by Pocket Books, a division of Simon & Schuster, Inc., 1230 Ave. of the Americas, New York, NY 10020. **PAGE 84** "How Did That Get There?": *FamilyFun* (August '99), © 1999 by FamilyFun, 244 Main St., Northampton, MA 01060. **PAGE 90** "The Cat Years": © 1996 by Adair Lara, *San Francisco Chronicle* (March 28, '96), 901 Mission St., San Francisco, CA 94103. **PAGE 98** "Time for the Talk": *Fathers, Sons, and Brothers,* © 1997 by Bret Lott. Reprinted by permission of Harcourt, Inc. **PAGE 108** "A Lineup of Fumbling Felons, Clumsy Crooks, and Bumbling Bad Guys": *America's Dumbest Criminals* by Daniel Butler, Alan Ray, and Leland Gregory, © 1995 The Entheos Group, L.L.C., published by Rutledge Hill Press, Inc., 211 Seventh Ave. North, Nashville, TN 37219. **PAGE 122** "The Know-It-All": *The Know-It-All: One Man's Humble Quest to Become the Smartest Person in the World,* © 2004 by A. J. Jacobs. Reprinted with permission of Simon & Schuster Adult Publishing Group. **PAGE 170** "What Women Want": *Boogers Are My Beat,* © 2003 by Dave Barry. Used by permission of Crown Publishers, a division of Random House, Inc. Originally appeared in *Miami Herald*. **PAGE 182** "Guys and Dolls Syndrome: When Men Go Ape, Women Go Shopping": © 2000 by Dave Barry, *Miami Herald* (July 2, '00), One Herald Plaza, Miami, FL 33132. **PAGE 188** "On Being Canadian: An Inventory": *Why I Hate Canadians,* © 1997 by William Stener Ferguson. Used by permission of Douglas & McIntyre Ltd., Publishers, 2323 Quebec Street, Suite 201, Vancouver, B.C. V5T 4S7. **PAGE 192** "Canada: Land of the Freeze," © 2006 by Josh Freed, first published in *The (Montreal) Gazette* (January 17, '04). **PAGE 194** "Canadian Humour: A Retrospective" by Nicholas Pashley, *A Beginner's Guide to Canadian Humour,* © 1986 by Eden Press. **PAGE 198** "Canadian Cuisine (And How to Avoid It...)": *How to Be a Canadian,* © 2001 by Will Ferguson and Ian Ferguson. Used by permission of Douglas & McIntyre Ltd., Publishers, 2323 Quebec Street, Suite 201, Vancouver, B.C. V5T 4S7. **PAGE 204** "How to Drink Like a Canadian": *How to Be a Canadian,* © 2001 by Will Ferguson and Ian Ferguson. Used by permission of Douglas & McIntyre Ltd., Publishers, 2323 Quebec Street, Suite 201, Vancouver, B.C. V5T 4S7. **PAGE 210** "How Boring Is Canada?" by Nicholas Pashley, *A Beginner's Guide to Canadian Humour,* © 1986 by Eden Press. **PAGE 212** "How Suzanne Remembered It?" by Nicholas Pashley, *A Beginner's Guide to Canadian Humour,* © 1986 by Eden Press. **PAGE 260** "The Great Hamster Caper": *Florida, the Sunday Magazine of the Orlando Sentinel* (July 6, '97), © 1997 by Sentinel Communications Co., 633 N. Orange Ave., Orlando, FL 32801. **PAGE 300** "A Biblical Traffic Jam" © 1995 By Bruce Carlson. *Funny Times* (November '95), P.O. Box 18530, Cleveland Heights, Ohio 44118.

art credits

Aislin *171, 197, 202, 207, 219, 328*
AM Alberts *29, 216*
Charles Almon *154, 257, 263, 317*
Mark Anderson *67, 102, 178*
Aaron Bacall *143, 221, 236*
Ian Baker *55, 112, 232, 289, 299, 314, 336, 348*
Paul Bommer *99*
Marty Bucella *134, 142, 286*
Patrick Byrnes *12, 49, 76, 91, 104*
John Caldwell *10, 40, 45, 57, 97, 118, 161, 243, 274, 280, 306, 325, 337*
Scott Calvert *31, 38*
Dave Carpenter *107, 160, 239, 303, 355*
Ken Catalino *48, 158, 283*
Len Chapman *218, 237*
Mike Cope *190, 191*
Roy Delgado *69, 78, 81, 101, 140, 148, 184, 185, 248, 251, 256, 265, 270, 272, 277, 293, 309, 310, 327, 351*
Susan Dewar *94, 196*
Dennis Dittrich/GID/RD *71*
Benita Epstein *80, 141, 225, 315*
Hadi Farahani *209*
Feggo *356*
Randy Glasbergen *56, 166, 220, 244*
Eric Godin *5*
John Grimes *60, 150, 186*
Joe Kohl *167*
Jeff Lok *30*
Mike Lynch *18, 22, 23, 43, 74, 93, 106, 130, 156, 162, 233, 246, 264, 294, 350*

Patricia Madigan *121, 137, 216*
Scott Arthur Masear *66, 169, 231, 241, 252, 258, 268, 284, 290, 316, 334, 340, 353*
Peter Mueller *34, 88, 96, 330*
Mary Nadler *175, 305, 332*
Adrian Raeside *203*
Dan Reynolds *15, 111, 116, 117, 128, 129, 226, 235, 275, 298, 304, 312, 318, 319, 331, 339, 341, 343, 346, 354*
Norm Rockwell *172, 345*
Harley Schwadron *24, 52, 58, 61, 73, 230, 292, 296, 302*
Mike Shapiro *135, 347*
Vahan Shirvanian *89, 114–115, 127, 179, 253, 259, 358*
Steve Smeltzer *82, 86, 181, 223, 342*
Elwood Smith *cover, 1, 6, 19, 20, 21, 26, 33, 37, 54, 63, 64, 65, 72, 83, 85, 95, 98, 109, 123, 124, 125, 136, 138, 139, 145, 151, 152, 153, 163, 177, 180, 195, 199, 201, 222, 227, 238, 250, 260, 271, 278, 295, 301, 320, 323, 344*
Thomas Bros. *35, 42, 147, 326*
Carla Ventresca *28, 262*
Kim Warp *13, 132*
WestMach *321, 324*

photo credits

Artville *255*
Classic *27, 47*
Corbis *17, 51, 144, 182, 193, 261*
Patrick Giardino/Corbis *37*
Photodisc *36, 62–63, 90, 138, 165, 189, 194–195, 211, 213*
RD/GID *176, 198, 205*
Stockbyte *229*